Sean O'Casey

by the same author

SEAN O'CASEY: PLAYS TWO

The Shadow of a Gunman
The Plough and the Stars
The Silver Tassie
Purple Dust
Hall of Healing

SEAN O'CASEY

Plays One

Juno and the Paycock

Within the Gates

Red Roses for Me

Cock-A-Doodle Dandy

Introduced by
Seamus Heaney

faber and faber

Juno and the Paycock and *Within the Gates*
were first published in 1949 by Macmillan London Ltd.
Red Roses for Me and *Cock-A-Doodle Dandy*
were first published in 1951 by Macmillan London Ltd.

First published in 1998 in this edition by
Faber and Faber Limited
3 Queen Square London WC1N 3AU

Photoset by Parker Typesetting Service, Leicester
Printed in England by Mackays of Chatham plc, Chatham, Kent

A CIP record for this book
is available from the British Library

ISBN 0-571-19181-9

2 4 6 8 10 9 7 5 3 1

Contents

Introduction, vii

Juno and the Paycock, 1

Within the Gates, 87

Red Roses for Me, 211

Cock-A-Doodle Dandy, 317

Introduction

The names of some writers work like spells to take us out of this world. Say Oscar Wilde or Samuel Beckett and everything else falls away: what remains is a word-place where reality has been successfully Wildified or Beckettized. However credible and recreational the worlds of *The Importance of Being Earnest* or *Waiting for Godot* may be, a citizen who wandered in off the street would surely find them unfamiliar.

Sean O'Casey's plays are different: a citizen who happened in off the street on to the set of *The Shadow of a Gunman* would be only one of several other wanderers-in. In O'Casey's theatre, to misquote one of his immortal lines, 'the blinds is up' and the world beyond the stage door seems to have gained direct access to the stage. His name belongs not with the great purists, but with the great impurists, poets like Hugh MacDiarmid and Pablo Neruda, for example, voluble and turbulent party-liners, disturbers of the literary peace, impatient provokers who provoke impatience, lenient-hearted layers-down of the law. Beloved of the many, problematical for a few, these writers make any stand-off between literature and politics look like over-anxiety, if not prissiness. Their function is to remain in spate, to overwhelm fastidiousness with a torrent of authorial energy.

O'Casey's genius is originally related to his ear for Dublin speech, an ability to go verbally over the top in order to get to the bottom of the matter, that unique mixture of the sardonic and the exultant which characterizes his dialogue. But the release of that genius had much to do with his being in the swim of Dublin

vii

culture and politics during an era of revolutionary change in Ireland. It was an era, in fact, when Dublin changed from being a locus of British imperial rule, symbolized by Dublin Castle, the military and administrative centre of power, and became identified with the fight for Irish independence, symbolized by the General Post Office where the leaders of the Easter Rising hung out their flag of war in 1916. Heretofore the struggle for national freedom had been imagined against a background of romantic landscapes; in spite of Robert Emmet's abortive insurrection in the city in 1803, the traditional images of resistance were situated beyond the Pale. Pikemen on the march in Wexford or Co. Down, French expeditions foundering in Co. Kerry or being defeated in Co. Leitrim, Fenians mustering in Munster – these were the dream images of the struggle.

O'Casey urbanized and demythologized all that. Yeats's poem 'Easter 1916' might also be set in contemporary Dublin with its clubs and its counters, its mockers and jesters, but in Yeats's imagination the city ends up on the Olympian heights. It is made to step back into what the poet called 'the tapestry', and is woven into his own history-defying phantasmagoria. But O'Casey's Dublin is at one with the Dublin of newsreel film and documentary recordings. You can hear the twentieth century beginning to rev its irreverent gears. The background music of the era is there all right, the sonorous and religiose rhetoric of Irish patriotism, but the voices broadcasting are indomitably urban working class, speaking a lingo that would have fairly discomfited Yeats's 'indomitable Irishry'. Yeats's 'lords and ladies gay' came riding on horseback, by his own admission, from 'other days'; O'Casey's citizens came in from the pub round the corner, whiskey on their breath, rags on their back and realism written all over them.

In his great trilogy – *The Shadow of a Gunman* (1923), *Juno and the Paycock* (1924) and *The Plough and the*

Stars (1926) – O'Casey's characters are both down to earth and larger than life. They could hold their own with Falstaff in Cheapside, and the Falstaff who dodged all heroics and pleaded for the weakness of 'mortal men, mortal men' would have been at home with both the boaster and the boozer in Captain Boyle. Equally, neither Falstaff nor the Captain can be confined within the category of 'low life scenes'; fundamentally, they and their associates are not part of the light relief but an expression of their creator's critical temper. O'Casey may not have had kings and feudal lords among his dramatis personae, but his democratic genius was at one with his tragic understanding, and his recoil from tyranny and his compassion for the oppressed were an essential – as opposed to a moral and thematic – element of his art. This is not to say that the doctrinal Marxist in him never got the upper hand over the demotic mimic, only to emphasize that his theatrical experiments and assaults were born of a desperation to get at life, to take the frame off the picture appearing on the picture-frame stage. *The Silver Tassie* (1928) and *Within the Gates* (1933) go head-on at big political subjects and have moral rage rather than artistic realism written all over them, but they still know one big artistic truth: that the drama, in spite of its covenant with the actuality and sorrow of what goes on outside the frame, is a thing made up in order to be played within.

It is a measure of O'Casey's achievement that these Shakespearean comparisons can be brought up without exaggeration or embarrassment. It is also a measure of his achievement to know that his origins as a playwright lie as much in the world of nineteenth-century melodrama as in high Elizabethan tragedy. If it makes sense to read the compassionate, anti-heroic understanding of guerrilla war demonstrated in the Dublin trilogy in the light of both parts of *Henry IV*, it is worth remembering too that the dramatist enjoyed the Irish fustian and Fenian antics of

Dion Boucicault's *The Shaughraun* (1875). In fact, O'Casey's theatrical instincts led him along a path half-way between The Globe and the music hall, a path at the frontier between send-up and the sublime, one that we can see him following first of all in the completely surefooted language of his masterpieces, and then in the shakier conventions of his later, more experimental works.

So perhaps it is wrong to make too fine a distinction between O'Casey and the other, very different Irish playwrights mentioned at the beginning. It is O'Casey's language, after all, that creates the illusion that he has drawn no line between the stage and the street. But just as surely as J. M. Synge, his fellow genius in the early history of the Abbey Theatre, composed a poetic idiom based upon the spoken idiom of the countryside, and wrote with a deliberation that would have pleased Ben Jonson, so too O'Casey rose to the poetic occasion by other, less deliberate methods and wrote with an unscholastic extravagance that would have pleased Jonson's rival. In fact, by characterizing himself later in life as 'a green crow', O'Casey, in his half-serious, half-send-uppy way, may have been identifying himself with that 'upstart crow' from Stratford-upon-Avon whom the Elizabethan theatrical establishment had long ago patronized as 'the only shake-scene in the country'. The history of O'Casey's ongoing popularity in Ireland, the adequacy of his tragi-comedy to the recent violent politics in the north and the recent postnationalist bewilderments in the Republic, the continuities between his work and the work of many of the new urban novelists, dramatists and film-makers who have made their international mark in the past decade – all this makes him as much if not more of an Irish shake-scene at the end of the century as he was when he wandered in off the street in the beginning.

Seamus Heaney
October 1997

JUNO AND THE PAYCOCK

A TRAGEDY IN THREE ACTS

Characters

'Captain' Jack Boyle
Juno Boyle, his wife
Johnny Boyle ⎤ their children
Mary Boyle ⎦
'Joxer' Daly
Mrs Maisie Madigan
'Needle' Nugent, a tailor
Mrs Tancred
Jerry Devine
Charles Bentham, a schoolteacher
An Irregular Mobilizer
Two Irregulars
A Coal-block Vendor
A Sewing-machine Man
Two Furniture-removal Men
Two Neighbours

Residents in the Tenement

Period of the play, 1922.

Act One

*The living-room of a two-room tenancy occupied by the
Boyle family in a tenement house in Dublin. Left, a door
leading to another part of the house; left of door a
window looking into the street; at back a dresser; farther
to right at back, a window looking into the back of the
house. Between the window and the dresser is a picture of
the Virgin; below the picture, on a bracket, is a crimson
bowl in which a floating votive light is burning. Farther to
the right is a small bed partly concealed by cretonne
hangings strung on a twine. To the right is the fireplace;
near the fireplace is a door leading to the other room.
Beside the fireplace is a box containing coal. On the
mantelshelf is an alarm clock lying on its face. In a corner
near the window looking into the back is a galvanized
bath. A table and some chairs. On the table are breakfast
things for one. A teapot is on the hob and a frying-pan
stands inside the fender. There are a few books on the
dresser and one on the table. Leaning against the dresser is
a long-handled shovel – the kind invariably used by
labourers when turning concrete or mixing mortar. Johnny
Boyle is sitting crouched beside the fire. Mary with her
jumper off – it is lying on the back of a chair – is arranging
her hair before a tiny mirror perched on the table. Beside
the mirror is stretched out the morning paper, which she
looks at when she isn't gazing into the mirror. She is a
well-made and good-looking girl of twenty-two. Two
forces are working in her mind – one, through the
circumstances of her life, pulling her back; the other,
through the influence of books she has read, pushing her
forward. The opposing forces are apparent in her speech*

*and her manners, both of which are degraded by her
environment, and improved by her acquaintance – slight
though it be – with literature. The time is early forenoon.*

Mary (*looking at the paper*) On a little bye-road, out
beyant Finglas, he was found.

> *Mrs Boyle enters by door on right; she has been
> shopping and carries a small parcel in her hand. She is
> forty-five years of age, and twenty years ago she must
> have been a pretty woman; but her face has now
> assumed that look which ultimately settles down upon
> the faces of the women of the working-class; a look of
> listless monotony and harassed anxiety, blending with
> an expression of mechanical resistance. Were
> circumstances favourable, she would probably be a
> handsome, active and clever woman.*

Mrs Boyle Isn't he come in yet?

Mary No, mother.

Mrs Boyle Oh, he'll come in when he likes; struttin' about
the town like a paycock with Joxer, I suppose. I hear all
about Mrs Tancred's son is in this mornin's paper.

Mary The full details are in it this mornin'; seven wounds
he had – one entherin' the neck, with an exit wound
beneath the left shoulder-blade; another in the left breast
penethratin' the heart, an' . . .

Johnny (*springing up from the fire*) Oh, quit that readin',
for God's sake! Are yous losin' all your feelin's? It'll soon
be that none of you'll read anythin' that's not about
butcherin'! (*He goes quickly into the room on left.*)

Mary He's gettin' very sensitive, all of a sudden!

Mrs Boyle I'll read it myself, Mary, by an' by, when I
come home. Everybody's sayin' that he was a Die-hard –

thanks be to God that Johnny had nothin' to do with him this long time . . . (*Opening the parcel and taking out some sausages, which she places on a plate.*) Ah, then, if that father o' yours doesn't come in soon for his breakfast, he may go without any; I'll not wait much longer for him.

Mary Can't you let him get it himself when he comes in?

Mrs Boyle Yes, an' let him bring in Joxer Daly along with him? Ay, that's what he'd like, an' that's what he's waitin' for – till he thinks I'm gone to work, an' then sail in with the boul' Joxer, to burn all the coal an' dhrink all the tea in the place, to show them what a good Samaritan he is! But I'll stop here till he comes in, if I have to wait till tomorrow mornin'.

Voice of Johnny (*inside*) Mother!

Mrs Boyle Yis?

Voice of Johnny Bring us in a dhrink o' wather.

Mrs Boyle Bring in that fella a dhrink o' wather, for God's sake, Mary.

Mary Isn't he big an' able enough to come out an' get it himself?

Mrs Boyle If you weren't well yourself you'd like somebody to bring you in a dhrink o' wather. (*She brings in drink and returns.*) Isn't it terrible to have to be waitin' this way! You'd think he was bringin' twenty poun's a week into the house the way he's going on. He wore out the Health Insurance long ago, he's afther wearin' out the unemployment dole, an', now, he's thryin' to wear out me! An' constantly singin', no less, when he ought always to be on his knees offerin' up a Novena for a job!

Mary (*tying a ribbon fillet-wise around her head*) I don't

7

like this ribbon, ma; I think I'll wear the green – it looks betther than the blue.

Mrs Boyle Ah, wear whatever ribbon you like, girl, only don't be botherin' me. I don't know what a girl on strike wants to be wearin' a ribbon round her head for, or silk stockins on her legs either; it's wearin' them things that make the employers think they're givin' yous too much money.

Mary The hour is past now when we'll ask the employers' permission to wear what we like.

Mrs Boyle I don't know why you wanted to walk out for Jennie Claffey; up to this you never had a good word for her.

Mary What's the use of belongin' to a Trades Union if you won't stand up for your principles? Why did they sack her? It was a clear case of victimization. We couldn't let her walk the streets, could we?

Mrs Boyle No, of course yous couldn't – yous wanted to keep her company. Wan victim wasn't enough. When the employers sacrifice wan victim, the Trades Unions go wan betther be sacrificin' a hundred.

Mary It doesn't matther what you say, ma – a principle's a principle.

Mrs Boyle Yis; an' when I go into oul' Murphy's tomorrow, an' he gets to know that, instead o' payin' all, I'm goin' to borry more, what'll he say when I tell him a principle's a principle? What'll we do if he refuses to give us any more on tick?

Mary He daren't refuse – if he does, can't you tell him he's paid?

Mrs Boyle It's lookin' as if he was paid, whether he refuses or no.

*Johnny appears at the door on left. He can be plainly
seen now; he is a thin, delicate fellow, something
younger than Mary. He has evidently gone through a
rough time. His face is pale and drawn; there is a
tremulous look of indefinite fear in his eyes. The left
sleeve of his coat is empty, and he walks with a slight
halt.*

Johnny I was lyin' down; I thought yous were gone. Oul'
Simon Mackay is thrampin' about like a horse over me
head, an' I can't sleep with him – they're like thunder-claps
in me brain! The curse o' – God forgive me for goin' to
curse!

Mrs Boyle There, now; go back an' lie down again, an' I'll
bring you in a nice cup o' tay.

Johnny Tay, tay, tay! You're always thinkin' o' tay. If a
man was dyin', you'd thry to make him swally a cup o'
tay! (*He goes back.*)

Mrs Boyle I don't know what's goin' to be done with him.
The bullet he got in the hip in Easter Week was bad
enough, but the bomb that shatthered his arm in the fight
in O'Connell Street put the finishin' touch on him. I knew
he was makin' a fool of himself. God knows I went down
on me bended knees to him not to go agen the Free State.

Mary He stuck to his principles, an', no matther how you
may argue, ma, a principle's a principle.

Voice of Johnny Is Mary goin' to stay here?

Mary No, I'm not goin' to stay here; you can't expect me
to be always at your beck an' call, can you?

Voice of Johnny I won't stop here be meself!

Mrs Boyle Amn't I nicely handicapped with the whole o'
yous! I don't know what any o' yous ud do without your

ma. (*To Johnny*) Your father'll be here in a minute, an' if you want anythin', he'll get it for you.

Johnny I hate assin' him for anythin' . . . He hates to be assed to stir . . . Is the light lightin' before the picture o' the Virgin?

Mrs Boyle Yis, yis! The wan inside to St Anthony isn't enough, but he must have another wan to the Virgin here!

Jerry Devine enters hastily. He is about twenty-five, well set, active and earnest. He is a type, becoming very common now in the Labour Movement, of a mind knowing enough to make the mass of his associates, who know less, a power, and too little to broaden that power for the benefit of all. Mary seizes her jumper and runs hastily into room left.

Jerry (*breathless*) Where's the Captain, Mrs Boyle, where's the Captain?

Mrs Boyle You may well ass a body that: he's wherever Joxer Daly is – dhrinkin' in some snug or another.

Jerry Father Farrell is just afther stoppin' to tell me to run up an' get him to go to the new job that's goin' on in Rathmines; his cousin is foreman o' the job, an' Father Farrell was speakin' to him about poor Johnny an' his father bein' idle so long, an' the foreman told Father Farrell to send the Captain up an' he'd give him a start – I wondher where I'd find him?

Mrs Boyle You'll find he's ayther in Ryan's or Foley's.

Jerry I'll run round to Ryan's – I know it's a great house o' Joxer's. (*He rushes out.*)

Mrs Boyle (*piteously*) There now, he'll miss that job, or I know for what! If he gets win' o' the word, he'll not come back till evenin', so that it'll be too late. There'll never be any good got out o' him so long as he goes with that shouldher-shruggin' Joxer. I killin' meself workin', an' he sthruttin' about from mornin' till night like a paycock!

The steps of two persons are heard coming up a flight of stairs. They are the footsteps of Captain Boyle and Joxer. Captain Boyle is singing in a deep, sonorous, self-honouring voice.

The Captain Sweet Spirit, hear me prayer! Hear . . . oh . . . hear . . . me prayer . . . hear, oh, hear . . . Oh, he . . . ar . . . oh, he. . . ar . . . me . . . pray . . . er!

Joxer (*outside*) Ah, that's a darlin' song, a daaarlin' song!

Mrs Boyle (*viciously*) Sweet spirit hear his prayer! Ah, then, I'll take me solemn affeydavey, it's not for a job he's prayin'!

She sits down on the bed so that the cretonne hangings hide her from the view of those entering.

The Captain comes in slowly. He is a man of about sixty; stout, grey-haired and stocky. His neck is short, and his head looks like a stone ball that one sometimes sees on top of a gate-post. His cheeks, reddish-purple, are puffed out, as if he were always repressing an almost irrepressible ejaculation. On his upper lip is a crisp, tightly cropped moustache; he carries himself with the upper part of his body slightly thrown back, and his stomach slightly thrust forward. His walk is a slow, consequential strut. His clothes are dingy, and he wears a faded seaman's-cap with a glazed peak.

Boyle (*to Joxer, who is still outside*) Come on, come on in, Joxer; she's gone out long ago, man. If there's nothing else to be got, we'll furrage out a cup o' tay, anyway. It's the only bit I get in comfort when she's away. 'Tisn't Juno should be her pet name at all, but Deirdre of the Sorras, for she's always grousin'.

*Joxer steps cautiously into the room. He may be
younger than the Captain but he looks a lot older. His
face is like a bundle of crinkled paper; his eyes have a
cunning twinkle; he is spare and loosely built; he has a
habit of constantly shrugging his shoulders with a
peculiar twitching movement, meant to be ingratiating.
His face is invariably ornamented with a grin.*

Joxer It's a terrible thing to be tied to a woman that's
always grousin'. I don't know how you stick it – it ud put
years on me. It's a good job she has to be so ofen away, for
(*with a shrug*) when the cat's away, the mice can play!

Boyle (*with a commanding and complacent gesture*) Pull
over to the fire, Joxer, an' we'll have a cup o' tay in a
minute.

Joxer Ah, a cup o' tay's a darlin' thing, a daaarlin' thing –
the cup that cheers but doesn't . . .

*Joxer's rhapsody is cut short by the sight of Juno
coming forward and confronting the two cronies. Both
are stupefied.*

Mrs Boyle (*with sweet irony – poking the fire, and turning
her head to glare at Joxer*) Pull over to the fire, Joxer Daly,
an' we'll have a cup o' tay in a minute! Are you sure, now,
you wouldn't like an egg?

Joxer I can't stop, Mrs Boyle; I'm in a desperate hurry, a
desperate hurry.

Mrs Boyle Pull over to the fire, Joxer Daly; people is
always far more comfortabler here than they are in their
own place.

*Joxer makes hastily for the door. Boyle stirs to follow
him; thinks of something to relieve the situation – stops.*

Boyle (*suddenly*) Joxer!

Joxer (*at door ready to bolt*) Yis?

Boyle You know the foreman o' that job that's goin' on down in Killesther, don't you, Joxer?

Joxer (*puzzled*) Foreman – Killesther?

Boyle (*with a meaning look*) He's a butty o' yours, isn't he?

Joxer (*the truth dawning on him*) The foreman at Killesther – oh yis, yis. He's an oul' butty o' mine – oh, he's a darlin' man, a daarlin' man.

Boyle Oh, then, it's a sure thing. It's a pity we didn't go down at breakfast first thing this mornin' – we might ha' been working now; but you didn't know it then.

Joxer (*with a shrug*) It's betther late than never.

Boyle It's nearly time we got a start, anyhow; I'm fed up knockin' round, doin' nothin'. He promised you – gave you the straight tip?

Joxer Yis. 'Come down on the blow o' dinner,' says he, 'an' I'll start you, an' any friend you like to brin' with you.' 'Ah,' says I, 'you're a darlin' man, a daarlin' man.'

Boyle Well, it couldn't come at a betther time – we're a long time waitin' for it.

Joxer Indeed we were; but it's a long lane that has no turnin'.

Boyle The blow up for dinner is at one – wait till I see what time it 'tis. (*He goes over to the mantelpiece, and gingerly lifts the clock.*)

Mrs Boyle Min' now, how you go on fiddlin' with that clock – you know the least little thing sets it asthray.

Boyle The job couldn't come at a betther time; I'm feelin' in great fettle, Joxer. I'd hardly believe I ever had a pain in me legs, an' last week I was nearly crippled with them.

Joxer That's betther an' betther; ah, God never shut wan door but He opened another!

Boyle It's only eleven o'clock; we've lashins o' time. I'll slip on me oul' moleskins afther breakfast, an' we can saunther down at our ayse. (*Putting his hand on the shovel.*) I think, Joxer, we'd betther bring our shovels?

Joxer Yis, Captain, yis; it's betther to go fully prepared an' ready for all eventualities. You bring your long-tailed shovel, an' I'll bring me navvy. We mighten' want them, an', then agen, we might: for want of a nail the shoe was lost, for want of a shoe the horse was lost, an' for want of a horse the man was lost – aw, that's a darlin' proverb, a daarlin' . . .

As Joxer is finishing his sentence, Mrs Boyle approaches the door and Joxer retreats hurriedly. She shuts the door with a bang.

Boyle (*suggestively*) We won't be long pullin' ourselves together agen when I'm working for a few weeks.

Mrs Boyle takes no notice.

The foreman on the job is an oul' butty o' Joxer's; I have an idea that I know him meself. (*Silence.*) . . . There's a button off the back o' me moleskin trousers . . . . If you leave out a needle an' thread I'll sew it on meself . . . . Thanks be to God, the pains in me legs is gone, anyhow!

Mrs Boyle (*with a burst*) Look here, Mr Jacky Boyle, them yarns won't go down with Juno. I know you an' Joxer Daly of an oul' date, an' if you think you're able to come it over me with them fairy tales, you're in the wrong shop.

Boyle (*coughing subduedly to relieve the tenseness of the situation*) U-u-u-ugh!

Mrs Boyle Butty o' Joxer's! Oh, you'll do a lot o' good as long as you continue to be a butty o' Joxer's!

Boyle U-u-u-ugh!

Mrs Boyle Shovel! Ah, then, me boyo, you'd do far more work with a knife an' fork than ever you'll do with a shovel! If there was e'er a genuine job goin' you'd be dh'other way about – not able to lift your arms with the pains in your legs! Your poor wife slavin' to keep the bit in your mouth, an' you gallivantin' about all the day like a paycock!

Boyle It ud be betther for a man to be dead, betther for a man to be dead.

Mrs Boyle (*ignoring the interruption*) Everybody callin' you 'Captain', an' you only wanst on the wather, in an oul' collier from here to Liverpool, when anybody, to listen or look at you, ud take you for a second Christo For Columbus!

Boyle Are you never goin' to give us a rest?

Mrs Boyle Oh, you're never tired o' lookin' for a rest.

Boyle D'ye want to dhrive me out o' the house?

Mrs Boyle It ud be easier to dhrive you out o' the house than to dhrive you into a job. Here, sit down an' take your breakfast – it may be the last you'll get, for I don't know where the next is goin' to come from.

Boyle If I get this job we'll be all right.

Mrs Boyle Did ye see Jerry Devine?

Boyle (*testily*) No, I didn't see him.

Mrs Boyle No, but you seen Joxer. Well, he was here lookin' for you.

Boyle Well, let him look!

Mrs Boyle Oh, indeed, he may well look, for it ud be hard for him to see you, an' you stuck in Ryan's snug.

Boyle I wasn't in Ryan's snug – I don't go into Ryan's.

Mrs Boyle Oh, is there a mad dog there? Well, if you weren't in Ryan's you were in Foley's.

Boyle I'm telling you for the last three weeks I haven't tasted a dhrop of intoxicatin' liquor. I wasn't in ayther wan snug or dh'other – I could swear that on a prayer-book – I'm as innocent as the child unborn!

Mrs Boyle Well, if you'd been in for your breakfast you'd ha' seen him.

Boyle (*suspiciously*) What does he want me for?

Mrs Boyle He'll be back any minute an' then you'll soon know.

Boyle I'll dhrop out an' see if I can meet him.

Mrs Boyle You'll sit down an' take your breakfast, an' let me go to me work, for I'm an hour late already waitin' for you.

Boyle You needn't ha' waited, for I'll take no breakfast – I've a little spirit left in me still!

Mrs Boyle Are you goin' to have your breakfast – yes or no?

Boyle (*too proud to yield*) I'll have no breakfast – yous can keep your breakfast. (*Plaintively*) I'll knock out a bit somewhere, never fear.

Mrs Boyle Nobody's goin' to coax you – don't think that.

(*She vigorously replaces the pan and the sausages in the press.*)

Boyle I've a little spirit left in me still.

Jerry Devine enters hastily.

Jerry Oh, here you are at last! I've been searchin' for you everywhere. The foreman in Foley's told me you hadn't left the snug with Joxer ten minutes before I went in.

Mrs Boyle An' he swearin' on the holy prayer-book that he wasn't in no snug!

Boyle (*to Jerry*) What business is it o' yours whether I was in a snug or no? What do you want to be gallopin' about afther me for? Is a man not to be allowed to leave his house for a minute without havin' a pack o' spies, pimps an' informers cantherin' at his heels?

Jerry Oh, you're takin' a wrong view of it, Mr Boyle; I simply was anxious to do you a good turn. I have a message for you from Father Farrell: he says that if you go to the job that's on in Rathmines, an' ask for Foreman Managan, you'll get a start.

Boyle That's all right, but I don't want the motions of me body to be watched the way an asthronomer ud watch a star. If you're folleyin' Mary aself, you've no pereeogative to be folleyin' me. (*Suddenly catching his thigh*) U-ugh, I'm afther gettin' a terrible twinge in me right leg!

Mrs Boyle Oh, it won't be very long now till it travels into your left wan. It's miraculous that whenever he scents a job in front of him, his legs begin to fail him! Then, me bucko, if you lose this chance, you may go an' furrage for yourself!

Jerry This job'll last for some time too, Captain, an' as soon as the foundations are in, it'll be cushy enough.

Boyle Won't it be a climbin' job? How d'ye expect me to be able to go up a ladder with these legs? An', if I get up aself, how am I goin' to get down agen?

Mrs Boyle (*viciously*) Get wan o' the labourers to carry you down in a hod! You can't climb a laddher, but you can skip like a goat into a snug!

Jerry I wouldn't let myself be let down that easy, Mr Boyle; a little exercise, now, might do you all the good in the world.

Boyle It's a docthor you should have been, Devine – maybe you know more about the pains in me legs than meself that has them?

Jerry (*irritated*) Oh, I know nothin' about the pains in your legs; I've brought the message that Father Farrell gave me, an' that's all I can do.

Mrs Boyle Here, sit down an' take your breakfast, an' go an' get ready; an' don't be actin' as if you couldn't pull a wing out of a dead bee.

Boyle I want no breakfast, I tell you; it ud choke me afther all that's been said. I've a little spirit left in me still.

Mrs Boyle Well, let's see your spirit, then, an' go in at wanst an' put on your moleskin trousers!

Boyle (*moving towards the door on left*) It ud be betther for a man to be dead! U-ugh! There's another twinge in me other leg! Nobody but meself knows the sufferin' I'm goin' through with the pains in these legs o' mine!

He goes into the room on left as Mary comes out with her hat in her hand.

Mrs Boyle I'll have to push off now, for I'm terrible late already, but I was determined to stay an' hunt that Joxer this time. (*She goes off.*)

Jerry Are you going out, Mary?

Mary It looks like it when I'm putting on my hat, doesn't it?

Jerry The bitther word agen, Mary.

Mary You won't allow me to be friendly with you; if I thry, you deliberately misundherstand it.

Jerry I didn't always misundherstand it; you were often delighted to have the arms of Jerry around you.

Mary If you go on talkin' like this, Jerry Devine, you'll make me hate you!

Jerry Well, let it be either a weddin' or a wake! Listen, Mary, I'm standin' for the Secretaryship of our Union. There's only one opposin' me; I'm popular with all the men, an' a good speaker – all are sayin' that I'll get elected.

Mary Well?

Jerry The job's worth three hundred an' fifty pounds a year, Mary. You an' I could live nice an' cosily on that; it would lift you out o' this place an' . . .

Mary I haven't time to listen to you now – I have to go.

She is going out, when Jerry bars the way.

Jerry (*appealingly*) Mary, what's come over you with me for the last few weeks? You hardly speak to me, an' then only a word with a face o' bittherness on it. Have you forgotten, Mary, all the happy evenins that were as sweet as the scented hawthorn that sheltered the sides o' the road as we sauntered through the country?

Mary That's all over now. When you get your new job, Jerry, you won't be long findin' a girl far betther than I am for your sweetheart.

Jerry Never, never, Mary! No matther what happens, you'll always be the same to me.

Mary I must be off; please let me go, Jerry.

Jerry I'll go a bit o' the way with you.

Mary You needn't, thanks; I want to be by meself.

Jerry (*catching her arm*) You're goin' to meet another fella; you've clicked with someone else, me lady!

Mary That's no concern o' yours, Jerry Devine; let me go!

Jerry I saw yous comin' out o' the Cornflower Dance Class, an' you hangin' on his arm – a thin, lanky strip of a Micky Dazzler, with a walkin'-stick an' gloves!

Voice of Johnny (*loudly*) What are you doin' there – pullin' about everything!

Voice of Boyle (*loudly and viciously*) I'm puttin' on me moleskin trousers!

Mary You're hurtin' me arm! Let me go, or I'll scream, an' then you'll have the oul' fella out on top of us!

Jerry Don't be so hard on a fella, Mary, don't be so hard.

Boyle (*appearing at the door*) What's the meanin' of all this hillabaloo?

Mary Let me go, let me go!

Boyle D'ye hear me – what's all this hillabaloo about?

Jerry (*plaintively*) Will you not give us one kind word, one kind word, Mary?

Boyle D'ye hear me talkin' to yous? What's all this hillabaloo for?

Jerry Let me kiss your hand, your little, tiny, white hand!

Boyle Your little, tiny, white hand – are you takin' leave o' your senses, man?

Mary breaks away and rushes out.

This is nice goins on in front of her father!

Jerry Ah, dhry up, for God's sake! (*He follows Mary.*)

Boyle Chiselurs don't care a damn now about their parents, they're bringin' their fathers' grey hairs down with sorra to the grave, an' laughin' at it, laughin' at it. Ah, I suppose it's just the same everywhere – the whole worl's in a state o' chassis! (*He sits by the fire.*) Breakfast! Well, they can keep their breakfast for me. Not if they were down on their bended knees would I take it – I'll show them I've a little spirit left in me still! (*He goes over to the press, takes out a plate and looks at it.*) Sassige! Well, let her keep her sassige. (*He returns to the fire, takes up the teapot and gives it a gentle shake.*) The tea's wet right enough. (*A pause; he rises, goes to the press, takes out the sausage, puts it on the pan, and puts both on the fire. He attends the sausage with a fork. Singing*)

> When the robins nest agen,
> And the flowers are in bloom,
> When the Springtime's sunny smile seems to banish all
> sorrow an' gloom;
> Then me bonny blue-ey'd lad, if me heart be true till
> then –
> He's promised he'll come back to me,
> When the robins nest agen!

(*He lifts his head at the high note, and then drops his eyes to the pan. Singing*)

When the . . .

Steps are heard approaching; he whips the pan off the fire and puts it under the bed, then sits down at the fire.

The door opens and a bearded man looks in.

Sewing-machine Man You don't happen to want a sewin' machine?

Boyle (*furiously*) No, I don't want e'er a sewin' machine! (*He returns the pan to the fire, and commences to sing again. Singing*)

> When the robins nest agen,
> And the flowers they are in bloom,
> He's . . .

A thundering knock is heard at the street door.

There's a terrible tatheraraa – that's a stranger – that's nobody belongin' to the house.

Another loud knock.

Joxer (*sticking his head in at the door*) Did ye hear them tatherarahs?

Boyle Well, Joxer, I'm not deaf.

Johnny (*appearing in his shirt and trousers at the door on left; his face is anxious and his voice is tremulous*) Who's that at the door; who's that at the door? Who gave that knock – d'ye yous hear me – are yous deaf or dhrunk or what?

Boyle (*to Johnny*) How the hell do I know who 'tis? Joxer, stick your head out o' the window an' see.

Joxer An' mebbe get a bullet in the kisser? Ah, none o' them thricks for Joxer! It's betther to be a coward than a corpse!

Boyle (*looking cautiously out of the window*) It's a fella in a thrench coat.

Johnny Holy Mary, Mother o' God, I . . .

Boyle He's goin' away – he must ha' got tired knockin'.

Johnny returns to the room on left.

Sit down an' have a cup o' tay, Joxer.

Joxer I'm afraid the missus ud pop in on us agen before we'd know where we are. Somethin's tellin' me to go at wanst.

Boyle Don't be superstitious, man; we're Dublin men, an' not boyos that's only afther comin' up from the bog o' Allen – though if she did come in, right enough, we'd be caught like rats in a thrap.

Joxer An' you know the sort she is – she wouldn't listen to reason – an' wanse bitten twice shy.

Boyle (*going over to the window at back*) If the worst came to the worst, you could dart out here, Joxer; it's only a dhrop of a few feet to the roof of the return room, an' the first minute she goes into dh'other room I'll give you the bend, an' you can slip in an' away.

Joxer (*yielding to the temptation*) Ah, I won't stop very long anyhow. (*Picking up a book from the table*) Whose is the buk?

Boyle Aw, one o' Mary's; she's always readin' lately – nothin' but thrash, too. There's one I was lookin' at dh'other day: three stories, *The Doll's House*, *Ghosts*, an' *The Wild Duck* – buks only fit for chiselurs!

Joxer Didja ever rade *Elizabeth, or Th' Exile o' Sibayria*? . . . Ah, it's a darlin' story, a daarlin' story!

Boyle You eat your sassige, an' never min' *Th' Exile o' Sibayria*.

Both sit down; Boyle fills out tea, pours gravy on Joxer's plate, and keeps the sausage for himself.

23

Joxer What are you wearin' your moleskin trousers for?

Boxer I have to go to a job, Joxer. Just afther you'd gone, Devine kem runnin' in to tell us that Father Farrell said if I went down to the job that's goin' on in Rathmines I'd get a start.

Joxer Be the holy, that's good news!

Boyle How is it good news? I wondher if you were in my condition, would you call it good news?

Joxer I thought . . .

Boyle You thought! You think too sudden sometimes, Joxer. D'ye know, I'm hardly able to crawl with the pains in me legs!

Joxer Yis, yis; I forgot the pains in your legs. I know you can do nothin' while they're at you.

Boyle You forgot; I don't think any of yous realize the state I'm in with the pains in me legs. What ud happen if I had to carry a bag o' cement?

Joxer Ah, any man havin' the like of them pains id be down an' out, down an' out.

Boyle I wouldn't mind if he had said it to meself; but, no, oh no, he rushes in an' shouts it out in front o' Juno, an' you know what Juno is, Joxer. We all know Devine knows a little more than the rest of us, but he doesn't act as if he did; he's a good boy, sober, able to talk an' all that, but still . . .

Joxer Oh ay; able to argufy, but still . . .

Boyle If he's runnin' afther Mary, aself, he's not goin' to be runnin' afther me. Captain Boyle's able to take care of himself. Afther all, I'm not gettin' brought up on Virol. I never heard him usin' a curse; I don't believe he was ever dhrunk in his life – sure he's not like a Christian at all!

Joxer You're afther takin' the word out o' me mouth – afther all, a Christian's natural, but he's unnatural.

Boyle His oul' fella was just the same – a Wicklow man.

Joxer A Wicklow man! That explains the whole thing. I've met many a Wicklow man in me time, but I never met wan that was any good.

Boyle 'Father Farrell,' says he, 'sent me down to tell you.' Father Farrell! . . . D'ye know Joxer, I never like to be beholden to any o' the clergy.

Joxer It's dangerous, right enough.

Boyle If they do anything for you, they'd want you to be livin' in the Chapel . . . . I'm goin' to tell you somethin', Joxer, that I wouldn't tell to anybody else – the clergy always had too much power over the people in this unfortunate country.

Joxer You could sing that if you had an air to it!

Boyle (*becoming enthusiastic*) Didn't they prevent the people in ' '47' from seizin' the corn, an' they starvin'; didn't they down Parnell; didn't they say that hell wasn't hot enough nor eternity long enough to punish the Fenians? We don't forget, we don't forget them things, Joxer. If they've taken everything else from us, Joxer, they've left us our memory.

Joxer (*emotionally*) For mem'ry's the only friend that grief can call its own, that grief . . . can . . . call . . . its own!

Boyle Father Farrell's beginnin' to take a great intherest in Captain Boyle; because of what Johnny did for his country, says he to me wan day. It's a curious way to reward Johnny be makin' his poor oul' father work. But that's what the clergy want, Joxer – work, work, work for

me an' you; havin' us mulin' from mornin' till night, so
that they may be in bChapter fettle when they come hoppin'
round for their dues! Job! Well, let him give his job to wan
of his hymn-singin', prayer-spoutin', craw-thumpin'
Confraternity men!

*The voice of a coal-block vendor is heard chanting in
the street.*

Voice of Coal Vendor Blocks . . . coal-blocks! Blocks . . .
coal-blocks!

Joxer God be with the young days when you were steppin'
the deck of a manly ship, with the win' blowin' a hurricane
through the masts, an' the only sound you'd hear was, 'Port
your helm!' an' the only answer, 'Port it is, sir!'

Boyle Them was days, Joxer, them was days. Nothin' was
too hot or too heavy for me then. Sailin' from the Gulf o'
Mexico to the Antanartic Ocean. I seen things, I seen
things, Joxer, that no mortal man should speak about that
knows his Catechism. Ofen, an' ofen, when I was fixed to
the wheel with a marlin-spike, an' the wins blowin' fierce
an' the waves lashin' an' lashin', till you'd think every
minute was goin' to be your last, an' it blowed, an' blowed
– blew is the right word, Joxer, but blowed is what the
sailors use . . .

Joxer Aw, it's a darlin' word, a daarlin' word.

Boyle An', as it blowed an' blowed, I ofen looked up at
the sky an' assed meself the question – what is the stars,
what is the stars?

Voice of Coal Vendor Any blocks, coal-blocks; blocks,
coal-blocks!

Joxer Ah, that's the question, that's the question – what is
the stars?

Boyle An' then, I'd have another look, an' I'd ass meself – what is the moon?

Joxer Ah, that's the question – what is the moon, what is the moon?

Rapid steps are heard coming towards the door. Boyle makes desperate efforts to hide everything; Joxer rushes to the window in a frantic effort to get out; Boyle begins to innocently lilt 'Oh, me darlin' Jennie, I will be thrue to thee', when the door is opened, and the black face of the Coal Vendor appears.

Coal Vendor D'yes want any blocks?

Boyle (*with a roar*) No, we don't want any blocks!

Joxer (*coming back with a sigh of relief*) That's afther puttin' the heart across me – I could ha' sworn it was Juno. I'd betther be goin', Captain; you couldn't tell the minute Juno'd hop in on us.

Boyle Let her hop in; we may as well have it out first as at last. I've made up me mind – I'm not goin' to do only what she damn well likes.

Joxer Them sentiments does you credit, Captain; I don't like to say anything as between man an' wife, but I say as a butty, as a butty, Captain, that you've stuck it too long, an' that it's about time you showed a little spunk.

How can a man die betther than facin' fearful odds,
For th' ashes of his fathers an' the temples of his gods?

Boyle She has her rights – there's no one denyin' it, but haven't I me rights too?

Joxer Of course you have – the sacred rights o' man!

Boyle Today, Joxer, there's goin' to be issued a proclamation be me, establishin' an independent Republic, an' Juno'll have to take an oath of allegiance.

Joxer Be firm, be firm, Captain; the first few minutes'll be the worst: – if you gently touch a nettle it'll sting you for your pains; grasp it like a lad of mettle, an' as soft as silk remains!

Voice of Juno (*outside*) Can't stop, Mrs Madigan – I haven't a minute!

Joxer (*flying out of the window*) Holy God, here she is!

Boyle (*packing the things away with a rush in the press*) I knew that fella ud stop till she was in on top of us!

> *He sits down by the fire. Juno enters hastily; she is flurried and excited.*

Juno Oh, you're in – you must have been only afther comin' in?

Boyle No, I never went out.

Juno It's curious, then, you never heard the knockin'. (*She puts her coat and hat on bed.*)

Boyle Knockin'? Of course I heard the knockin'.

Juno An' why didn't you open the door, then? I suppose you were so busy with Joxer that you hadn't time.

Boyle I haven't seen Joxer since I seen him before. Joxer! What ud bring Joxer here?

Juno D'ye mean to tell me that the pair of yous wasn't collogin' together here when me back was turned?

Boyle What ud we be collogin' together about? I have somethin' else to think of besides collogin' with Joxer. I can swear on all the holy prayer-books . . .

Mrs Boyle That you weren't in no snug! Go on in at wanst now, an' take off that moleskin trousers o' yours,

an' put on a collar an' tie to smarten yourself up a bit.
There's a visitor comin' with Mary in a minute, an' he has
great news for you.

Boyle A job, I suppose; let us get wan first before we start
lookin' for another.

Mrs Boyle That's the thing that's able to put the win' up
you. Well, it's no job, but news that'll give you the chance
o' your life.

Boyle What's all the mystery about?

Mrs Boyle G'win an' take off the moleskin trousers when
you're told!

> *Boyle goes into room on left. Mrs Boyle tidies up the
> room, puts the shovel under the bed, and goes to the
> press.*

Oh, God bless us, looka the way everything's thrun about!
Oh, Joxer was here, Joxer was here!

> *Mary enters with Charlie Bentham; he is a young man
> of twenty-five, tall, good-looking, with a very high
> opinion of himself generally. He is dressed in a brown
> coat, brown knee-breeches, grey stockings, a brown
> sweater, with a deep blue tie; he carries gloves and a
> walking-stick.*

(*Fussing round*) Come in, Mr Bentham; sit down, Mr
Bentham, in this chair; it's more comfortabler than that,
Mr Bentham. Himself'll be here in a minute; he's just
takin' off his trousers.

Mary Mother!

Bentham Please don't put yourself to any trouble, Mrs
Boyle – I'm quite all right here, thank you.

Mrs Boyle An' to think of you knowin' Mary, an' she

knowin' the news you had for us, an' wouldn't let on; but it's all the more welcomer now, for we were on our last lap!

Voice of Johnny (*inside*) What are you kickin' up all the racket for?

Boyle (*roughly*) I'm takin' off me moleskin trousers!

Johnny Can't you do it, then, without lettin' th' whole house know you're takin off your trousers? What d'ye want puttin' them on an' takin' them off again?

Boyle Will you let me alone, will you let me alone? Am I never goin' to be done thryin' to please th' whole o' yous?

Mrs Boyle (*to Bentham*) You must excuse th' state o' th' place, Mr Bentham; th' minute I turn me back that man o' mine always makes a litther o' th' place, a litther' o' th' place.

Bentham Don't worry, Mrs Boyle; it's all right, I assure . . .

Boyle (*inside*) Where's me braces; where in th' name o' God did I leave me braces? . . . Ay, did you see where I put me braces?

Johnny (*inside, calling out*) Ma, will you come in here an' take da away ou' o' this or he'll dhrive me mad.

Mrs Boyle (*going towards the door*) Dear, dear, dear, that man'll be lookin' for somethin' on th' day o' Judgement. (*Looking into room and calling to Boyle*) Look at your braces, man, hangin' round your neck!

Boyle (*inside*) Aw, Holy God!

Mrs Boyle (*calling*) Johnny, Johnny, come out here for a minute.

Johnny Ah, leave Johnny alone, an' don't be annoyin' him!

Mrs Boyle Come on, Johnny, till I inthroduce you to Mr Bentham. (*to Bentham*) My son, Mr Bentham; he's afther goin' through the mill. He was only a chiselur of a Boy Scout in Easter Week, when he got hit in the hip; and his arm was blew off in the fight in O'Connell Street. (*Johnny comes in.*) Here he is, Mr Bentham; Mr Bentham, Johnny. None can deny he done his bit for Irelan', if that's goin' to do him any good.

Johnny (*boastfully*) I'd do it agen, ma, I'd do it agen; for a principle's a principle.

Mrs Boyle Ah, you lost your best principle, me boy, when you lost your arm; them's the only sort o' principles that's any good to a workin' man.

Johnny Ireland only half free'll never be at peace while she has a son left to pull a trigger.

Mrs Boyle To be sure, to be sure – no bread's a lot betther than half a loaf. (*Calling loudly in to Boyle*) Will you hurry up there?

Boyle enters in his best trousers, which aren't too good, and looks very uncomfortable in his collar and tie.

This is me husband; Mr Boyle, Mr Bentham.

Bentham Ah, very glad to know you, Mr Boyle. How are you?

Boyle Ah, I'm not too well at all; I suffer terrible with pains in me legs. Juno can tell you there what . . .

Mrs Boyle You won't have many pains in your legs when you hear what Mr Bentham has to tell you.

Bentham Juno! What an interesting name! It reminds one of Homer's glorious story of ancient gods and heroes.

Boyle Yis, doesn't it? You see, Juno was born an'

31

christened in June; I met her in June; we were married in
June, an' Johnny was born in June, so wan day I says to
her, 'You should ha' been called Juno,' an' the name stuck
to her ever since.

Mrs Boyle Here, we can talk o' them things agen; let Mr
Bentham say what he has to say now.

Bentham Well, Mr Boyle, I suppose you'll remember a Mr
Ellison of Santry – he's a relative of yours, I think.

Boyle (*viciously*) Is it that prognosticator an' procrastinator! Of course I remember him.

Bentham Well, he's dead, Mr Boyle . . .

Boyle Sorra many'll go into mournin' for him.

Mrs Boyle Wait till you hear what Mr Bentham has to
say, an' then, maybe, you'll change your opinion.

Bentham A week before he died he sent for me to write his
will for him. He told me that there were two only that he
wished to leave his property to: his second cousin, Michael
Finnegan of Santry, and John Boyle, his first cousin, of
Dublin.

Boyle (*excitedly*) Me, is it me, me?

Bentham You, Mr Boyle; I'll read a copy of the will that
I have here with me, which has been duly filed in the
Court of Probate. (*He takes a paper from his pocket and
reads.*)

> *6th February 1922*
> This is the last Will and Testament of William Ellison,
> of Santry, in the County of Dublin. I hereby order and
> wish my property to be sold and divided as follows:
> £20 to the St Vincent de Paul Society.
> £60 for Masses for the repose of my soul (5s. for each
> Mass).

The rest of my property to be divided between my first and second cousins.

I hereby appoint Timothy Buckly, of Santry, and Hugh Brierly, of Coolock, to be my Executors.

> (*Signed*)   WILLIAM ELLISON.
> HUGH BRIERLY.
> TIMOTHY BUCKLY.
> CHARLES BENTHAM, N.T.

Boyle (*eagerly*) An' how much'll be comin' out of it, Mr Bentham?

Bentham The Executors told me that half of the property would be anything between £1,500 and £2,000.

Mary A fortune, father, a fortune!

Johnny We'll be able to get out o' this place now, an' go somewhere we're not known.

Mrs Boyle You won't have to trouble about a job for awhile, Jack.

Boyle (*fervently*) I'll never doubt the goodness o' God agen.

Bentham I congratulate you, Mr Boyle.

They shake hands.

Boyle An' now, Mr Bentham, you'll have to have a wet.

Bentham A wet?

Boyle A wet – a jar – a boul!

Mrs Boyle Jack, you're speakin' to Mr Bentham, an' not to Joxer.

Boyle (*solemnly*) Juno . . . Mary . . . Johnny . . . we'll have to go into mournin' at wanst . . . . I never expected that poor Bill ud die so sudden . . . . Well, we all have to die some day . . . you, Juno, today . . . an' me, maybe, tomorrow . . . . It's sad, but it can't be helped . . . . Requiescat in pace . . . or, usin' our oul' tongue like St Patrick or St Bridget, Guh sayeree jeea ayera!

Mary Oh, father, that's not Rest in Peace; that's God save Ireland.

Boyle U-u-ugh, it's all the same – isn't it a prayer? . . . Juno, I'm done with Joxer; he's nothin' but a prognosticator an' a . . .

Joxer (*climbing angrily through the window and bounding into the room*) You're done with Joxer, are you? Maybe you thought I'd stop on the roof all the night for you! Joxer out on the roof with the win' blowin' through him was nothin' to you an' your friend with the collar an' tie!

Mrs Boyle What in the name o' God brought you out on the roof; what were you doin' there?

Joxer (*ironically*) I was dhreamin' I was standin' on the bridge of a ship, an' she sailin' the Antartic Ocean, an' it blowed, an' blowed, an' I lookin' up at the sky an' sayin', what is the stars, what is the stars?

Mrs Boyle (*opening the door and standing at it*) Here, get ou' o' this, Joxer Daly; I was always thinkin' you had a slate off.

Joxer (*moving to the door*) I have to laugh every time I look at the deep-sea sailor; an' a row on a river ud make him sea-sick!

Boyle Get ou' o' this before I take the law into me own hands!

Joxer (*going out*) Say aw rewaeawr, but not good-bye.

Lookin' for work, an' prayin' to God he won't get it! (*He goes.*)

Mrs Boyle I'm tired tellin' you what Joxer was; maybe now you see yourself the kind he is.

Boyle He'll never blow the froth off a pint o' mine agen, that's a sure thing. Johnny . . . Mary . . . you're to keep yourselves to yourselves for the future. Juno, I'm done with Joxer . . . . I'm a new man from this out . . . (*Clasping Juno's hand, and singing emotionally*)

O, me darlin' Juno, I will be thrue to thee;
Me own, me darlin' Juno, you're all the world to me.

Curtain.

Act Two

*The same, but the furniture is more plentiful, and of a
vulgar nature. A glaringly upholstered armchair and
lounge; cheap pictures and photos everywhere. Every
available spot is ornamented with huge vases filled with
artificial flowers. Crossed festoons of coloured paper chains
stretch from end to end of ceiling. On the table is an old
attaché case. It is about six in the evening, and two days
after the First Act. Boyle, in his shirt-sleeves, is
voluptuously stretched on the sofa; he is smoking a clay
pipe. He is half asleep. A lamp is lighting on the table. After
a few moments' pause the voice of Joxer is heard singing
softly outside at the door – 'Me pipe I'll smoke, as I dhrive
me moke – are you there, Mor . . . ee . . . ar . . . i . . . teee!'*

Boyle (*leaping up, takes a pen in his hand and busies
himself with papers*) Come along, Joxer, me son, come
along.

Joxer (*putting his head in*) Are you be yourself?

Boyle Come on, come on; that doesn't matther; I'm
masther now, an' I'm goin' to remain masther.

Joxer comes in.

Joxer How d'ye feel now, as a man o' money?

Boyle (*solemnly*) It's a responsibility, Joxer, a great
responsibility.

Joxer I suppose 'tis now, though you wouldn't think it.

Boyle Joxer, han' me over that attackey case on the table
there.

36

Joxer hands the case.

Ever since the Will was passed I've run hundhreds o' dockyments through me hans – I tell you, you have to keep your wits about you. (*He busies himself with papers.*)

Joxer Well, I won't disturb you; I'll dhrop in when . . .

Boyle (*hastily*) It's all right, Joxer, this is the last one to be signed today. (*He signs a paper, puts it into the case, which he shuts with a snap, and sits back pompously in the chair.*) Now, Joxer, you want to see me; I'm at your service – what can I do for you, me man?

Joxer I've just dhropped in with the £3:5s. that Mrs Madigan riz on the blankets an' table for you, an' she says you're to be in no hurry payin' it back.

Boyle She won't be long without it; I expect the first cheque for a couple o' hundhred any day. There's the five bob for yourself – go on, take it, man; it'll not be the last you'll get from the Captain. Now an' agen we have our differ, but we're there together all the time.

Joxer Me for you, an' you for me, like the two Musketeers.

Boyle Father Farrell stopped me today an' tole me how glad he was I fell in for the money.

Joxer He'll be stoppin' you ofen enough now; I suppose it was 'Mr' Boyle with him?

Boyle He shuk me be the han' . . .

Joxer (*ironically*) I met with Napper Tandy, an' he shuk me be the han'!

Boyle You're seldom asthray, Joxer, but you're wrong shipped this time. What you're sayin' of Father Farrell is very near to blasfeemey. I don't like any one to talk disrespectful of Father Farrell.

Joxer You're takin' me up wrong, Captain; I wouldn't let a word be said agen Father Farrell – the heart o' the rowl, that's what he is; I always said he was a darlin' man, a daarlin' man.

Boyle Comin' up the stairs who did I meet but that bummer, Nugent. 'I seen you talkin' to Father Farrell,' says he, with a grin on him. 'He'll be folleyin' you,' says he, 'like a Guardian Angel from this out' – all the time the oul' grin on him, Joxer.

Joxer I never seen him yet but he had that oul' grin on him!

Boyle 'Mr Nugent,' says I, 'Father Farrell is a man o' the people, an', as far as I know the History o' me country, the priests was always in the van of the fight for Irelan's freedom.'

Joxer (*fervently*)
  Who was it led the van, Soggart Aroon?
  Since the fight first began, Soggart Aroon?

Boyle 'Who are you tellin'?' says he. 'Didn't they let down the Fenians, an' didn't they do in Parnell? An' now . . .' 'You ought to be ashamed o' yourself,' says I, interruptin' him, 'not to know the History o' your country.' An' I left him gawkin' where he was.

Joxer Where ignorance 's bliss 'tis folly to be wise; I wondher did he ever read the Story o' Irelan'.

Boyle Be J. L. Sullivan? Don't you know he didn't.

Joxer Ah, it's a darlin' buk, a daarlin' buk!

Boyle You'd betther be goin', now, Joxer; his Majesty, Bentham, 'll be here any minute, now.

Joxer Be the way things is lookin', it'll be a match between him an' Mary. She's thrun over Jerry altogether.

Well, I hope it will, for he's a darlin' man.

Boyle I'm glad you think so – I don't. (*irritably*) What's darlin' about him?

Joxer (*nonplussed*) I only seen him twiced; if you want to know me, come an' live with me.

Boyle He's too dignified for me – to hear him talk you'd think he knew as much as a Boney's Oraculum. He's given up his job as teacher, an' is goin' to become a solicitor in Dublin – he's been studyin' law. I suppose he thinks I'll set him up, but he's wrong shipped. An' th' other fella – Jerry's as bad. The two o' them ud give you a pain in your face, listenin' to them; Jerry believin' in nothin', an' Bentham believin' in everythin'. One that says all is God an' no man; an' th' other that says all is man an' no God!

Joxer Well, I'll be off now.

Boyle Don't forget to dhrop down afther awhile; we'll have a quiet jar, an' a song or two.

Joxer Never fear.

Boyle An' tell Mrs Madigan that I hope we'll have the pleasure of her organization at our little enthertainment.

Joxer Righto; we'll come down together.

He goes out. Johnny comes from room on left, and sits down moodily at the fire. Boyle looks at him for a few moments, and shakes his head. He fills his pipe.

Voice of Juno (*at the door*) Open the door, Jack; this thing has me nearly kilt with the weight.

Boyle opens the door. Juno enters carrying the box of a gramophone, followed by Mary carrying the horn and some parcels. Juno leaves the box on the table and flops into a chair.

Juno Carryin' that from Henry Street was no joke.

Boyle U-u-ugh, that's a grand-lookin' insthrument – how much was it?

Juno Pound down, an' five to be paid at two shillins a week.

Boyle That's reasonable enough.

Juno I'm afraid we're runnin' into too much debt; first the furniture, an' now this.

Boyle The whole lot won't be much out of £2,000.

Mary I don't know what you wanted a gramophone for – I know Charlie hates them; he says they're destructive of real music.

Boyle Desthructive of music – that fella ud give you a pain in your face. All a gramophone wants is to be properly played; its thrue wondher is only felt when everythin's quiet – what a gramophone wants is dead silence!

Mary But, father, Jerry says the same; afther all, you can only appreciate music when your ear is properly trained.

Boyle That's another fella ud give you a pain in your face. Properly thrained! I suppose you couldn't appreciate football unless your fut was properly thrained.

Mrs Boyle (*to Mary*) Go on in ower that an' dress, or Charlie 'll be in on you, an' tea nor nothing 'll be ready.

    Mary goes into room left.

(*Arranging table for tea*) You didn't look at our new gramophone, Johnny?

Johnny 'Tisn't gramophones I'm thinking of.

Mrs Boyle An' what is it you're thinkin' of, allanna?

Johnny Nothin', nothin', nothin'.

Mrs Boyle Sure, you must be thinkin' of somethin'; it's yourself that has yourself the way y'are; sleepin' wan night in me sisther's, an' the nex' in your father's brother's – you'll get no rest goin' on that way.

Johnny I can rest nowhere, nowhere, nowhere.

Mrs Boyle Sure, you're not thryin' to rest anywhere.

Johnny Let me alone, let me alone, let me alone, for God's sake.

A knock at street door.

Mrs Boyle (*in a flutter*) Here he is; here's Mr Bentham!

Boyle Well, there's room for him; it's a pity there's not a brass band to play him in.

Mrs Boyle We'll han' the tea round, an' not be clusthered round the table, as if we never seen nothin'.

Steps are heard approaching, and Juno, opening the door, allows Bentham to enter.

Juno Give your hat an' stick to Jack, there . . . sit down, Mr Bentham . . . no, not there . . . in th' easy chair be the fire . . . there, that's betther. Mary'll be out to you in a minute.

Boyle (*solemnly*) I seen be the paper this mornin' that Consols was down half per cent. That's serious, min' you, an' shows the whole counthry's in a state o' chassis.

Mrs Boyle What's Consols, Jack?

Boyle Consols? Oh, Consols is – oh, there's no use tellin' women what Consols is – th' wouldn't undherstand.

Bentham It's just as you were saying, Mr Boyle . . .

Mary enters, charmingly dressed.

Oh, good evening, Mary; how pretty you're looking!

Mary (*archly*) Am I?

Boyle We were just talkin' when you kem in, Mary; I was tellin' Mr Bentham that the whole counthry's in a state o' chassis.

Mary (*to Bentham*) Would you prefer the green or the blue ribbon round me hair, Charlie?

Mrs Boyle Mary, your father's speakin'.

Boyle (*rapidly*) I was jus' tellin' Mr Bentham that the whole counthry's in a state o' chassis.

Mary I'm sure you're frettin', da, whether it is or no.

Mrs Boyle With all our churches an' religions, the worl's not a bit the betther.

Boyle (*with a commanding gesture*) Tay!

Mary and Mrs Boyle dispense the tea.

Mrs Boyle An' Irelan's takin' a leaf out o' the worl's buk; when we got the makin' of our own laws I thought we'd never stop to look behind us, but instead of that we never stopped to look before us! If the people ud folley up their religion betther there'd be a betther chance for us – what do you think, Mr Bentham?

Bentham I'm afraid I can't venture to express an opinion on that point, Mrs Boyle; dogma has no attraction for me.

Mrs Boyle I forgot you didn't hold with us: what's this you said you were?

Bentham A Theosophist, Mrs Boyle.

Mrs Boyle An' what in the name o' God's a Theosophist?

Boyle A Theosophist, Juno, 's a – tell her, Mr Bentham, tell her.

Bentham It's hard to explain in a few words: Theosophy's founded on The Vedas, the religious books of the East. Its central theme is the existence of an all-pervading Spirit – the Life-Breath. Nothing really exists but this one Universal Life-Breath. And whatever even seems to exist separately from this Life-Breath, doesn't really exist at all. It is all vital force in man, in all animals, and in all vegetation. This Life-Breath is called the Prawna.

Mrs Boyle The Prawna! What a comical name!

Boyle Prawna; yis, the Prawna. (*Blowing gently through his lips*) That's the Prawna!

Mrs Boyle Whist, whist, Jack.

Bentham The happiness of man depends upon his sympathy with this Spirit. Men who have reached a high state of excellence are called Yogi. Some men become Yogi in a short time, it may take others millions of years.

Boyle Yogi! I seen hundhreds of them in the streets o' San Francisco.

Bentham It is said by these Yogi that if we practise certain mental exercises that we would have powers denied to others – for instance, the faculty of seeing things that happen miles and miles away.

Mrs Boyle I wouldn't care to meddle with that sort o' belief; it's a very curious religion, altogether.

Boyle What's curious about it? Isn't all religions curious? – if they weren't, you wouldn't get any one to believe them. But religions is passin' away – they've had their day like everything else. Take the real Dublin people, f'rinstance: they know more about Charlie Chaplin an'

Tommy Mix than they do about SS Peter an' Paul!

Mrs Boyle You don't believe in ghosts, Mr Bentham?

Mary Don't you know he doesn't, mother?

Bentham I don't know that, Mary. Scientists are beginning to think that what we call ghosts are sometimes seen by persons of a certain nature. They say that sensational actions, such as the killing of a person, demand great energy, and that that energy lingers in the place where the action occurred. People may live in the place and see nothing, when someone may come along whose personality has some peculiar connection with the energy of the place, and, in a flash, the person sees the whole affair.

Johnny (*rising swiftly, pale and affected*) What sort o' talk is this to be goin' on with? Is there nothin' better to be talkin' about but the killin' o' people? My God, isn't it bad enough for these things to happen without talkin' about them! (*He hurriedly goes into the room on left.*)

Bentham Oh, I'm very sorry, Mrs Boyle; I never thought . . .

Mrs Boyle (*apologetically*) Never mind, Mr Bentham, he's very touchy.

A frightened scream is heard from Johnny inside.

Mrs Boyle Mother of God, what's that?

He rushes out again, his face pale, his lips twitching, his limbs trembling.

Johnny Shut the door, shut the door, quick, for God's sake! Great God, have mercy on me! Blessed Mother o' God, shelter me, shelther your son!

Mrs Boyle (*catching him in her arms*) What's wrong with

you? What ails you? Sit down, sit down, here, on the bed
. . . there now . . . there now.

Mary Johnny, Johnny, what ails you?

Johnny I seen him, I seen him . . . kneelin' in front o' the
statue . . . merciful Jesus, have pity on me!

Mrs Boyle (*to Boyle*) Get him a glass o' whiskey . . .
quick, man, an' don't stand gawkin'.

  Boyle gets the whiskey.

Johnny Sit here, sit here, mother . . . between me an' the
door.

Mrs Boyle I'll sit beside you as long as you like, only tell
me what was it came across you at all?

Johnny (*after taking some drink*) I seen him . . . . I seen
Robbie Tancred kneelin' down before the statue . . . an'
the red light shinin' on him . . . an' when I went in . . . he
turned an' looked at me . . . an' I seen the wouns bleedin'
in his breast . . . . Oh, why did he look at me like that?
. . . it wasn't my fault that he was done in . . . . Mother o'
God, keep him away from me!

Mrs Boyle There, there, child, you've imagined it all.
There was nothin' there at all – it was the red light you
seen, an' the talk we had put all the rest into your head.
Here, dhrink more o' this – it'll do you good . . . An', now,
stretch yourself down on the bed for a little. (*to Boyle*) Go
in, Jack, an' show him it was only in his own head it was.

Boyle (*making no move*) E-e-e-e-eh; it's all nonsense; it
was only a shadda he saw.

Mary Mother o' God, he made me heart lep!

Bentham It was simply due to an over-wrought
imagination – we all get that way at times.

45

Mrs Boyle There, dear, lie down in the bed, an' I'll put the quilt across you . . . e-e-e-eh, that's it . . . you'll be as right as the mail in a few minutes.

Johnny Mother, go into the room an' see if the light's lightin' before the statue.

Mrs Boyle (*to Boyle*) Jack, run in an' see if the light's lightin' before the statue.

Boyle (*to Mary*) Mary, slip in an' see if the light's lightin' before the statue.

Mary hesitates to go in.

Bentham It's all right; Mary, I'll go. (*He goes into the room; remains for a few moments, and returns.*) Everything's just as it was – the light burning bravely before the statue.

Boyle Of course; I knew it was all nonsense.

A knock at the door.

(*Going to open the door*) E-e-e-e-eh.

He opens it, and Joxer, followed by Mrs Madigan, enters. Mrs Madigan is a strong, dapper little woman of about forty-five; her face is almost always a widespread smile of complacency. She is a woman who, in manner at least, can mourn with them that mourn, and rejoice with them that do rejoice. When she is feeling comfortable, she is inclined to be reminiscent; when others say anything, or following a statement made by herself, she has a habit of putting her head a little to one side, and nodding it rapidly several times in succession, like a bird pecking at a hard berry. Indeed, she has a good deal of the bird in her, but the bird instinct is by no means a melodious one. She is ignorant, vulgar and forward, but her heart is generous withal. For instance, she would help a

neighbour's sick child; she would probably kill the child,
but her intention would be to cure it; she would be more
at home helping a drayman to lift a fallen horse. She is
dressed in a rather soiled grey dress and a vivid purple
blouse; in her hair is a huge comb, ornamented with huge
coloured beads. She enters with a gliding step, beaming
smile and nodding head. Boyle receives them effusively.

Come on in, Mrs Madigan; come on in; I was afraid you
weren't comin' . . . (*Slyly*) There's some people able to
dhress, ay, Joxer?

Joxer Fair as the blossoms that bloom in the May, an'
sweet as the scent of the new-mown hay . . . Ah, well she
may wear them.

Mrs Madigan (*looking at Mary*) I know some as are as
sweet as the blossoms that bloom in the May – oh, no
names, no pack dhrill!

Boyle An' now I'll inthroduce the pair o' yous to Mary's
intended: Mr Bentham, this is Mrs Madigan, an oul' back-
parlour neighbour, that, if she could help it at all, ud never
see a body shuk!

Bentham (*rising, and tentatively shaking the hand of Mrs*
Madigan) I'm sure, it's a great pleasure to know you, Mrs
Madigan.

Mrs Madigan An' I'm goin' to tell you, Mr Bentham,
you're goin' to get as nice a bit o' skirt in Mary, there, as
ever you seen in your puff. Not like some of the dhressed
up dolls that's knockin' about lookin' for men when it's a
skelpin' they want. I remember, as well as I remember
yestherday, the day she was born – of a Tuesday, the 25th
o' June, in the year 1901, at thirty-three minutes past wan
in the day be Foley's clock, the pub at the corner o' the
street. A cowld day it was too, for the season o' the year,
an' I remember sayin' to Joxer, there, who I met comin' up

th' stairs, that the new arrival in Boyle's ud grow up a hardy chiselur if it lived, an' that she'd be somethin' one o' these days that nobody suspected, an' so signs on it, here she is today, goin' to be married to a young man lookin' as if he'd be fit to commensurate in any position in life it ud please God to call him!

Boyle (*effusively*) Sit down, Mrs Madigan, sit down, me oul' sport. (*To Bentham*) This is Joxer Daly, Past Chief Ranger of the Dear Little Shamrock Branch of the Irish National Foresters, an oul' front-top neighbour, that never despaired, even in the darkest days of Ireland's sorra.

Joxer Nil desperandum, Captain, nil desperandum.

Boyle Sit down, Joxer, sit down. The two of us was ofen in a tight corner.

Mrs Boyle Ay, in Foley's snug!

Joxer An' we kem out of it flyin', we kem out of it flyin', Captain.

Boyle An' now for a dhrink – I know yous won't refuse an oul' friend.

Mrs Madigan (*to Juno*) Is Johnny not well, Mrs . . .

Mrs Boyle (*warningly*) S-s-s-sh.

Mrs Madigan Oh, the poor darlin'.

Boyle Well, Mrs Madigan, is it tea or what?

Mrs Madigan Well, speakin' for meself, I jus' had me tea a minute ago, an' I'm afraid to dhrink any more – I'm never the same when I dhrink too much tay. Thanks, all the same, Mr Boyle.

Boyle Well, what about a bottle o' stout or a dhrop o' whiskey?

Mrs Madigan A bottle o' stout ud be a little too heavy for me stummock afther me tay . . . A-a-ah, I'll thry the ball o' malt.

Boyle prepares the whiskey.

There's nothin' like a ball o' malt occasional like – too much of it isn't good. (*To Boyle, who is adding water*) Ah, God, Johnny, don't put too much wather on it! (*She drinks.*) I suppose yous'll be lavin' this place.

Boyle I'm looking for a place near the sea; I'd like the place that you might say was me cradle, to be me grave as well. The sea is always callin' me.

Joxer She is callin', callin', callin', in the win' an' on the sea.

Boyle Another dhrop o' whiskey, Mrs Madigan?

Mrs Madigan Well, now, it ut be hard to refuse seein' the suspicious times that's in it.

Boyle (*with a commanding gesture*) Song! . . . Juno . . . Mary . . . 'Home to Our Mountains'!

Mrs Madigan (*enthusiastically*) Hear, hear!

Joxer Oh, tha's a darlin' song, a daarlin' song!

Mary (*bashfully*) Ah no, da; I'm not in a singin' humour.

Mrs Madigan Gawn with you, child, an' you only goin' to be marrid; I remember as well as I remember yestherday, – it was on a lovely August evenin', exactly, accordin' to date, fifteen years ago, come the Tuesday folleyin' the nex' that's comin' on, when me own man - *the Lord be good to him* – an' me was sittin' shy together in a doty little nook on a counthry road, adjacent to The Stiles. 'That'll scratch your lovely, little white neck,' says he, ketchin' hould of a danglin' bramble branch, holdin' clusters of the loveliest flowers you ever seen, an' breakin' it off, so that his arm fell, accidental like, roun' me waist, an' as I felt it tightenin', an' tightenin', an' tightenin', I thought me buzzom was every minute goin' to burst out into a roystherin' song about

The little green leaves that were shakin' on the threes,
The gallivantin' buttherflies, an' buzzin' o' the bees!

Boyle Ordher for the song!

Juno Come on, Mary – we'll do our best.

Juno and Mary stand up, and choosing a suitable position, sing simply 'Home to Our Mountains'. They bow to company, and return to their places.

Boyle (*emotionally, at the end of song*) Lull . . . me . . . to . . . rest!

Joxer (*clapping his hands*) Bravo, bravo! Darlin' girulls, darlin' girulls!

Mrs Madigan Juno, I never seen you in bether form.

Bentham Very nicely rendered indeed.

Mrs Madigan A noble call, a noble call!

Mrs Boyle What about yourself, Mrs Madigan?

After some coaxing, Mrs Madigan rises, and in a quavering voice sings.

Mrs Madigan
If I were a blackbird I'd whistle and sing;
I'd follow the ship that my thrue love was in;
An' on the top riggin', I'd there build me nest,
An' at night I would sleep on me Willie's white breast!

Becoming husky, amid applause, she sits down.

Ah, me voice is too husky now, Juno; though I remember the time when Maisie Madigan could sing like a

nightingale at matin' time. I remember as well as I
remember yestherday, at a party given to celebrate the
comin' of the first chiselur to Annie an' Benny Jimeson –
who was the barber, yous may remember, in Henrietta
Street, that, afther Easter Week, hung out a green, white
an' orange pole, an', then, when the Tans started their jazz
dancin', whipped it in agen, an' stuck out a red, white an'
blue wan instead, givin' as an excuse that a barber's pole
was strictly non-political – singin' 'An' You'll Remember
Me', with the top notes quiverin' in a dead hush of
pethrified attention, folleyed be a clappin' o' hans that
shuk the tumblers on the table, an' capped by Jimeson, the
barber, sayin' that it was the best rendherin' of 'You'll
Remember Me' he ever heard in his natural!

Boyle (*peremptorily*) Ordher for Joxer's song!

Joxer Ah no, I couldn't; don't ass me, Captain.

Boyle Joxer's song, Joxer's song – give us wan of your
shut-eyed wans.

*Joxer settles himself in his chair; takes a drink; clears his
throat; solemnly closes his eyes, and begins to sing in a
very querulous voice.*

Joxer
She is far from the lan' where her young hero sleeps,
An' lovers around her are sighing (*He hesitates.*)
An' lovers around her are sighin' . . . sighin' . . .
sighin' . . .

A pause.

Boyle (*imitating Joxer*)
And lovers around her are sighing!

What's the use of you thryin' to sing the song if you don't
know it?

Mary Thry another one, Mr Daly – maybe you'd be more fortunate.

Mrs Madigan Gawn, Joxer; thry another wan.

Joxer (*starting again*)
I have heard the mavis singin' his love song to the morn;
I have seen the dew-dhrop clingin' to the rose jus'
newly   born; but . . . but . . . (*Frantically*) To the rose
jus'   newly born . . . newly born . . . born.

Johnny Mother, put on the gramophone, for God's sake, an' stop Joxer's bawlin'.

Boyle (*commandingly*) Gramophone! . . . I hate to see fellas thryin' to do what they're not able to do.

Boyle arranges the gramophone, and is about to start it, when voices are heard of persons descending the stairs.

Mrs Boyle (*warningly*) Whisht, Jack, don't put it on, don't put it on yet; this must be poor Mrs Tancred comin' down to go to the hospital – I forgot all about them bringin' the body to the church tonight. Open the door, Mary, an' give them a bit o' light.

Mary opens the door, and Mrs Tancred – a very old woman, obviously shaken by the death of her son – appears, accompanied by several neighbours. The first few phrases are spoken before they appear.

First Neighbour It's a sad journey we're goin' on, but God's good, an' the Republicans won't be always down.

Mrs Tancred Ah, what good is that to me now? Whether they're up or down – it won't bring me darlin' boy from the grave.

Mrs Boyle Come in an' have a hot cup o' tay, Mrs Tancred, before you go.

Mrs Tancred Ah, I can take nothin' now, Mrs Boyle – I won't be long afther him.

First Neighbour Still an' all, he died a noble death, an' we'll bury him like a king.

Mrs Tancred An' I'll go on livin' like a pauper. Ah, what's the pains I suffered bringin' him into the world to carry him to his cradle, to the pains I'm sufferin' now, carryin' him out o' the world to bring him to his grave!

Mary It would be better for you not to go at all, Mrs Tancred, but to stay at home beside the fire with some o' the neighbours.

Mrs Tancred I seen the first of him, an' I'll see the last of him.

Mrs Boyle You'd want a shawl, Mrs Tancred; it's a cowld night, an' the win's blowin' sharp.

Mrs Madigan (*rushing out*) I've a shawl above.

Mrs Tancred Me home is gone now; he was me only child, an' to think that he was lyin' for a whole night stretched out on the side of a lonely counthry lane, with his head, his darlin' head, that I often kissed an' fondled, half hidden in the wather of a runnin' brook. An' I'm told he was the leadher of the ambush where me nex' door neighbour, Mrs Mannin', lost her Free State soldier son. An' now here's the two of us oul' women, standin' one on each side of a scales o' sorra, balanced be the bodies of our two dead darlin' sons.

Mrs Madigan returns, and wraps a shawl around her.

God bless you, Mrs Madigan . . . . (*She moves slowly towards the door.*) Mother o' God, Mother o' God, have pity on the pair of us! . . . O Blessed Virgin, where were you when me darlin' son was riddled with bullets, when

me darlin' son was riddled with bullets! . . . Sacred Heart
of the Crucified Jesus, take away our hearts o' stone . . .
an' give us hearts o' flesh! . . . Take away this murdherin'
hate . . . an' give us Thine own eternal love!

They pass out of the room.

Mrs Boyle (*explanatorily to Bentham*) That was Mrs
Tancred of the two-pair back; her son was found, e'er
yestherday, lyin' out beyant Finglas riddled with bullets. A
Die-hard he was, be all accounts. He was a nice quiet boy,
but lattherly he went to hell, with his Republic first, an'
Republic last an' Republic over all. He ofen took tea with
us here, in the oul' days, an' Johnny, there, an' him used to
be always together.

Johnny Am I always to be havin' to tell you that he was
no friend o' mine? I never cared for him, an' he could
never stick me. It's not because he was Commandant of
the Battalion that I was Quarther-Masther of, that we
were friends.

Mrs Boyle He's gone now – the Lord be good to him! God
help his poor oul' creature of a mother, for no matther
whose friend or enemy he was, he was her poor son.

Bentham The whole thing is terrible, Mrs Boyle; but the
only way to deal with a mad dog is to destroy him.

Mrs Boyle An' to think of me forgettin' about him bein'
brought to the church tonight, an' we singin' an' all, but it
was well we hadn't the gramophone goin', anyhow.

Boyle Even if we had aself. We've nothin' to do with these
things, one way or t'other. That's the Government's
business, an' let them do what we're payin' them for doin'.

Mrs Boyle I'd like to know how a body's not to mind
these things; look at the way they're afther leavin' the
people in this very house. Hasn't the whole house, nearly,

been massacreed? There's young Dougherty's husband with his leg off; Mrs Travers that had her son blew up be a mine in Inchegeela, in Co. Cork; Mrs Mannin' that lost wan of her sons in ambush a few weeks ago, an' now, poor Mrs Tancred's only child gone west with his body made a collandher of. Sure, if it's not our business, I don't know whose business it is.

Boyle Here, there, that's enough about them things; they don't affect us, an' we needn't give a damn. If they want a wake, well, let them have a wake. When I was a sailor, I was always resigned to meet with a wathery grave; an' if they want to be soldiers, well, there's no use o' them squealin' when they meet a soldier's fate.

Joxer Let me like a soldier fall – me breast expandin' to th' ball!

Mrs Boyle In wan way, she deserves all she got; for lately, she let th' Die-hards make an open house of th' place; an' for th' last couple of months, either when th' sun was risin' or when th' sun was settin', you had CID men burstin' into your room, assin' you where were you born, where were you christened, where were you married, an' where would you be buried!

Johnny For God's sake, let us have no more o' this talk.

Mrs Madigan What about Mr Boyle's song before we start th' gramophone?

Mary (*getting her hat, and putting it on*) Mother, Charlie and I are goin' out for a little sthroll.

Mrs Boyle All right, darlin'.

Bentham (*going out with Mary*) We won't be long away, Mrs Boyle.

Mrs Madigan Gwan, Captain, gwan.

Boyle E-e-e-e-eh, I'd want to have a few more jars in me, before I'd be in fettle for singin'.

Joxer Give us that poem you writ t'other day. (*To the rest*) Aw, it's a darlin' poem, a daarlin' poem.

Mrs Boyle God bless us, is he startin' to write poetry!

Boyle (*rising to his feet*) E-e-e-e-eh. (*He recites in an emotional, consequential manner the following verses:*)

> Shawn an' I were friends, sir, to me he was all in all.
> His work was very heavy and his wages were very small.
> None betther on th' beach as Docker, I'll go bail,
> 'Tis now I'm feelin' lonely, for today he lies in jail.
> He was not what some call pious – seldom at church or   prayer;
> For the greatest scoundrels I know, sir, goes every Sunday there.
> Fond of his pint – well, rather, but hated the Boss by creed
> But never refused a copper to comfort a pal in need.

E-e-e-e-eh. (*He sits down.*)

Mrs Madigan Grand, grand; you should folly that up, you should folly that up.

Joxer It's a daarlin' poem!

Boyle (*delightedly*) E-e-e-e-eh.

Johnny Are yous goin' to put on th' gramophone tonight, or are yous not?

Mrs Boyle Gwan, Jack, put on a record.

Mrs Madigan Gwan, Captain, gwan.

Boyle Well, yous'll want to keep a dead silence.

He sets a record, starts the machine, and it begins to play 'If you're Irish, come into the Parlour'. As the tune is in full blare, the door is suddenly opened by a brisk, little bald-headed man, dressed circumspectly in a black suit; he glares fiercely at all in the room; he is 'Needle Nugent', a tailor. He carries his hat in his hand.

Nugent (*loudly, above the noise of the gramophone*) Are yous going' to have that thing bawlin' an' the funeral of Mrs Tancred's son passin' the house? Have none of yous any respect for the Irish people's National regard for the dead?

Boyle stops the gramophone.

Mrs Boyle Maybe, Needle Nugent, it's nearly time we had a little less respect for the dead, an' a little more regard for the livin'.

Mrs Madigan We don't want you, Mr Nugent, to teach us what we learned at our mother's knee. You don't look yourself as if you were dyin' of grief; if y'ass Maisie Madigan anything, I'd call you a real thrue Die-hard an' live-soft Republican, attendin' Republican funerals in the day, an' stoppin' up half the night makin' suits for the Civic Guards!

Persons are heard running down to the street, some saying, 'Here it is, here it is.' Nugent withdraws, and the rest, except Johnny, go to the window looking into the street, and look out. Sounds of a crowd coming nearer are heard; a portion are singing:

To Jesus' Heart all burning
With fervent love for men,
My heart with fondest yearning
Shall raise its joyful strain.
While ages course along,
Blest be with loudest song

The Sacred Heart of Jesus
By every heart and tongue.

Mrs Boyle Here's the hearse, here's the hearse!

Boyle There's t'oul' mother walkin' behin' the coffin.

Mrs Madigan You can hardly see the coffin with the wreaths.

Joxer Oh, it's a darlin' funeral, a daarlin' funeral!

Mrs Madigan We'd have a betther view from the street.

Boyle Yes – this place ud give you a crick in your neck.

They leave the room, and go down. Johnny sits moodily by the fire. A young man enters; he looks at Johnny for a moment.

Young Man Quarther-Masther Boyle.

Johnny (*with a start*) The Mobilizer!

Young Man You're not at the funeral?

Johnny I'm not well.

Young Man I'm glad I've found you; you were stoppin' at your aunt's; I called there but you'd gone. I've to give you an ordher to attend a Battalion Staff meetin' the night afther tomorrow.

Johnny Where?

Young Man I don't know; you're to meet me at the Pillar at eight o'clock; then we're to go to a place I'll be told of tonight; there we'll meet a mothor that'll bring us to the meeting. They think you might be able to know somethin' about them that gave the bend where Commandant Tancred was shelterin'.

Johnny I'm not goin', then. I know nothing about Tancred.

Young Man (*at the door*) You'd betther come for your own sake – remember your oath.

Johnny (*passionately*) I won't go! Haven't I done enough for Ireland! I've lost me arm, an' me hip's desthroyed so that I'll never be able to walk right agen! Good God, haven't I done enough for Ireland?

Young Man Boyle, no man can do enough for Ireland!

He goes. Faintly in the distance the crowd is heard saying:

Hail, Mary, full of grace, the Lord is with Thee; Blessed art Thou amongst women, and blessed, etc.

Curtain.

Act Three

The same as Act Two. It is about half-past six on a November evening; a bright fire burns in the grate; Mary, dressed to go out, is sitting on a chair by the fire, leaning forward, her hands under her chin, her elbows on her knees. A look of dejection, mingled with uncertain anxiety, is on her face. A lamp, turned low, is lighting on the table. The votive light under the picture of the Virgin gleams more redly than ever. Mrs Boyle is putting on her hat and coat. It is two months later.

Mrs Boyle An' has Bentham never even written to you since – not one line for the past month?

Mary (*tonelessly*) Not even a line, mother.

Mrs Boyle That's very curious . . . What came between the two of yous at all? To leave you so sudden, an' yous so great together. . . . To go away t' England, an' not to even leave you his address . . . . The way he was always bringin' you to dances, I thought he was mad afther you. Are you sure you said nothin' to him?

Mary No, mother – at least nothing that could possibly explain his givin' me up.

Mrs Boyle You know you're a bit hasty at times, Mary, an' say things you shouldn't say.

Mary I never said to him what I shouldn't say, I'm sure of that.

Mrs Boyle How are you sure of it?

Mary Because I love him with all my heart and soul,

mother. Why, I don't know; I often thought to myself that he wasn't the man poor Jerry was, but I couldn't help loving him, all the same.

Mrs Boyle But you shouldn't be frettin' the way you are; when a woman loses a man, she never knows what she's afther losin', to be sure, but, then, she never knows what she's afther gainin', either. You're not the one girl of a month ago – you look like one pinin' away. It's long ago I had a right to bring you to the doctor, instead of waitin' till tonight.

Mary There's no necessity, really, mother, to go to the doctor; nothing serious is wrong with me – I'm run down and disappointed, that's all.

Mrs Boyle I'll not wait another minute; I don't like the look of you at all . . . I'm afraid we made a mistake in throwin' over poor Jerry . . . He'd have been betther for you than that Bentham.

Mary Mother, the best man for a woman is the one for whom she has the most love, and Charlie had it all.

Mrs Boyle Well, there's one thing to be said for him – he couldn't have been thinkin' of the money, or he wouldn't ha' left you . . . it must ha' been somethin' else.

Mary (*wearily*) I don't know . . . I don't know, mother . . . only I think . . .

Mrs Boyle What d'ye think?

Mary I imagine . . . he thought . . . we weren't . . . good enough for him.

Mrs Boyle An' what was he himself, only a school teacher? Though I don't blame him for fightin' shy of people like that Joxer fella an' that oul' Madigan wan – nice sort o' people for your father to inthroduce to a man like Mr Bentham. You might have told me all about this before now, Mary; I don't know why you like to hide everything from your mother; you knew Bentham, an' I'd ha' known nothin' about it if it hadn't bin for the Will; an' it was only today, afther long coaxin', that you let out that he's left you.

Mary It would have been useless to tell you – you wouldn't understand.

Mrs Boyle (*hurt*) Maybe not . . . . Maybe I wouldn't understand . . . . Well, we'll be off now. (*She goes over to door left, and speaks to Boyle inside.*)

We're goin' now to the doctor's. Are you goin' to get up this evenin'?

Boyle (*from inside*) The pains in me legs is terrible! It's me should be poppin' off to the doctor instead o' Mary, the way I feel.

Mrs Boyle Sorra mend you! A nice way you were in last night – carried in in a frog's march, dead to the world. If that's the way you'll go on when you get the money it'll be the grave for you, an asylum for me and the Poorhouse for Johnny.

Boyle I thought you were goin'?

Mrs Boyle That's what has you as you are – you can't bear to be spoken to. Knowin' the way we are, up to our ears in debt, it's a wondher you wouldn't ha' got up to go to th' solicitor's an' see if we could ha' gotten a little o' the money even.

Boyle (*shouting*) I can't be goin' up there night, noon an' mornin' can I? He can't give the money till he gets it, can he? I can't get blood out of a turnip, can I?

Mrs Boyle It's nearly two months since we heard of the

Will, an' the money seems as far off as ever . . . . I suppose you know we owe twenty pouns to oul' Murphy?

Boyle I've a faint recollection of you tellin' me that before.

Mrs Boyle Well, you'll go over to the shop yourself for the things in future – I'll face him no more.

Boyle I thought you said you were goin'?

Mrs Boyle I'm goin' now; come on, Mary.

Boyle Ey, Juno, ey!

Mrs Boyle Well, what d'ye want now?

Boyle Is there e'er a bottle o' stout left?

Mrs Boyle There's two o' them here still.

Boyle Show us in one o' them an' leave t'other there till I get up. An' throw us in the paper that's on the table, an' the bottle o' Sloan's Liniment that's in th' drawer.

Mrs Boyle (*getting the liniment and the stout*) What paper is it you want – the *Messenger*?

Boyle *Messenger*! The *News o' the World*!

Mrs Boyle brings in the things asked for, and comes out again.

Mrs Boyle (*at door*) Mind the candle, now, an' don't burn the house over our heads. I left t'other bottle o' stout on the table.

She puts bottle of stout on table. She goes out with Mary. A cork is heard popping inside. A pause; then outside the door is heard the voice of Joxer lilting softly: 'Me pipe I'll smoke, as I dhrive me moke . . . are you . . . there . . . Mor . . . ee . . . ar . . . i . . . teee!' A gentle knock is heard, and after a pause the door opens, and Joxer, followed by Nugent, enters.

Joxer Be God, they must be all out; I was thinkin' there was somethin' up when he didn't answer the signal. We seen Juno an' Mary goin', but I didn't see him, an' it's very seldom he escapes me.

Nugent He's not goin' to escape me – he's not goin' to be let go to the fair altogether.

Joxer Sure, the house couldn't hould them lately; an' he goin' about like a mastherpiece of the Free State counthry; forgettin' their friends; forgettin' God – wouldn't even lift his hat passin' a chapel! Sure they were bound to get a dhrop! An' you really think there's no money comin' to him afther all?

Nugent Not as much as a red rex, man; I've been a bit anxious this long time over me money, an' I went up to the solicitor's to find out all I could – ah, man, they were goin' to throw me down the stairs. They toul' me that the oul' cock himself had the stairs worn away comin' up afther it, an' they black in the face tellin' him he'd get nothin'. Some way or another that the Will is writ he won't be entitled to get as much as a make!

Joxer Ah, I thought there was somethin' curious about the whole thing; I've bin havin' sthrange dhreams for the last couple o' weeks. An' I notice that that Bentham fella doesn't be comin' here now – there must be somethin' on the mat there too. Anyhow, who, in the name o' God, ud leave anythin' to that oul' bummer? Sure it ud be unnatural. An' the way Juno an' him's been throwin' their weight about for the last few months! Ah, him that goes a borrowin' goes a sorrowin'!

Nugent Well, he's not goin' to throw his weight about in the suit I made for him much longer. I'm tellin' you seven pouns aren't to be found growin' on the bushes these days.

Joxer An' there isn't hardly a neighbour in the whole

street that hasn't lent him money on the strength of what he was goin' to get, but they're after backing the wrong horse. Wasn't it a mercy o' God that I'd nothin' to give him! The softy I am, you know, I'd ha' lent him me last juice! I must have had somebody's good prayers. Ah, afther all, an honest man's the noblest work o' God!

Boyle coughs inside.

Whisht, damn it, he must be inside in bed.

Nugent Inside o' bed or outside of it, he's goin' to pay me for that suit, or give it back – he'll not climb up my back as easily as he thinks.

Joxer Gwan in at wanst, man, an' get it off him, an' don't be a fool.

Nugent (*going to door left, opening it and looking in*) Ah, don't disturb yourself, Mr Boyle; I hope you're not sick?

Boyle Th' oul' legs, Mr Nugent, the oul' legs.

Nugent I just called over to see if you could let me have anything off the suit?

Boyle E-e-e-eh, how much is this it is?

Nugent It's the same as it was at the start – seven pouns.

Boyle I'm glad you kem, Mr Nugent; I want a good heavy top-coat – Irish frieze, if you have it. How much would a top-coat like that be, now?

Nugent About six pouns.

Boyle Six pouns – six an' seven, six an' seven is thirteen – that'll be thirteen pouns I'll owe you.

Joxer slips the bottle of stout that is on the table into his pocket. Nugent rushes into the room, and returns with suit on his arm; he pauses at the door.

Nugent You'll owe me no thirteen pouns. Maybe you think you're betther able to owe it than pay it!

Boyle (*frantically*) Here, come back to hell ower that – where're you goin' with them clothes o' mine?

Nugent Where am I goin' with them clothes o' yours? Well, I like your damn cheek!

Boyle Here, what am I going' to dhress meself in when I'm goin' out?

Nugent What do I care what you dhress yourself in! You can put yourself in a bolsther cover, if you like. (*He goes towards the other door, followed by Joxer.*)

Joxer What'll he dhress himself in! Gentleman Jack an' his frieze coat!

  They go out.

Boyle (*inside*) Ey, Nugent; ey, Mr Nugent, Mr Nugent! (*After a pause he enters hastily, buttoning the braces of his moleskin trousers; his coat and vest are on his arm; he throws these on a chair and hurries to the door on right.*) Ey, Mr Nugent, Mr Nugent!

Joxer (*meeting him at the door*) What's up, what's wrong, Captain?

Boyle Nugent's been here an' took away me suit – the only things I had to go out in!

Joxer Tuk your suit – for God's sake! An' what were you doin' while he was takin' them?

Boyle I was in bed when he stole in like a thief in the night, an' before I knew even what he was thinkin' of, he whipped them from the chair an' was off like a redshank!

Joxer An' what, in the name o' God, did he do that for?

Boyle What did he do it for? How the hell do I know what he done it for? – jealousy an' spite, I suppose.

Joxer Did he not say what he done it for?

Boyle Amn't I afther tellin' you that he had them whipped up an' was gone before I could open me mouth?

Joxer That was a very sudden thing to do; there mus' be somethin' behin' it. Did he hear anythin', I wondher?

Boyle Did he hear anythin'? – you talk very queer, Joxer – what could he hear?

Joxer About you not gettin' the money, in some way or t'other?

Boyle An' what ud prevent me from gettin' th' money?

Joxer That's jus' what I was thinkin' – what ud prevent you from gettin' the money – nothin', as far as I can see.

Boyle (*looking round for bottle of stout, with an exclamation*) Aw, holy God!

Joxer What's up, Jack?

Boyle He must have afther lifted the bottle o' stout that Juno left on the table!

Joxer (*horrified*) Ah no, ah no; he wouldn't be afther doin' that now.

Boyle An' who done it then? Juno left a bottle o' stout here, an' it's gone – it didn't walk, did it?

Joxer Oh, that's shockin'; ah, man's inhumanity to man makes countless thousands mourn!

Mrs Madigan (*appearing at the door*) I hope I'm not disturbin' you in any discussion on your forthcomin' legacy – if I may use the word – an' that you'll let me have a barny for a minute or two with you, Mr Boyle.

Boyle (*uneasily*) To be sure, Mrs Madigan – an oul' friend's always welcome.

Joxer Come in the evenin', come in th' mornin'; come when you're assed, or come without warnin', Mrs Madigan.

Boyle Sit down, Mrs Madigan.

Mrs Madigan (*ominously*) Th' few words I have to say can be said standin'. Puttin' aside all formularies, I suppose you remember me lendin' you some time ago three pouns that I raised on blankets an' furniture in me uncle's?

Boyle I remember it well. I have it recorded in me book – three pouns five shillins from Maisie Madigan, raised on articles pawned; an', item: fourpence, given to make up the price of a pint, on th' principle that no bird ever flew on wan wing; all to be repaid at par, when the ship comes home.

Mrs Madigan Well, ever since I shoved in the blankets I've been perishing with th' cowld, an' I've decided, if I'll be too hot in th' nex' world aself, I'm not goin' to be too cowld in this wan; an' consequently, I want me three pouns, if you please.

Boyle This is a very sudden demand, Mrs Madigan, an' can't be met; but I'm willin' to give you a receipt in full, in full.

Mrs Madigan Come on, out with th' money, an' don't be jack-actin'.

Boyle You can't get blood out of a turnip, can you?

Mrs Madigan (*rushing over and shaking him*) Gimme me money, y'oul' reprobate, or I'll shake the worth of it out of you!

Boyle Ey, houl' on, there; houl' on, there! You'll wait for your money now, me lassie!

Mrs Madigan (*looking around the room and seeing the gramophone*) I'll wait for it, will I? Well, I'll not wait long; if I can't get th' cash, I'll get th' worth of it. (*She catches up the gramophone.*)

Boyle Ey, ey, there, wher'r you goin' with that?

Mrs Madigan I'm goin' to th' pawn to get me three quid five shillins; I'll brin' you th' ticket, an' then you can do what you like, me bucko.

Boyle You can't touch that, you can't touch that! It's not my property, an' it's not ped for yet!

Mrs Madigan So much th' betther. It'll be an ayse to me conscience, for I'm takin' what doesn't belong to you. You're not goin' to be swankin' it like a paycock with Maisie Madigan's money – I'll pull some o' th' gorgeous feathers out o' your tail! (*She goes off with the gramophone.*)

Boyle What's th' world comin' to at all? I ass you, Joxer Daly, is there any morality left anywhere?

Joxer I wouldn't ha' believed it, only I seen it with me own two eyes. I didn't think Maisie Madigan was that sort of woman; she has either a sup taken, or she's heard somethin'.

Boyle Heard somethin' – about what, if it's not any harm to ass you?

Joxer She must ha' heard some rumour or other that you weren't goin' to get th' money.

Boyle Who says I'm not goin' to get th' money?

Joxer Sure, I don't know – I was only sayin'.

Boyle Only sayin' what?

Joxer Nothin'.

Boyle You were goin' to say somethin' – don't be a twisther.

Joxer (*angrily*) Who's a twisther?

Boyle Why don't you speak your mind, then?

Joxer You never twisted yourself – no, you wouldn't know how!

Boyle Did you ever know me to twist; did you ever know me to twist?

Joxer (*fiercely*) Did you ever do anythin' else! Sure, you can't believe a word that comes out o' your mouth.

Boyle Here, get out, ower o' this; I always knew you were a prognosticator an' a procrastinator!

Joxer (*going out as Johnny comes in*) The anchor's weighed, farewell, ree . . . mem . . . ber . . . me. Jacky Boyle, Esquire, infernal rogue an' damned liar.

Johnny Joxer an' you at it agen? – when are you goin' to have a little respect for yourself, an' not be always makin' a show of us all?

Boyle Are you goin' to lecture me now?

Johnny Is mother back from the doctor yet, with Mary?

Mrs Boyle enters; it is apparent from the serious look on her face that something has happened. She takes off her hat and coat without a word and puts them by. She then sits down near the fire, and there is a few moments' pause.

Boyle Well, what did the doctor say about Mary?

Mrs Boyle (*in an earnest manner and with suppressed agitation*) Sit down here, Jack; I've something to say to you . . . about Mary.

Boyle (*awed by her manner*) About . . . Mary?

Mrs Boyle Close that door there and sit down here.

Boyle (*closing the door*) More throuble in our native land, is it? (*He sits down.*) Well, what is it?

Mrs Boyle It's about Mary.

Boyle Well, what about Mary – there's nothin' wrong with her, is there?

Mrs Boyle I'm sorry to say there's a gradle wrong with her.

Boyle A gradle wrong with her! (*Peevishly*) First Johnny an' now Mary; is the whole house goin' to become an hospital! It's not consumption, is it?

Mrs Boyle No . . . it's not consumption . . . it's worse.

Johnny Worse! Well, we'll have to get her into some place ower this, there's no one here to mind her.

Mrs Boyle We'll all have to mind her now. You might as well know now, Johnny, as another time. (*To Boyle*) D'ye know what the doctor said to me about her, Jack?

Boyle How ud I know – I wasn't there, was I?

Mrs Boyle He told me to get her married at wanst.

Boyle Married at wanst! An' why did he say the like o' that?

Mrs Boyle Because Mary's goin' to have a baby in a short time.

Boyle Goin' to have a baby! – my God, what'll Bentham say when he hears that?

Mrs Boyle Are you blind, man, that you can't see that it was Bentham that has done this wrong to her?

Boyle (*passionately*) Then he'll marry her, he'll have to marry her!

Mrs Boyle You know he's gone to England, an' God knows where he is now.

Boyle I'll folly him, I'll folly him, an' bring him back, an' make him do her justice. The scoundrel, I might ha' known what he was, with his yogees an' his prawna!

Mrs Boyle We'll have to keep it quiet till we see what we can do.

Boyle Oh, isn't this a nice thing to come on top o' me, an' the state I'm in! A pretty show I'll be to Joxer an' to that oul' wan, Madigan! Amn't I afther goin' through enough without havin' to go through this!

Mrs Boyle What you an' I'll have to go through'll be nothin' to what poor Mary'll have to go through; for you an' me is middlin' old, an' most of our years is spent; but Mary'll have maybe forty years to face an' handle, an' every wan of them'll be tainted with a bitther memory.

Boyle Where is she? Where is she till I tell her off? I'm tellin' you when I'm done with her she'll be a sorry girl!

Mrs Boyle I left her in me sister's till I came to speak to you. You'll say nothin' to her, Jack; ever since she left school she's earned her livin', an' your fatherly care never throubled the poor girl.

Boyle Gwan, take her part agen her father! But I'll let you see whether I'll say nothin' to her or no! Her an' her readin'! That's more o' th' blasted nonsense that has the house fallin' down on top of us! What did th' likes of her, born in a tenement house, want with readin'? Her readin's afther bringin' her to a nice pass – oh, it's madnin', madnin', madnin'!

Mrs Boyle When she comes back say nothin' to her, Jack, or she'll leave this place.

Boyle Leave this place! Ay, she'll leave this place, an' quick too!

Mrs Boyle If Mary goes, I'll go with her.

Boyle Well, go with her! Well, go, th' pair o' yous! I lived before I seen yous, an' I can live when yous are gone. Isn't this a nice thing to come rollin' in on top o' me afther all your prayin' to St Anthony an' The Little Flower! An' she's a Child o' Mary, too – I wonder what'll the nuns think of her now? An' it'll be bellows'd all over th' disthrict before you could say Jack Robinson; an' whenever I'm seen they'll whisper, 'That's th' father of Mary Boyle that had th' kid be th' swank she used to go with; d'ye know, d'ye know?' To be sure they'll know – more about it than I will meself!

Johnny She should be dhriven out o' th' house she's brought disgrace on!

Mrs Boyle Hush, you, Johnny. We needn't let it be bellows'd all over the place; all we've got to do is to leave this place quietly an' go somewhere where we're not known, an' nobody'll be th' wiser.

Boyle You're talkin' like a two-year-oul', woman. Where'll we get a place ou' o' this? – places aren't that easily got.

Mrs Boyle But, Jack, when we get the money . . .

Boyle Money – what money?

Mrs Boyle Why, oul' Ellison's money, of course.

Boyle There's no money comin' from oul' Ellison, or any one else. Since you've heard of wan throuble, you might as well hear of another. There's no money comin' to us at all – the Will's a wash-out!

Mrs Boyle What are you sayin', man – no money?

Johnny How could it be a wash-out?

Boyle The boyo that's afther doin' it to Mary done it to me as well. The thick made out the Will wrong; he said in th' Will, only first cousin an' second cousin, instead of mentionin' our names, an' now any one that thinks he's a first cousin or second cousin t'oul' Ellison can claim the money as well as me, an' they're springin' up in hundreds, an' comin' from America an' Australia, thinkin' to get their whack out of it, while all the time the lawyers is gobblin' it up, till there's not as much as ud buy a stockin' for your lovely daughter's baby!

Mrs Boyle I don't believe it, I don't believe it, I don't believe it!

Johnny Why did you say nothin' about this before?

Mrs Boyle You're not serious, Jack; you're not serious!

Boyle I'm tellin' you the scholar, Bentham, made a banjax o' th' Will; instead o' sayin', 'th' rest o' me property to be divided between me first cousin, Jack Boyle, an' me second cousin, Mick Finnegan, o' Santhry', he writ down only, 'me first an' second cousins', an' the world an' his wife are afther th' property now.

Mrs Boyle Now I know why Bentham left poor Mary in th' lurch; I can see it all now – oh, is there not even a middlin' honest man left in th' world?

Johnny (*to Boyle*) An' you let us run into debt, an' you borreyed money from everybody to fill yourself with beer!

An' now you tell us the whole thing's a wash-out! Oh, if it's thrue, I'm done with you, for you're worse than me sisther Mary!

Boyle You hole your tongue, d'ye hear? I'll not take any lip from you. Go an' get Bentham if you want satisfaction for all that's afther happenin' us.

Johnny I won't hole me tongue, I won't hole me tongue! I'll tell you what I think of you, father an' all as you are . . . you . . .

Mrs Boyle Johnny, Johnny, Johnny, for God's sake, be quiet!

Johnny I'll not be quiet, I'll not be quiet; he's a nice father, isn't he? Is it any wondher Mary went asthray, when . . .

Mrs Boyle Johnny, Johnny, for my sake be quiet – for your mother's sake!

Boyle I'm goin' out now to have a few dhrinks with th' last few makes I have, an' tell that lassie o' yours not to be here when I come back; for if I lay me eyes on her, I'll lay me hans on her, an' if I lay me hans on her, I won't be accountable for me actions!

Johnny Take care somebody doesn't lay his hands on you – y'oul' . . .

Mrs Boyle Johnny, Johnny!

Boyle (*at door, about to go out*) Oh, a nice son, an' a nicer daughter, I have. (*Calling loudly upstairs*) Joxer, Joxer, are you there?

Joxer (*from a distance*) I'm here. More . . . ee . . . aar . . . i . . . tee!

Boyle I'm goin' down to Foley's – are you comin'?

Joxer Come with you? With that sweet call me heart is

stirred; I'm only waiting for the word, an' I'll be with you, like a bird!

Boyle and Joxer pass the door going out.

Johnny (*throwing himself on the bed*) I've a nice sisther, an' a nice father, there's no bettin' on it. I wish to God a bullet or a bomb had whipped me ou' o' this long ago! Not one o' yous, not one o' yous, have any thought for me!

Mrs Boyle (*with passionate remonstrance*) If you don't whisht, Johnny, you'll drive me mad. Who has kep' th' home together for the past few years – only me? An' who'll have to bear th' biggest part o' this throuble but me? – but whinin' an' whingin' isn't goin' to do any good.

Johnny You're to blame yourself for a gradle of it – givin' him his own way in everything, an' never assin' to check him, no matther what he done. Why didn't you look afther th' money? Why . . .

There is a knock at the door; Mrs Boyle opens it; Johnny rises on his elbow to look and listen; two men enter.

First Man We've been sent up be th' Manager of the Hibernian Furnishing Co., Mrs Boyle, to take back the furniture that was got a while ago.

Mrs Boyle Yous'll touch nothin' here – how do I know who yous are?

First Man (*showing a paper*) There's the ordher, ma'am. (*Reading*) A chest o' drawers, a table, wan easy an' two ordinary chairs; wan mirror; wan chestherfield divan, an' a wardrobe an' two vases. (*To his comrade*) Come on, Bill, it's afther knockin'-off time already.

Johnny For God's sake, mother, run down to Foley's an'

bring father back, or we'll be left without a stick.

The men carry out the table.

Mrs Boyle What good would it be? – you heard what he said before he went out.

Johnny Can't you thry? He ought to be here, an' the like of this goin' on.

Mrs Boyle puts a shawl around her, as Mary enters.

Mary What's up, mother? I met men carryin' away the table, an' everybody's talking about us not gettin' the money after all.

Mrs Boyle Everythin's gone wrong, Mary, everythin'. We're not gettin' a penny out o' the Will, not a penny – I'll tell you all when I come back; I'm goin' for your father. (*She runs out.*)

Johnny (*to Mary, who has sat down by the fire*) It's a wondher you're not ashamed to show your face here, afther what has happened.

Jerry enters slowly; there is a look of earnest hope on his face. He looks at Mary for a few moments.

Jerry (*softly*) Mary!

Mary does not answer.

Mary, I want to speak to you for a few moments, may I?

Mary remains silent; Johnny goes slowly into room on left.

Your mother has told me everything, Mary, and I have come to you . . . . I have come to tell you, Mary, that my love for you is greater and deeper than ever . . . .

Mary (*with a sob*) Oh, Jerry, Jerry, say no more; all that is over now; anything like that is impossible now!

Jerry Impossible? Why do you talk like that, Mary?

Mary After all that has happened.

Jerry What does it matter what has happened? We are young enough to be able to forget all those things. (*He catches her hand.*) Mary, Mary, I am pleading for your love. With Labour, Mary, humanity is above everything; we are the Leaders in the fight for a new life. I want to forget Bentham, I want to forget that you left me – even for a while.

Mary Oh, Jerry, Jerry, you haven't the bitter word of scorn for me after all.

Jerry (*passionately*) Scorn! I love you, love you, Mary!

Mary (*rising, and looking him in the eyes*) Even though . . .

Jerry Even though you threw me over for another man; even though you gave me many a bitter word!

Mary Yes, yes, I know; but you love me, even though . . . even though . . . I'm . . . goin' . . . goin' . . .

He looks at her questioningly, and fear gathers in his eyes.

Ah, I was thinkin' so . . . . You don't know everything!

Jerry (*poignantly*) Surely to God, Mary, you don't mean that . . . that . . . that . . .

Mary Now you know all, Jerry; now you know all!

Jerry My God, Mary, have you fallen as low as that?

Mary Yes, Jerry, as you say, I have fallen as low as that.

Jerry I didn't mean it that way, Mary . . . it came on me so sudden, that I didn't mind what I was sayin' . . . . I never expected this – your mother never told me . . . . I'm sorry . . . God knows, I'm sorry for you, Mary.

Mary Let us say no more, Jerry; I don't blame you for thinkin' it's terrible . . . . I suppose it is . . . Everybody'll think the same . . . it's only as I expected – your humanity is just as narrow as the humanity of the others.

Jerry I'm sorry, all the same . . . . I shouldn't have troubled you . . . . I wouldn't if I'd known . . . . If I can do anything for you . . . Mary . . . . I will. (*He turns to go, and halts at the door.*)

Mary Do you remember, Jerry, the verses you read when you gave the lecture in the Socialist Rooms some time ago, on Humanity's Strife with Nature?

Jerry The verses - no; I don't remember them.

Mary I do. They're runnin' in me head now –

An' we felt the power that fashion'd
All the lovely things we saw,
That created all the murmur
Of an everlasting law,
Was a hand of force an' beauty,
With an eagle's tearin' claw.

Then we saw our globe of beauty
Was an ugly thing as well,
A hymn divine whose chorus
Was an agonizin' yell;
Like the story of a demon,
That an angel had to tell;

Like a glowin' picture by a
Hand unsteady, brought to ruin;
Like her craters, if their deadness
Could give life unto the moon;
Like the agonizing horror
Of a violin out of tune.

There is a pause, and Devine goes slowly out.

Johnny (*returning*) Is he gone?

Mary Yes.

The two men re-enter.

First Man We can't wait any longer for t'oul' fella – sorry, Miss, but we have to live as well as th' nex' man.

They carry out some things.

Johnny Oh, isn't this terrible! . . . I suppose you told him everything . . . couldn't you have waited for a few days? . . . he'd have stopped th' takin' of the things, if you'd kep' your mouth shut. Are you burnin' to tell every one of the shame you've brought on us?

Mary (*snatching up her hat and coat*) Oh, this is unbearable! (*She rushes out.*)

First Man (*re-entering*) We'll take the chest o' drawers next – it's the heaviest.

The votive light flickers for a moment, and goes out.

Johnny (*in a cry of fear*) Mother o' God, the light's afther goin' out!

First Man You put the win' up me the way you bawled that time. The oil's all gone, that's all.

Johnny (*with an agonizing cry*) Mother o' God, there's a shot I'm afther gettin'!

First Man What's wrong with you, man? Is it a fit you're takin'?

Johnny I'm afther feelin' a pain in me breast, like the tearin' by of a bullet!

First Man He's goin' mad – it's a wondher they'd leave a chap like that here by himself.

Two Irregulars enter swiftly; they carry revolvers; one goes over to Johnny; the other covers the two furniture men.

First Irregular (*to the men, quietly and incisively*) Who are you? – what are yous doin' here? – quick!

First Man Removin' furniture that's not paid for.

First Irregular Get over to the other end of the room an' turn your faces to the wall – quick!

The two men turn their faces to the wall, with their hands up.

Second Irregular (*to Johnny*) Come on, Sean Boyle, you're wanted; some of us have a word to say to you.

Johnny I'm sick, I can't – what do you want with me?

Second Irregular Come on, come on; we've a distance to go, an' haven't much time – come on.

Johnny I'm an oul' comrade – yous wouldn't shoot an oul' comrade.

Second Irregular Poor Tancred was an oul' comrade o' yours, but you didn't think o' that when you gave him away to the gang that sent him to his grave. But we've no time to waste; come on – here, Dermot, ketch his arm. (*to Johnny*) Have you your beads?

Johnny Me beads! Why do you ass me that, why do you ass me that?

Second Irregular Go on, go on, march!

Johnny Are yous goin' to do in a comrade? – look at me arm, I lost it for Ireland.

Second Irregular Commandant Tancred lost his life for Ireland.

Johnny Sacred Heart of Jesus, have mercy on me! Mother o' God, pray for me – be with me now in the agonies o' death! . . . Hail, Mary, full o' grace . . . the Lord is . . . with Thee.

> *They drag out Johnny Boyle, and the curtain falls. When it rises again the most of the furniture is gone. Mary and Mrs Boyle, one on each side, are sitting in a darkened room, by the fire; it is an hour later.*

Mrs Boyle I'll not wait much longer . . . what did they bring him away in the mothor for? Nugent says he thinks they had guns . . . is me throubles never goin' to be over? . . . If anything ud happen to poor Johnny, I think I'd lose me mind . . . I'll go to the Police Station, surely they ought to be able to do somethin'.

> *Below is heard the sound of voices.*

Whisht, is that something? Maybe, it's your father, though when I left him in Foley's he was hardly able to lift his head. Whisht!

> *A knock at the door, and the voice of Mrs Madigan, speaking very softly.*

Mrs Madigan Mrs Boyle, Mrs Boyle.

> *Mrs Boyle opens the door.*

Oh, Mrs Boyle, God an' His Blessed Mother be with you this night!

Mrs Boyle (*calmly*) What is it, Mrs Madigan? It's Johnny – something about Johnny.

Mrs Madigan God send it's not, God send it's not Johnny!

Mrs Boyle Don't keep me waitin', Mrs Madigan; I've gone through so much lately that I feel able for anything.

Mrs Madigan Two polismen below wantin' you.

Mrs Boyle Wantin' me; an' why do they want me?

Mrs Madigan Some poor fella's been found, an' they think it's, it's . . .

Mrs Boyle Johnny, Johnny!

Mary (*with her arms round her mother*) Oh, mother, mother, me poor, darlin' mother.

Mrs Boyle Hush, hush, darlin'; you'll shortly have your own throuble to bear. (*To Mrs Madigan*) An' why do the polis think it's Johnny, Mrs Madigan?

Mrs Madigan Because one o' the doctors knew him when he was attendin' with his poor arm.

Mrs Boyle Oh, it's thrue, then; it's Johnny, it's me son, me own son!

Mary Oh, it's thrue, it's thrue what Jerry Devine says – there isn't a God, there isn't a God; if there was He wouldn't let these things happen!

Mrs Boyle Mary, Mary, you mustn't say them things. We'll want all the help we can get from God an' His Blessed Mother now! These things have nothin' to do with the Will o' God. Ah, what can God do agen the stupidity o' men!

Mrs Madigan The polis want you to go with them to the hospital to see the poor body – they're waitin' below.

Mrs Boyle We'll go. Come, Mary, an' we'll never come back here agen. Let your father furrage for himself now; I've done all I could an' it was all no use – he'll be hopeless till the end of his days. I've got a little room in me sisther's where we'll stop till your throuble is over, an' then we'll work together for the sake of the baby.

Mary My poor little child that'll have no father!

Mrs Boyle It'll have what's far betther – it'll have two mothers.

A Rough Voice (*shouting from below*) Are yous goin' to keep us waitin' for yous all night?

Mrs Madigan (*going to the door, and shouting down*) Take your hour, there, take your hour! If yous are in such a hurry, skip off, then, for nobody wants you here – if they did yous wouldn't be found. For you're the same as yous were undher the British Government – never where yous are wanted! As far as I can see, the Polis as Polis, in this city, is Null an' Void!

Mrs Boyle We'll go, Mary, we'll go; you to see your poor dead brother, an' me to see me poor dead son!

Mary I dhread it, mother, I dhread it!

Mrs Boyle I forgot, Mary, I forgot; your poor oul' selfish mother was only thinkin' of herself. No, no, you mustn't come – it wouldn't be good for you. You go on to me sisther's an I'll face th' ordeal meself. Maybe I didn't feel sorry enough for Mrs Tancred when her poor son was found as Johnny's been found now – because he was a Die-hard! Ah, why didn't I remember that then he wasn't a Diehard or a Stater, but only a poor dead son! It's well I remember all that she said – an' it's my turn to say it now: What was the pain I suffered, Johnny, bringin' you into the world to carry you to your cradle, to the pains I'll suffer carryin' you out o' the world to bring you to your grave! Mother o' God, Mother o' God, have pity on us all! Blessed Virgin, where were you when me darlin' son was riddled with bullets, when me darlin' son was riddled with bullets? Sacred Heart o' Jesus, take away our hearts o' stone, and give us hearts o' flesh! Take away this murdherin' hate, an' give us Thine own eternal love!

They all go slowly out. There is a pause; then a sound of

84

*shuffling steps on the stairs outside. The door opens and
Boyle and Joxer, both of them very drunk, enter.*

Boyle I'm able to go no farther. . . . Two polis, ey . . .
what were they doin' here, I wondher? . . . Up to no good,
anyhow . . . an' Juno an' that lovely daughter o' mine with
them. (*Taking a sixpence from his pocket and looking at
it*) Wan single, solitary tanner left out of all I borreyed
. . . . (*He lets it fall.*) The last o' the Mohicans . . . . The
blinds is down, Joxer, the blinds is down!

Joxer (*walking unsteadily across the room, and anchoring
at the bed*) Put all . . . your throubles . . . in your oul' kit-
bag . . . an' smile . . . smile . . . smile!

Boyle The counthry'll have to steady itself . . . it's goin'
. . . to hell . . . . Where'r all . . . the chairs . . . gone to . . .
steady itself, Joxer. . . . Chairs'll . . . have to . . . steady
themselves . . . . No matther . . . what any one may . . .
say . . . . Irelan' sober . . . is Irelan' . . . free.

Joxer (*stretching himself on the bed*) Chains . . . an' . . .
slaveree . . . that's a darlin' motto . . . a daaarlin' . . .
motto!

Boyle If th' worst comes . . . to th' worse . . . I can join a
. . . flyin' . . . column . . . . I done . . . me bit . . . in
Easther Week . . . had no business . . . to . . . be . . . there
. . . but Captain Boyle's Captain Boyle!

Joxer Breathes there a man with soul . . . so . . . de . . . ad
. . . this . . . me . . . o . . . wn, me nat . . . ive l . . . an'!

Boyle (*subsiding into a sitting posture on the floor*)
Commandant Kelly died . . . in them . . . arms . . . Joxer
. . . . Tell me Volunteer Butties . . . says he . . . that . . . I
died for . . . Irelan'!

Joxer D'jever rade Willie . . . Reilly . . . an' his own . . .
Colleen . . . Bawn? It's a darlin' story, a daarlin' story!

Boyle I'm telling you . . . Joxer . . . th' whole worl's . . . in a terr . . . ible state o' . . . chassis!

Curtain.

WITHIN THE GATES

If possible, the Curtain intervening between the opening of the play and the scenes following, should be one showing the Park Gates, stiff and formal, dignified and insolent. The bars should shine with the silver gleam of aluminium paint, and cross or diagonal bars should be a deep and sombre black. All space between the bars should be dark – but not too dark – green. The gates proper are flanked by generous panels of a vivid yellow, representing the piers, lower than the bars, and topped by copings of orange-coloured panels. This curtain, when it is pulled back, represents the opening of the gates; and, when it falls back into its place, represents the closing of the gates; or, the outline of the gates may be suggested on the curtain.

The above idea of a front curtain was derived from Eugene O'Neill's suggestion of a front curtain for his great play, *Mourning Becomes Electra*.

Characters

The Dreamer
Older Chair Attendant
Younger Chair Attendant
The Bishop
The Bishop's Sister
The Atheist
The Policewoman
1st Nursemaid
2nd Nursemaid
A Guardsman
A Gardener
1st Evangelist
2nd Evangelist
The Young Woman
A Young Salvation Army Officer
The Old Woman
A Man Wearing a Bowler Hat
The Man with the Stick (afterwards, an umbrella)
Man Wearing a Trilby Hat
Man Wearing a Straw One (afterwards, a cap)
A Crowd of the Down-and-Out
A Chorus of Young Men and Maidens

Scene One

Spring. Morning.
Within a park on a spring morning.
A clear, light-blue sky, against which is shown, in
places, the interlaced dark brown branches of trees, dotted
with green, yellow, and red buds.
The green sward in front slopes up towards the back,
but in no way high enough to prevent a view of the
spaciousness of the Park behind. In the centre of the slope
are a few wide steps leading to the top, where, a little to
one side, stands a War Memorial in the form of a steel-
helmeted soldier, the head bent on the breast, skeleton-like
hands leaning on the butt-end of a rifle. Bushes allow the
figure to be seen only from the waist up. The body and
arms of the figure are shaped in a sharply defined way; the
hat a wide circle; and the features are cut in long, sharp
and angular lines. The figure stands out grey against the
blue sky and the green shrubs, and seems to be shrinking
back from the growing interests brought into being by new
life and her thrusting activities.
The rise of the slope is sprinkled with large, formalized
figures of daffodils.
At the foot of the slope are paths branching to the right
and to the left, that on the left flowing into a wider one
encircling the Park lake, from which can be occasionally
heard the cries of the water-fowl swimming on the water
or preening themselves on the banks.
Birds are heard singing in a subdued but busy way, as
they search for food or build their nests.
Formally shaped chairs are here and there, and one or
two stiff and dignified-looking benches are near the foot of

*the slope. They are painted so as to mingle with the
colours of the scene, and are hardly noticeable. The
scheme of colour is a delicate green and light blue,
patterned by the yellow daffodils and the bare, bud-dotted
branches of the trees.*

*As the gates are opening, the Dreamer enters, and passes
through them into the Park. He is gazing with an intensely
dreaming expression at a paper which he holds in his left
hand. His right hand, holding a short pencil, moves in a
gentle, dreamy way, beating time, as he murmurs the
opening bars of 'Our Mother the Earth is a Maiden Again'.
He crosses out as the Chorus enters, singing, followed by
various people, who move about at the back, up, down,
and about the paths, without jostle or confusion.*

*A Chorus of Young Boys and Girls, representing trees
and flowers, enters singing.*

*First, a girl whose skirt represents a white crocus, veined
with blue; next, a boy in black on whose breast is a
stylized pattern of a beech tree leaf; then a girl whose skirt
represents a blue cornflower; next, a boy on whose breast
is a formally shaped oak leaf; then a girl whose skirt
represents a daffodil; next, a boy on whose breast is the
pattern of a maple leaf.*

*The Chorus remains in front, while the crowd move
about as they listen, or when they join in the singing.*

Chorus (*singing*)
> Our mother, the earth, is a maiden again, young, fair,
>   and a maiden again.
> Our mother, the earth, is a maiden again, she's young,
>   fair, and a maiden again.
> Her thoughts are a dance as she seeks out her
>   Bridegroom, the Sun, through the lovely confusion of
>   singing of birds, and of blossom and bud.
> She feels the touch of his hand on her hair, on her
>   cheeks; in the budding of trees,

She feels the kiss of his love on her mouth, on her
    breast, as she dances along,

Crowd (*joining in*)
Through the lovely confusion of singing of birds, and of
    blossom and bud.
Her thoughts are a dance as she seeks out her
    Bridegroom, the Sun, through the lovely confusion of
    singing of birds, and of blossom and bud.

Chorus
She hears the fiercely sung song of the birds, busy
    building new homes in the hedge;
She hears a challenge to life and to death as she dances
    along,

Crowd (*joining in*)
Through the lovely confusion of singing of birds, and of
    blossom and bud.
Her thoughts are a dance as she seeks out her
    Bridegroom, the Sun, through the lovely confusion of
    singing of birds, and of blossom and bud.

Chorus and Crowd
Our mother, the earth, is a maiden again, young, fair,
    and a maiden again.

*While the last line is being sung, the Crowd and the
Chorus go out by different ways, leaving only the two
Chair Attendants dusting the chairs and arranging them.
One is young and thin and the other is old and stocky,
and both are in the last lap of physical decay. One has a
stiff right leg, and the other has a stiff left one. They are
dressed in long, khaki-coloured cotton coats, and wear
peaked caps.*

Older One 'Ow's the poor old leg, todye, 'Erbert?

Young One Oh Gord! 'Ow's yours?

Older One Aw – sime wye, with honours! I seen thet poet chap atryin' to cadge a chire again; sits dahn on one till 'ee sees me comin' in the distance.

Young One (*not listening – pensively*) Wot'll we do when we file to be able to walk! 'En this singin' gets me dahn. 'Eartless for a crahwd to sing when a man's in misery.

Older One (*testily*) Don't let us think of them things! It's our destiny. But I 'ates that poet chap; I 'ates 'im! 'Ate 'is liveliness. Fair cheek 'ee 'as. A bum – that's wot 'ee 'is. Wouldn't do a dye's work for Gord Almighty. I'd say it to 'is fice, I would.

Young One Look aht! 'Ere 'ee is.

The Dreamer comes down the grass slope, crosses over, and sits down on a bench. He watches the Two Attendants. He is a young man, lithely built, though a little thin and pale now from a hard time; but he carries himself buoyantly. His features are rugged; his eyes bright, sometimes flashing in an imaginative mood, but usually quiet and dreamy-looking. His head is covered with a soft black, broad-brimmed hat, and he is wearing a tightly belted trench mackintosh. Outside the trench coat, around his neck, is a light, vivid orange scarf.

Dreamer (*suddenly*) Here, you two derelict worshippers of fine raiment – when are you going to die?

Older One (*angrily*) Mind your own business, see! We 'as more right to life than you 'as. We work – you don't – eh, Godfrey?

Young One My oath, we 'as!

Dreamer No one has a right to life who doesn't fight to make it greater. I've watched you fawning on the bishop and on every good coat that sits down on a chair.

Young One You mind your own business!

*The Young Woman comes down the slope and crosses
the sward to go out to the left. She has a preoccupied
and rather anxious look on her face, and appears to be
searching for someone.*

*She is very pretty, and her figure would make most
young men immediately forget the seventh
commandment. Her face is a little pale, but this paleness
is hidden by a cautious and clever make-up. She has an
intelligent look, which is becoming a little worn by
contact with the selfishness and meanness of the few
clients that have patronized her; for these, though
unable to resist the desire to have her, hate her
subconsciously before they go with her, and consciously
detest her when their desires have been satisfied. She has
read a little, but not enough; she has thought a little, but
not enough; she is deficient in self-assurance, and is too
generous and sensitive to be a clever whore, and her
heart is not in the business.*

*Convent tales of punishments reserved for the
particular sins tangled round sex expression have left in
her mind lusty images of hellfire. She is dressed in a black
tailored suit, topped by a scarlet hat. On the hat is an
ornament, in black, of a crescent; and the hip of her dress
is decorated with a scarlet one. The Dreamer sees her,
rises, and is about to follow her. She stops and faces him.*

Young Woman I am troubled; I am anxious; please don't
follow me.

Dreamer I shall follow after loveliness all the days of my
life.

Young Woman Not just now, please; I do not want you.

*She turns to go; he follows slowly. She turns, to say
hysterically:*

Go away, please!

> *She goes out. He returns, crestfallen, to his seat on the*
> *bench. The Attendants snigger.*

Older One The likes of 'er ain't for the likes of 'im.

Young One (*to the Dreamer*) A fine choke-off, wha'?

> *Dreamer rises, catches each by the coat-collar, and*
> *shakes them.*

Dreamer (*roughly*)Ye lost ones! Will ye starve and droop
and die without a dream? Even the lame and the halt can
hunt out a shrine! Will ye mock at the better ones who
refuse to die like sheep?

Attendants (*together*) Eh, there, leggo! Someone call a
perliceman!

> *The Atheist comes in from a path above, sees the angry*
> *scene, and hurries down to stop it.*

Atheist (*catching the Dreamer by the arm*) Now then,
friend, now then; let withered life die in its own sour way,
without pushing it to a sudden and unprovided end!

Dreamer (*pushing the Attendants from him – one to the*
right, the other to the left) Away, and cower in your
corner, till life hoodooes you out of the misery you both
love! Away, the pair of you, who make a nightmare of the
dream of God!

> *The Attendants slink off, one to the right, the other to*
> *the left. The Dreamer and the Atheist sit on the bench*
> *together.*

Atheist (*warningly*) Take care, friend: you'd pay as high a
penalty for hurting hopelessness as you would for a life of
promise or one of proved production.

Dreamer I know; I lost my temper. Never mind that now.

I've seen her; she passed by here just before you came.

Atheist (*rising*) Passed by 'ere? I'm off in the opposite direction.

Dreamer (*stopping him*) No fear of meeting her; she won't come back. I tried to keep her, but she wouldn't stay a second.

Atheist Oh, lay off the young lass, Dreamer. Let 'er go 'er own wye – up the hill of life or dahn it.

Dreamer She's too lonely to be left alone, Ned; and too pretty; intelligent, too, as you say.

Atheist (*impatiently*) I know all that! She 'as a fine mind, if she'd only use it the right way. But it's forever darting forward, back; to the left today, to the right tomorrow – no 'uman being could stand it. I'm glad I'm only her step-da.

Dreamer Who is, and where is, her real daddy?

Atheist Stoodent of theology, the story goes: fell in love with a pretty housemaid, and she responded. When the mother knew what was abaht to happen, she knocked at the college gate, but was driven off. When a few years old, the kid was shoved into a church institootion, where the nuns, being what she was – a child of sin –, paid her special attention; an' the terrors an' dangers of hell became the child's chief enjoyment!

Dreamer Good God! (*Earnestly*) Ned, we must never ease off the fight for a life that is free from fear!

Atheist Never, Dreamer, never. Then the mother married an Irish dragoon, a brave, decent man, Dreamer, home from the front on leave; had a starlit time with the warrior for a week; then the dragoon disappeared in one of those vanishing advances from the front line an' the widow settles dahn on 'er pension.

Dreamer Then she fastened on to you, eh?

Atheist To tell the truth, it was I fastened on to 'er. Even when I met 'er, she was still the kind of woman would make a man long for something to 'appen – you know, Dreamer?

Dreamer Ay, I know – too damned well!

Atheist Then I delivered the child from the church institootion, sayin' I was the father. I did my best for 'er, takin' awye a supernatural 'eaven from over 'er 'ead, an' an unnatural 'ell from under 'er feet; but she never quite escaped. D'ye know, one time, the lass near knew the whole of Pine's *Age of Reason* off by 'eart!

Dreamer And did you bring her into touch with song?

Atheist Song? Oh, I had no time for song!

Dreamer You led her from one darkness into another, man. (*He rises and walks about. Angrily*) Will none of you ever guess that man can study man, or worship God, in dance and song and story! (*Appealingly*) Ah, Ned, if you could but see her with the eyes of youth, you would not let her live so lonely.

Atheist I helped her all I could. Out of the earnings of a first-class carpenter, I gave 'er a good education, an' taught 'er a lot myself; but it was all no good – she refused to think as I did. The 'ome's broken up, now, and I'm not eager to try to get it together agine.

Dreamer How broken up?

Atheist You see, when the maid came close to womanhood, the mother turned religious, an' begun to 'ate the kid, sayin' that while the kid was there, 'er sin was ever in front of 'er fice. Then she took to drink an' violence.

Dreamer A sweet home for a girl coming also to womanhood!

Atheist After a long time of patient endoorance, one day the girl ups an', withaht a word, goes; an' a month after, I goes too; so 'ere she is, her whole life a desire for a bright time of it; an' 'ere I am, a speaker rending the strands of superstition's web thet keeps poor men from movin'.

Dreamer Give the lovely lass one more chance, speaker; live the last years of your life with loveliness.

Atheist Not damn likely; the longer I'm by myself, the more I likes it.

While they have been speaking the last few words, the Man with the Stick has appeared on the slope above.

Man with Stick (*calling down to Atheist*) 'Ave you got tonight's speech ready, Ned?

Atheist (*taking notebook from a pocket*) Not yet, Bill.

Man with Stick Get a move on: we 'as to bounce the idea of a Gord from men's minds, so make it strong.

The Two Chair Attendants limp in, carrying a chair between them. They set it down, stand panting for a while, then the Older One begins to give it a dust, the Man with the Stick watching them contemptuously, and dubiously shaking his grey head.

(*Going close to Older Attendant*) 'Ere, 'ave you an inquirin' mind, friend?

Older One Eh? Wot?

Man with Stick I asks if you 'as an inquirin' mind. (*He taps the chair with the stick.*) Wot is this? A chair. Does thet tell you all abaht it? No. Wot's it myde of? Wood. Nah, if it was myde of cork it would be lighter; but if it was myde of lead it would be 'eavier – see?

Older one Ay?

Man with Stick Ay? Not ay, but wye?

Older One Wye? Wot wye?

Man with Stick (*impatiently*) Wot wye! Listen, man. (*hitting the chair with stick*) Wood; 'ard. Nah wye's the chair 'ard? Is it doo to density, or is it not?

Older One I don't ask no questions of chairs.

Young One We 'as to attend to our werk, see?

Man with Stick (*woe in his voice*) No brrine!

The two Nursemaids, the Under One pushing the fine pram, appear behind the Man with the Stick.

Under Nursemaid (*imperiously*) Gangway there!

The pram strikes his heels, and he jumps aside, his mouth opening for an angry exclamation; but when he sees the splendid pram, he closes it without saying a word. The Upper Nursemaid picks out a chair farthest from the others. The Chair Attendants run over bearing a chair between them for the Under Maid, and the Older One dusts both the chairs vigorously.

Older One (*after dusting*) Now, miss. Nice day, miss.

Upper Nursemaid (*shortly*) Very nice.

Older One To cart such a byeby abaht's a responsible thing, I'd say, miss.

Upper Nursemaid (*stiffly*) I suppose so. I don't feel it. (*She sees his dirty hand is resting on the pram.*) Take that dirty paw off the pram at once! This is a countess's baby!

Older One (*pulling his hand away as if the pram was red-hot*) Oh, excuse me, miss. I forgot for the minute!

Upper Nursemaid (*loftily*) Go away; we're season tickets; go away!

The Attendant slinks off from the pram as the Bishop, followed by his Sister, appears coming down the slope from behind the Memorial. The Policewoman strolls in from the path on the left.

Atheist (*mockingly – over to the Nursemaids*) Must be careful of a countess's byeby!

Upper Nursemaid (*with great dignity*) A countess's byeby's a considerytion. I'd like you all to know.

The Bishop and his Sister come down among the crowd. The Bishop is a heavily built man of sixty or so. His head, his feet, and hands are large; his voice, once deep and sonorous, has become a little husky. The pretentious briskness of his movements is an attempt to hide from others the fact that he is beginning to fail. He is anxious to show to all he meets that he is an up-to-the-present-minute clergyman, and that those who wear the stole are, on the whole, a lusty, natural, broad-minded, cheery crowd. He is in a black cassock, wears a purple stock round his neck, and his head is covered with a purple biretta or a scarlet one. A black ribbon is round his neck, and from the ends of this, which meet on his chest, hangs a large red cross, on which is a white figure of the Saviour.

His Sister is a few years younger, grey-haired, stiff, and formal. She has more common sense than her brother, but, while there is a suggestion of good-nature about the Bishop, there is no suggestion whatever of softness about the form or manner of his Sister. Her dress is of grey stuff, stiff like steel.

Bishop (*breezily*) Hello, boys; good morning, Constable. (*To Nursemaids*) Hello, girls!

Attendants (*together*) 'Ello, your reverence.

Policewoman (*with a dignified salute*) Morning, sir.

Bishop (*buoyantly*) Glorious nip of crispness in the air of a Spring morning, isn't there?

Policewoman Exhilarating, I'd say.

Older One Gits a man goin'.

Young One (*lilting*) Yes, let me like a soldier fall, dideray diderum dideree.

Bishop Flowers appear on the earth; the time of singing of birds is come, and the voice of the turtle is heard in the land – God speaking of Spring, friends!

Policewoman Quate, sir.

Young One 'Its it off nacely, sir.

Dreamer (*to the Bishop*) Not God, but a poet speaking of Spring, sir. Render to God the things that are God's and to the poet the things that are his.

Bishop (*to the Dreamer – smilingly*) God is in all, and God is all things, sir.

Atheist (*combatively*) Would the reverend en' learned gentleman tell us poor people 'oo is Gord, wot 'e is, en' where 'e is located?

Policewoman (*to the Atheist, stiffly*) You keep your almighty arguments for your meetings.

Older One (*viciously*) 'Ear, 'ear!

Bishop (*to Policewoman – graciously*) Never mind, Constable; there are always those who never will give thanks to God for life.

Dreamer Always, when there are those who have no life for which to thank Him.

*Two prowling Evangelists come shuffling in. Each has a
frame strapped to his body from which rise two upright
pieces between which is a poster, looking like a square
banner over their heads. On the first one, in red, is the
phrase Once to Die, and on the second, in black, Then
the Judgment.*

*The First Evangelist has a lemon-shaped head,
staring, stupid-looking eyes, shrunken cheeks, surly lines
round a wide mouth, and ears that stick out from the
side of his head.*

*The Second has a big head, coarse face, heavy,
hanging lips, and a small snubby nose. As he chants, he
continually blinks his eyes. Both are shabbily dressed,
and look, for all the world, like sullen, long-forgotten
clowns. They shuffle in among the disputants, each
pointing to the warning posters over their heads.*

1st Evangelist   Once to Die.

2nd Evangelist   After that The Judgement.

1st Evangelist (*chanting*)
Is it well with thy soul?
Is it well, is it well with thy soul?

2nd Evangelist (*chanting*)
It is well with my soul.
It is well, it is well with my soul.

*They chant themselves out, looking back to gather the
others into the warning they give.*

Atheist (*mockingly – to the Bishop*) Two more Richmonds
in the field!

Young One (*encouraging the Bishop*) Never you mind 'im
or them, sir; go on torking abaht the spring en' the birds!

The birds sing merrily.

Bishop (*joyously*) Listen! The busy birds warbling a
sylvan sonata. Facing out life with a song! No shaking of
the head here in denial of God's goodness and glory.
Sursum corda – lift up your hearts!

Dreamer We lift them up unto the birds.

Older One (*gushingly*) The birds bring a man 'ope. Even
with the doo 'eavy on the grass, a feller begins to feel spry
en' elevated when they stert their chirruping.

Policewoman Not a daht abaht it.

Bishop's Sister Gilbert, come and look at the swans.

Bishop (*with conviction – to the Policewoman*) Do you
know, Constable, that, to an observing mind, it seems to
be conclusive that the most beautiful part of God's
creation – apart from man, of course –

Policewoman Quate – setting man en' woman aside for a
moment.

Bishop Quite. The most beautiful part of God's manifold
creation is, undoubtedly, the birds!

> *The Bishop lifts his head and looks up at the sky; then
> the Policewoman does the same, and, lastly, the two
> Chair Attendants lift their heads and crane their necks
> in an upward look.*

Brave little birds.

Policewoman Beautiful little birds.

Attendants (*together*) Beautiful, innocent little birds.

Man with Stick (*suddenly leaning forward – imperatively*)
'Ere, 'ow do birds resist the lawrs of gravitation? Come,
quick – the lot of you – think!

> *They all lower their heads again, together.*

Young One (*enthusiastically*) Never you mind 'im, sir. Wot you says reminds man that Gord watches even over the fall of the sparrer!

Atheist (*mockingly*) Ay, an' the fall of the 'awk on the sparrer to tear it to pieces!

Older One (*hotly*) You shut your rotten mouth, will you! Warnt to 'ear yourself torkin', torkin', do you? Try to look at things in perspective, carn't you? Wot's you or me in the general scheme of things, eh? Speck o' dust, blide o' grass, a nought, a nothing. Wish Jimmy Douglas of the *Daily Express* was 'ere to 'ear you. 'Ee's the man would stun you both with truth! (*to his fellow Attendant*) Wot d'ye sye, Godfrey?

Young One 'Ee's a man as knows 'oo's 'oo en' wot's wot.

Older One You bet 'ee does. 'Ow on a 'olidye, sitting by the sea, under the stars, wot 'ee sawr en' wot 'ee 'eard. 'Ow 'ee marvelled at the star dust 'ee could see en' the star dust 'ee couldn't see; en' 'ow 'ee was filled with terror en' fear as 'ee 'eard the clock of eternity ticking!

Dreamer It won't be long, old man, till you hear the clock of eternity ticking!

Older One (*stormily*)Wot if it won't? It ain't the end, is it?

Dreamer (*rising from the bench – fervently*) Kill off the withered mind, the violently stupid, O Lord, who having nothing to give, have nothing to get!

Bishop's Sister (*pulling Bishop's cassock*) Gilbert, do come to watch the swans!

Older One (*catching hold of Dreamer's sleeve – violently*) Thinkin' thet life doesn't keep agoing on when it ends! I yells it aht, I yells it aht – death's only the gytewye to a fuller en' a nobler life!

Dreamer (*angrily shaking off the Attendant's hold*) Take that dead hand off me! There are some here equal in value to a countess's baby. (*He shoves the Attendant roughly from him so that he lurches back against the pram.*) Be off, and die, and keep a holy distance from the quick and the lively!

Young One (*bawling to the Older One*) 'Erbert, eh, mind the countess's byeby!

Atheist (*mockingly – to the Nursemaid*) Lady, lady, this is no place for a countess's byeby!

Policewoman (*going to the Nursemaid*) 'Ee's right; better conduct it to a calmer locality.

> The two Nursemaids rise hurriedly, cross over the sward, preceded by the Policewoman, and disappear with the pram behind the trees to the left.

Bishop's Sister (*plucking at his cassock*) You see, Gilbert! A bishop should be in the midst of the incense, in the sanctuary, safe away from the sour touch of common humanity.

Bishop (*jovially*) Nonsense, dear! I lose no dignity in getting close to the common people. Get them to talk with us; laugh and joke with us; and then we can expect them to pray with us.

Atheist (*over to the Bishop*) Prayer? For what? To whom?
Old memories, faiths infirm and dead,
Ye fools; for which among you deems
His prayer can alter green to red,
Or stones to bread?

Bishop's Sister (*pulling the Bishop away*) You but mould mockery from the profane thoughts of others. Come and watch the swans. Remember what happened to you in your student days!

The Bishop, at the last phrase, stiffens, his face clenches, and he goes off with his Sister without another word.

Atheist (*as the Bishop is pulled out*) He 'as a better charnce with the swans than 'ee 'as with us!

Man with Stick (*calling from top of slope*) 'Ere, are you comin' to look up wot it says in *The Origin of the Idea of a God*?

Atheist (*rising to go*) Must be off, Dreamer. Will you come a bit of the way?

Dreamer No; I've got a song shaping in my mind, and I must think it out: Song of the Down-and-Out.

Atheist (*indifferently*) Oh, hymn for the unemployed?

Dreamer No, no; not the unemployed. They remain men in their misfortune. I keen those who whine through today and dread tomorrow; who would for ever furl the flag of life; who fear any idea common thought hasn't had time to bless; those who have a sigh for a song and a sad sigh for a drumbeat.

Atheist A fair crowd, Dreamer. Well, so-long for the present.

Dreamer See you at the old place, and we'll have coffee and a sandwich?

Atheist I'll be there.

He goes off with the Man with the Stick. The Dreamer takes out a notebook, and writes in it. The Gardener appears behind, trimming the shrubs with a pair of shears. The Dreamer then strolls up to watch him, the two Chair Attendants put some chairs in order.

Older One (*attempting brightness*) I listened to the wireless last night, Godfrey.

Young One 'Eard anything worthwhile?

Older One Part of Pageant of England. Wunnerful! Mide me feel prahd to be en' Englishman!

Young One Wot was it abaht?

Older One The guys as was once kings en stytesmen wot mide us all wot we is. Mide me thrill, it did, to 'ear the sahnd of Drike's drum!

Young One 'Oo's drum?

Older One Drike's. The bloke wot beat the Spanish Armyda, en' drove them back to Spine. A ghost-drum is alwyes 'eard beatin' whenever England's in dineger.

Young One (*scornfully*) Superstition!

In the distance are heard faint sounds of the sombre music of the Down-and-Out chant, saddened with the slow beat of a muffled drum. The Attendants stand stiff, a look of fright on their faces.

Attendants (*together*) The drum-beat of the Down-and-Out!

Older One (*to his companion*) Wot'r you stiffenin' for?

Young One (*tensely*) I warn't stiffenin'. (*Pause.*) Wot'r you styrin' at?

Older One (*tensely*) I warnt styrin'. Didja hear anything?

Young One (*tensely*) No, nothing; did you?

Older One Nothing.

They go slowly by each other, one to the left, the other to the right, and go out – a deeper limp coming into each lame leg, keeping time to the distant chant and drumbeat.

The Dreamer is watching the Gardener working, handling the blossoms.

Dreamer Happy man to be handling the purple, blue, and yellow of the blossoms.

Gardener Let them live and let them die, for I'm not thinking of blossoms at all.

Dreamer What are you thinking of then?

Gardener Of a dance I take a sweet little lass to, when the sun goes in and the stars come out.

Dreamer I envy you the handling of a flower by day and of a girl by night.

Gardener When the dance ends, I go to her little flat, her very own flat, where (*he lilts*) She'll be the honeysuckle, I'll be the bee!

Dreamer I hope a bee that never leaves a sting behind.

Gardener You should see her – a beauty! Thinks I'll marry her; I'm too young to marry yet. Mad to have a kid – matrimony's signature tune; but not for me, though. An odd lass. A little too serious. Says she wants a chance sometimes to sit and wonder.

Dreamer (*musingly*) I hear a song in what you've said.

Gardener (*surprised*) A song? In what?

Dreamer In the flowers, heaven, and the girl.

Gardener You do, do you? Funny!

The Gardener goes on arranging the flowers, while the Dreamer slowly goes off till he is hidden behind the shrubs. After a pause, the Gardener begins to sing.

A fig for th' blossoms th' biggest vase can hold,
The flow'rs that face the world shy, the ones that face it bold.
Men may praise them and worship them as something fine and rare,

Lounging through their gorgeous perfumes so deftly
    hidden there.
But I'll never wonder though some in glee disclose
The white of whitest lily, the red of reddest rose;
For I'll fold in my arms a girl as bright as she is gay,
And tonight the primrose path of love will be a wonder
    way!

*Couples, linking arms, enter from different points, mix
and cross by each other, parade about, keeping time
with the tune as they join in the singing. The Gardener
moves out of sight. The Young Woman is seen moving
hurriedly among the couples, taking no heed of the
singing, weaving a way through the couples without
spoiling the ordered movements, but she doesn't keep in
time with the lilt. She looks anxious, and appears to be
searching for someone. She disappears while the song is
being sung.*

Crowd of Couples (*singing*)
When Adam first corner'd Eve, he stood bewildered
    there,
For he saw beauty shining through a mist of golden
    hair;
But Eve quickly coaxed him on, and show'd him
    woman's way,
And so the lover and his lass are king and queen today!

So here's to the lasses who bow in beauty's fane,
Who kiss in costly parlour or kiss in country lane;
Let man bend his back to work or bend down his knee
    to pray,
Still the primrose path of love will ever be a wonder
    way!

*When the couples go, the only ones left are the
Guardsman and the Nursemaid, and the Man with the
Stick. The Nursemaid and the Guardsman, who has his*

arm round her, go to a bench. He sits down, and as the
Nursemaid proceeds to do the same, he catches her, and
sweeps her on to his knee. The Man with the Stick, who
has been at the butt of the slope shaking his head
contemptuously at the singing, now comes down to
where the couple is seated, and swings his stick in
disdain.

Man with Stick (*scornfully – swinging the stick*)
Nonsense! A lot of it is all nonsense, nonsense!

Guardsman Lot of wot?

Man with Stick Babble abaht life! Life, man, life! Before
we can get sense into it, we've gotta know its meaning:
wot it is, where it came from, where it goes.

Guardsman Where wot goes?

Man with Stick Life, man, life!

Nursemaid (*indignantly*) You push off. We want to be left
alone. We've important things to talk abaht, so push off,
please!

Man with Stick (*taken aback*) Oh? If you ain't eager to
learn the truth, I'll push off – (*He sees the Two Evangelists
approaching, displaying their placards.*) now! (*Muttering
as he goes*) Bumptious, brazen ignorance!

The Two Evangelists prowl forward, looking left and
right for sinners. They spy the Guardsman and the
Nursemaid, and shuffle over slowly to them.

1st Evangelist (*to the Couple*) Remember, brother and
sister, it's a terrible thing when it comes.

Guardsman Wot is? When wot comes?

1st Evangelist Death, brother, death!

2nd Evangelist An' after death The Judgement!

1st Evangelist Oh, be converted before it is too late.

2nd Evangelist Before it is too, too late, too late.

1st Evangelist It may be upon you today, in an hour, in a moment.

Guardsman Wot mye?

1st Evangelist Death, brother, death!

Nursemaid (*indignantly*) We want to be left alone. We've important business to talk about an' do, so push off, please.

1st Evangelist Left alone! Devil's desire that, sister. You won't be left alone in hell.

Guardsman (*rising angrily, and pushing them away*) Here, git! We wants privacy, so git!

Nursemaid (*rising from bench as he is about to sit down again, having got rid of the Evangelists*) Let's sit dahn on th' grass, 'Arry – it's more comfortable.

Guardsman So it is.

They recline on the slope. He puts his arms round her, kisses her, and is about to kiss again, when the Policewoman appears opposite, and stares reprovingly at them. She goes over to them.

Policewoman You can't do the like of that 'ere. Control yourselves. It doesn't allow such conduct in a public place.

Guardsman (*embarrassed, but trying to be defiant*) Wot dorsen't?

Policewoman (*sharply*) Th' lawr, young man, the lawr!

The Couple rise, and go off embarrassed, followed by the Policewoman. As they go off, the Young Woman and the Atheist appear at the top of the slope, and come down it.

Guardsman (*to the Nursemaid, as they go off*) As I was asayein', th' orderly officer says to me, Private Odgerson, says 'ee, seein' as you're a man of intelligence, says 'ee, en' th' best shot in the battalion, 'ee says, we warnt your edvice, 'ee says, in a kinda fix we're in –

They disappear.

Young Woman (*indicating a bench to the Atheist*) I'll sit down on a seat, Dad, for a minute. My legs are giving way under me. Let me sit down a second.

Atheist (*irritably – as they sit down*) You shouldn't have rushed after me the way you did. En' 'urry up – I've gotta read up some things in *The Origin of the Idea of a God*.

Young Woman (*between breaths*) I was afraid, if I didn't run, I'd lose sight of you, and I wanted to see you.

Atheist (*as he helps the Young Woman to sit down*) Damn stupid to rush yourself into a heart attack.

Young Woman (*frightened*) There's a shadow passing over my eyes again! (*Grasping the Atheist's arm*) Dad, I'm afraid I'm far from well.

Atheist (*soothingly*) Just a little flutter from over-exertion, that's all. All our hearts jump at times.

Young Woman (*vehemently*) I tell you it's deeper than that, an' I'll croak suddenly, sooner or later. The other night I had a man with me, an' when I was half stripped it came on me as he was coming over to paw me. In a mist I saw the fright in his eyes, saw him huddling his clothes on an' hurrying away. Then I fell down. In a faint I fell down, till the morning came an' brought up the woman below to find me still in a faint where I fell down.

Atheist Excitement, over-excitement.

Young Woman (*hysterically*) If I have to die, I'll die game; I'll die dancing!

Atheist Hush! Not so loud – we're in a park.

Young Woman (*persuasively catching hold of his arm*) I want you to help me, Dad; I'll go mad if I have to live alone any longer.

Atheist (*firmly*) No, no; no more of that. Live your own life. I'm not your father, so cut out the daddy business.

Young Woman (*moving closer to him*) You crept into a father's place when you took me away from the nuns who were moulding my life round the sin of my mother. You made me call you Dad when you saved me from their crosses, their crowns, and their canes, and lifted my hands up in salute to the sun and the moon and the stars. (*She puts an arm around him.*) You'll give me one more chance, won't you? You will, you will!

Atheist (*restlessly*) I did that twice before, and, as soon as you felt well, you hurried off, leaving me with rooms I didn't want and furniture I couldn't sell.

Young Woman (*leaning wearily against his shoulder*) I can't live alone any longer, Dad. When I lie down in bed and stretch out in search of sleep, the darkness reddens into a glow from the fire that can never be quenched.

Atheist (*impatiently*) Oh, the old, false, foolish fear again!

Young Woman Green-eyed, barrel-bellied men glare and grin at me; huge-headed, yellow-eyed women beckon to me out of the glow from the fire that can never be quenched. Black-feathered owls, with eyes like great white moons, peck at me as they fly through the glow from the fire that can never be quenched. Save me, Dad, oh, save me!

Atheist (*scornful and angry*) The hell en' red-fire for ever talk of the nuns! They frame the world en' fill life with it, till we eat, sleep, work, en' play for ever in the smoke of hell!

Young Woman (*humbly*) It will be only for awhile, Dad, for I'm going to marry the Gardener. He's not much, but, at least, he is safety, and, maybe, peace too.

Atheist (*impatiently*) For Gord's sike, put 'im aht of your little 'ead, girl! 'Ee 'as as much intention of marryin' you as I have.

Young Woman We're to go to a dance tonight, and afterwards we'll settle everything.

Atheist (*positively*) I'm tellin' you all 'ee wants is a good en' warm time free o' cost.

> *A handsome young Salvation Army Officer enters from the right above, crosses slope, and comes down towards a seat some distance away from the Young Woman and the Atheist. He is trying to read a book as he walks along. He is wearing a yellow mackintosh, which is open, showing the red jersey of a Staff Officer. The Officer glances at the Young Woman as he passes, and she returns the look. He sits down on a seat and steals a furtive look at the Young Woman. He meets her eyes and lowers his glance to the ground. He again glances at her, at her face, and then at her legs.*

Young Woman (*turning her thoughts away from the Officer, and pressing close to the Atheist, as she puts an arm coaxingly round his neck*) You'll do what I ask you, this once, Dad, only this once, won't you?

Atheist (*firmly removing her arm from around his neck*) No, never again. Swing along on your own sweet way, and leave your dad out of it.

Young Woman (*tensely*) You won't? You won't, Dad?

Atheist (*in a tone of finality*) No, I won't!

There is a pause, during which the Young Woman, with tightened lips and a sullen look in her eyes, stares in front of her.

Young Woman (*suddenly thrusting her face close to the Atheist's*) I believe in God, see! And that in the beginning He created heaven and earth.

Atheist (*moving his face away from the Young Woman's*) I see, I see.

Young Woman (*following the face of the Atheist with her own, while the Salvation Army Officer listens intently to what she is saying*) And in the resurrection of the dead, when they that have done good shall go into life everlasting, and they that have done evil into everlasting fire!

The Atheist rises from the bench without a word, and goes up the centre path to the slope, and passes out.

Young Woman (*rising, follows him part of the way, and speaks loudly after him*) And I believe that God's near them who need His help, and helps them who ask His help – see!

S.A. Officer (*softly and prayerfully*) God be praised!

The Young Woman returns to the bench, sinks down on it, and begins to cry softly and resentfully. The Salvation Army Officer after a moment's hesitation comes over, looking with a shy interest at the pretty legs displayed by a disarranged skirt, and then slowly sits down beside her.

(*Earnestly*) No need to cry, sister, for no one trusts to God in vain.

Young Woman (*resentfully*) Oh, go away; I'm miserable, for he that's gone is the only real friend I have in the world.

S.A. Officer God is your only friend.

Young Woman I've not called upon Him for years, and He will not hasten to hear me now.

S.A. Officer (*putting his hand gently on her knee*) God would empty heaven of His angels rather than let the humblest penitent perish.

Young Woman (*in low tones*) If I ask for help, will He hear?

S.A. Officer He will hear.

Young Woman And hearing, will He listen?

S.A. Officer Hearing, He will listen.

Young Woman (*grasping his arm appealingly*) And listening, will He grant what the sinner asks, to save the sinner from a life of sin?

S.A. Officer (*fervently, as he caresses her knee*) God is able to save to the uttermost all them that come to Him.

Young Woman (*earnestly, after a few moments' thought*) I'll pray and pray and pray till all that's done's annulled, and all that is to do is blessed by God's agreement.

S.A. Officer (*fervently and softly*) God be praised, sister!

Young Woman (*becoming conscious that he is caressing her knee*) Oh, God, don't do that, please! You'll make a ladder, and silk stockings aren't easy to get.

She pushes his hand away, pulls down her skirt, and looks at him questioningly. He stands up, embarrassed, and fidgets with his cap.

S.A. Officer (*nervously*) I must go on, now, to our meeting. Will you come?

She is silent.

No? Some other time, then. I should like to keep in touch with you. Very much indeed. Sister, you are not very far from God. Goodbye.

Young Woman (*in a tired voice, void of interest*) Goodbye.

He turns up the centre path, looks back for a moment at the Young Woman, then crosses the slope, and goes out. She leans her arm on the arm of the bench, and shades her eyes wearily with her hand. After a few moments have passed, the Gardener enters carrying a tall, slender Maypole, painted black. On the top of the pole is a hoop from which hang long green, blue, and rich yellow ribbons. He fixes it in the centre of the sward. The Young Woman, with a long sigh, raises her head, sees the Gardener. She runs over to him, and flings her arms around his neck.

Gardener (*astonished*) What has brought you here? Aren't you working?

Young Woman No, I've given it up.

Gardener Why?

Young Woman You know well enough, you know well enough. How often have I told you that the swine of a manager brings good-looking girls, one at a time, to a silent storeroom to sort chemises, and then sends his slimy paw flickering around under their skirts. When he made a clutch at me, I came away.

Gardener (*peevishly*) Oh, you should have fenced him off as every girl does with a man like that. What are you going to do if you can't get another job?

Young Woman (*coaxingly*) That's why I wanted to speak to you. You'll have to live with me; I'm frightened, I'm frightened to live alone any longer.

Gardener (*suspiciously*) Live with you – how live with you?

Young Woman (*with calm confidence*) Marry me, Ned. You want me or you do not want me. I'm not going to be just a dance number for you any longer. Do you want me or do you not?

Gardener (*nervously*) Look here, Jannice, I'm busy getting ready for some damned fools to practise folk-dancing. They're trying to make England merry again. So I've no time to talk to you now, dear.

Young Woman (*impetuously*) Do you want me or do you not want me?

Gardener (*coaxingly*) Of course, I want you, but we can talk about this tonight.

Young Woman No, now; what we say now will last our lives out. There will only be our two selves – for awhile; we needn't have a kid till we can afford one. (*Appealingly*) You will, you will, Ned; this means everything to me, everything.

At the beginning of the Young Woman's appeal, the Man with the Stick appears on the slope above, and halts to listen.

Gardener A kid! Oh, be sensible, woman, for God's sake! We can't talk of these things here.

Young Woman (*vehemently*) Oh, be a man, Ned, be a man, and, if you want a thing, take a risk to get it! I want something for what I mean to give. Answer me – is it yes or no!

Gardener (*roughly removing her arms*) Buzz off, I tell you. I'll see you tonight.

Young Woman Answer the question: yes or no, yes or no, yes or no!

Gardener (*with a shout*) No!

> The Young Woman looks at him silently for a few moments, then turns away, and goes out, her face tense, but her lips quivering. The Gardener returns his attention to the Maypole.

Man with Stick (*from top of slope*) You've lost something, friend, you've lost a lot. If I was young as you, I'd ha' carried 'er 'ome!

Gardener (*resentfully*) Mind your own affairs. I've got my werk to do.

Man with Stick (*extending the stick towards the Maypole*) 'Ere, d'ye know what that there pole is a symbol of – what it represents?

Gardener (*surlily*) No, en' don't want to know.

Man with Stick You oughter then; knowledge is power, my friend. It represents life, new life about to be born; fertility; th' urge wot was in the young lass you hunted away.

Gardener (*mockingly*) You don't say!

Man with Stick Ay; en' Pharaoh 'ad one, en' on May Day used to pull it up with golden cords, en' orl the people darnced rahnd it.

Gardener 'Ow d'ye know? You weren't there.

Man with Stick Scholars were, man. Ask any scholar, en' 'ee'll tell you the sime.

Gardener (*stepping back to view the Maypole*) I'm not concerned with what Pharaoh did or didn't do.

A group of lively Boys and Girls run in, and catch in their hands the ribbons hanging from the Maypole. They are dressed in fancy folk-dress. They dance round the pole, keeping time to the first part of the folk-tune 'Haste to the Wedding'. Then they suddenly stop as the Young Woman enters from the direction by which she left, closely followed by the Policewoman. The Young Woman is sobbing softly. The Gardener and the Man with the Stick stare at them. They cross over.

Policewoman (*complacently*) I caught you in the act that time, my lyedy.

Young Woman (*sobbing*) It was he spoke to me, miss; on my word of honour, it was he spoke to me first.

Policewoman On your word of honour! Tell that to the magistrite when you're in front of 'im. If I'm eny kind of a guesser, you'll not solicit eny more young 'en innocent men for a month to come.

The two of them pass out. The Gardener and the Man with the Stick stare after them. The Folk-Dancers begin again, and dance through the second part of the tune, 'Haste to the Wedding'.
The gates close.

Scene Two

Summer noon. The same as the preceding one on a noonday in summer. The colours now are mainly golden glows, tinged with a gentle red. The green on the sward still lingers, but it, too, is tinted with a golden yellow. Instead of daffodils, big-faced hollyhocks, yellow, white, and red, peep out at life from the shrubbery. The Memorial, touched by the sun, now resembles a giant clad in gleaming steel.

The Dreamer enters as the gates open, and passes through them into the Park. He has a thoughtful look on his face, and is gazing at a piece of manuscript in his hand. His right hand moves gently as he beats time with the song that is being sung. People are moving about, all gay with a sensuous enjoyment of the loveliness of the day. They are singing at the top of their bent. The Dreamer passes through them, and goes out.

People (*singing*)
  Ye who are haggard and giddy with care, busy counting
     your profit and losses,
  Showing the might of your name unto God in the gay-
     coloured page of a cheque book;
  Storing the best of your life in a drawer of your desk at
     the office:

  Bellow goodbye to the buggerin' lot 'n come out
  To bow down the head 'n bend down the knee to the
     bee, the bird, 'n the blossom,
  Bann'ring the breast of the earth with a wonderful
     beauty!

Ye who are twisting a prayer from your thoughts in the
    dimness and gloom of the churches,
Lighting your candle-petitions away to chalk-coloured
    virgins and martyrs,
Racking your life for the hope of a cosy corner in
    heaven:

All Crowd Together
Bellow, etc.

Some of the Crowd
Ye who in senates, 'n Parliaments, talk, talk on through
    the day 'n the night-time,
Talk, and still talk, and still talk, and talk on through
    the hundreds of centuries passing,
Till the wide ear of the wide world is deafen'd with
    wisdom!

Bellow, etc.

*When the song has ended, the Atheist, the Man wearing
the Trilby Hat, and the Man with the Stick are seen
arguing together. On a bench towards the back sit the
two Nursemaids, between them the pram enfolding the
countess's baby. The Bishop is on a seat nearer the front.
He has been reading a book, but this is now lying open
on his knee, and he is bending forward to hear the better
what is being said by the disputants. The two Chair
Attendants are lying, half asleep, at the foot of the slope.*

Man wearing Trilby An 'eathen song! Say wot you like,
you'll find every man at 'eart is religious.

Atheist Look, brother, no question can be solved by a
generalization. All men are not religious no more'n all men
are liars. The more a man uses 'is mind, the less 'ee uses
Gord.

Man wearing Trilby If we was to set aside Deity, we'd let loose all manner of evil among ourselves – everyone knows that. There'd be no authority nowhere.

Bishop (*speaking over to them*) Our friend is right: there must be the few who rule and the many whose duty it is to obey, or there would be an end to order.

Atheist (*to the Bishop*) It 'as been the few rebels life gave us, the ones who forget to obey, that have rushed the world ahead! You think of Copernicus, Galileo, en' Darwin – rebels against the thought en' dooty of the time. (*He points an accusing finger at the Bishop.*) There isn't a single rebel in your calendar of saints!

Bishop Nonsense, friend.

Man with Stick (*with a long-drawn, impatient sigh*) Aw, wot's the use of arguin' with 'im!

Atheist (*to Bishop*) 'Ere, d'ye believe that the ten commandments constitoot a competent rule of life en' conduct?

Bishop (*smiling indulgently*) I'd venture to say they do, sir.

Man wearing Trilby I'd sye so, too.

Nursemaid (*joining in*) Of course they does.

Atheist (*mockingly*) Christian countries don't seem to think so, then, for even England, dooring the last thirty years, 'as myde over two thousand lawrs, covering sixteen thousand pages of cep imperial octavo, a tidy addition to the lawr of loving your neighbour as yourself, sir.

Man with Stick (*gleefully*) En' they ain't finished mikeing them yet!

Man wearing Trilby Where's your authority for thet?

Man with Stick (*angrily*) Where's your authority for wot you sye?

Man wearing Trilby (*firmly*) The Bible, sir; the 'Oly Book, every word inspired, every verse infallible.

Attendants (*together*) 'Ear, 'ear!

Nursemaid (*with calm conviction*) Even from time immemorial, the Bible 'as myde truth pline to all people.

Man with Stick (*taking a few steps to go in disgust, and returning to thrust his face close to that of the Man wearing the Trilby*) Aw, come on, Jenner; I'm off – no brrains! (*He taps his stick heatedly on the ground, and makes to go; he hesitates for a moment, then returns and comes close to Man wearing Trilby.*) 'Ere, d'ye believe the Bible where it syes the whyle swallowed Jonah?

Man wearing Trilby 'Course I does.

Man with Stick You does!

Nursemaid En' wye wouldn't 'ee?

Man wearing Trilby (*tapping Man with Stick on the chest*) If the Bible said Jonah swallowed the whyle, I'd believe it; but I'm not asked to believe anything so absurd.

Man with Stick (*catching the Atheist's arm, and drawing him away*) Aw, come on, man! We're just wastin' our knowledge 'ere.

   They go off.

Attendants (*as they are going – together*) Booh!

Bishop (*raising a hand to silence the boohing*) Friends, let our misguided brothers go in peace. (*to Man wearing Trilby*) I shouldn't harp too much on the whale story, friend; it's but an allegory, you know.

Man wearing Trilby (*indignantly*) Is that all you know about it! The Bible says the whyle swallowed Jonah, son of Amittae. It's a plyne fact, en' you should be ashymed to derny it. (*He crosses to go out; halts; and turns to glare at the Bishop.*) Tyke warnin' you at wot 'appened to Jonah, son of Amittae, for you're worse 'n 'ee was! (*He goes out.*)

Nursemaid (*consolingly – to Bishop*) Never mind 'im, sir; 'ee don't know wot 'ee's asaying of.

Older One Ignorance torkin'.

Young One Just ignorance.

Bishop (*cheerfully*) Never mind! (*He goes over to the Nursemaids.*) Aha, here we have the fair countess's baby. No guile here. The world hasn't been long enough yet with the young lamb. (*To Upper Nursemaid*) And where's your boy-friend – that gallant guardsman I've seen you with so often?

Upper Nursemaid (*after a moment's hesitation*) We ain't on speaking terms, sir; he misbehaved himself by takin' walks with another girl.

The head and half the body of the Guardsman has appeared above the bushes at top of the slope. He stares down at the Nursemaid, dodging down whenever he thinks anyone might see him.

Bishop Oh? Maybe he is sorry.

Under Nursemaid (*to Bishop*) 'Ee is, sir. It's agettin' 'im dahn. (*To Upper Nursemaid*) I'd try to forgive 'im, Greeta, even if 'ee was to blime. You never knows wot a quarrel'll lead to – mye mean a parting for ever!

Bishop In this life, we have to forgive many things.

Under Nursemaid Besides, 'ee asserted thet it was 'is sister.

Upper Nursemaid (*indignantly*) 'Is sister! I seen them in the bushes when 'ee was atuckin' 'er into 'im. No; I'm determined to be adamant. I don't allow for deception.

When 'ee knew how to respect me, 'ee 'ad me; when 'ee doesn't, 'ee 'asn't; en' I'm determined to be adamant!

Under Nursemaid (*catching a glimpse of the soldier's head as it pops up and down – excitedly*) 'Ee's behind the 'edge awatching us, Greeta! Oh, 'is fice 'as altered, worn en' unhappy like – Greeta, 'ave a 'eart: 'ee is suffering!

Bishop Do be kind to him, dear.

Under Nursemaid I feel for 'im when I see the sorrowful look in 'is eyes. You are 'ard, Greeta.

Upper Nursemaid (*rising and tidying the pram, preparatory to moving away*) A little suffering'll do 'im good. No, Reeta; unless 'ee writes en' apologizes humbly; unless 'ee writes en' explines; unless 'ee writes en' asks me to forgive 'im, 'ee'll never 'ave a chance of being with yours truly agine!

She goes off, pushing the pram, stiff and dignified, never glancing at where the head of the Guardsman is gaping over the bushes. She is followed by the other Nursemaid, shaking her head, and sending a sympathetic glance to the soldier. When they have gone, the Guardsman comes down the slope to follow; but the Bishop halts him by catching his arm in a friendly way.

Bishop (*sympathetically*) Friend, a little kindly advice to you: write a humble letter of apology to your sweetheart. Then there'll be harmony, and everything in the garden'll look lovely. (*smilingly*) Your conduct calls for an apology, you know.

Guardsman (*coldly*) Ow, does it? (*Angrily*) En' wot the 'ell is it to you wether it does or not? Powkin' your big nose into other people's business. You keep off my affyres, see!

He goes angrily off after the Nurses, leaving the good Bishop embarrassed.

Older One (*with almost tearful sympathy*) Wot a shime, sir! You see wot 'appens when religion's lost. Upsets the mind. There ought to be some lawr to mike people respect religion.

Young One We goes to church reglar, don't we, 'Erbert? We was brought up thet wye, wasn't we, 'Erbert? Respectful like.

Bishop (*feelingly*) I know; I guessed it from the first.

Older One (*slyly*) Where's the lyedy as is always with you, sir?

Bishop (*slyly, too*) I gave her – what do you call it? – I gave her the slip, today. My sister, you know; she's too cautious; afraid I'll come to harm by being familiar with the common people.

Older One Harm! Ahar har! (*He chuckles at the idea.*) Harm!

Young One Nice thing to see a clergyman merry an' bright, an' ready to tork to 'umble men, like us – isn't it, 'Erbert?

Older One I cencur with thet.

Bishop (*gaily*) Oh, the Church isn't altogether so solemn an institution as many people seem to think – she can laugh, sing, and skip – at a suitable time, at a suitable time.

Older One I always said the clergy was 'uman – didn't I, Godfrey?

Young One Often en' often.

Older One (*confidently*) We've a friend 'ere – d'ye know thet, Godfrey?

Young One The gentleman's got a kind 'eart, I'd sye.

Older One You've only got to look at 'is fine fice to see thet. (*Affectionately linking his arm in that of the Bishop's, an act which makes the Bishop stiffen a little in doubt.*) At the moment, sir, the pire of us is in a bad wye, a bad wye; we 'ave lost our jobs, en' don't know wot to do. A pahnd or two, now, would 'elp a lot – wouldn't it, Godfrey?

Young One I'd sye so.

Bishop (*growing stiffer, and withdrawing his arm from the contact of the Older Attendant's*) No, no, please. My sister deals with all matters of help to the needy. Apply to her. If she approves, she'll assist you. One must be careful in the dispensation of charity.

Older One (*peevishly*) Aw, your sister wouldn't be no good to us! She wouldn't listen right. She'd warnt to know the why en' wherefore of everything.

Bishop (*firmly*) And rightly so, friend. The giving away of money is a great responsibility. She'd be very angry if I did what you ask.

Older One She'd never know, sir. Me nor Godfrey would never sye a word – would we, Godfrey?

Young One We'd keep it dark, orlright.

Bishop (*decisively*) No no; a rule is a rule, so let us change the subject.

   A silent pause.

Older One (*bitterly*) Chynge the subject! En' why did you coax innercent people into queuein' up behind the idea of the clergy bein' 'uman? (*hotly*) Whaja warnt to force your company on them as didn't warnt it!

Young One I knew it all along. The clergy alwyes fail when they're asked a pline question.

Older One (*indignantly*) 'Op en' skip en' jump! Here's one as 'opes they'll 'op outa this place!

The Bishop sits down on a bench, takes out his book, and begins to read again.

Ow, we're goin' to read, are we? Well, if we was asittin' on a bench, en' got a 'int to go, I'd push off – wouldn't you, Godfrey?

Young One Quick!

Bishop (*with quiet determination*) I choose this place in which to rest, and I shall go when I think it dignified to do so. (*He resumes his reading.*)

Older One (*recklessly and loudly – to the Young One*) Know wot I'd like to do, Godfrey, honest? Gambol a gime with en 'eifer in front of a clergyman, strite, I would! Show 'im a little of the gaiety of life, strite, I would!

Young One Don't know as it would shock them, 'Erbert – I bet they 'as their 'ectic moments on the sly!

Older One You bet they 'as! Wot do they do in their palaces when the lamps is lighted en' the blinds is drawn? We eats, they eats; we drinks, they drinks; we sleeps, they sleeps; but wot do they do in their palaces when the lamps is lighted en' the blinds is drawn?

The Young Woman enters, and, after a glance at the Bishop, sits down on a bench directly opposite him. She takes out mirror and puff from her handbag, and gives her face a few deft touches.

Young One (*giving a few stiff steps of a dance – echoing the Older Attendant*) Ay, wot do they do in their palaces when the lamps is lighted en' the blinds is drawn!

Older One (*poking him in the side to draw his attention to the Young Woman*) Look, Godfrey, oh, look! Wot a

peach! 'Ow would you like to tuck 'er up at night,
Godfrey?

*Lines of ugly joy swarm over their faces at the delightful
thought, while they stare brazenly at the Young
Woman. Suddenly, in the near distance, is heard the roll
of a muffled drum, and the mournful chant of the
Down-and-Out. The scene seems to grow dark and the
air chilly. The two Attendants stiffen, and lines of fright
chase away the lines of joy from their faces. The Young
Woman, frightened too, turns pale, half rises from her
seat, and stares into the distance.*

Down-and-Out (*chanting in the near distance*)
Life has pass'd us by to the loud roll of her drum,
With her waving flags of green and yellow held high,
All starr'd with the golden, flaming names of her most
    mighty children.

The chant fades away.
    *The two Attendants slink out, bent-backed and silent,
one to the right, the other to the left, as the chant fades
away. The Young Woman, shivering, sinks slowly down
on to the seat again. There is a pause. She is very
attractive, sitting there in her tailor-made coat and her
bright hat. Her slim legs looking slimmer in their elegant
silk stockings are for all to see from the knees down.
The Bishop suddenly sighs, closes the book he has been
reading, puts it in his pocket, and, turning a little round,
sees the Young Woman. He looks at her pretty face,
thoughtfully bent towards the ground, at her neatly
dressed body, and, finally, his eyes linger a little over the
slim legs visible from the knees down. An old interest
seems to stir in him as he looks at her. Ashamed, he
turns his head away for a few moments. He looks at her
again, first at her face, then at her body, and then, more
consciously, at her legs. He turns his gaze away again*

*and moves uneasily in his seat, lets his head sink
forward till his chin rests on his breast. He lifts his head
and looks at her; she turns at the same time, and they
stare at each other for a moment; then the Bishop's head
sinks down on his breast again.*

 *Suddenly the Young Woman rises swiftly, as if she
had come to a sudden resolution, hurries to where the
Bishop is, sits down on the bench beside him, and,
catching his arm, speaks to him imploringly.*

Young Woman (*appealingly*) I want you to help me. You
are near to God, but I am out of reach.

Bishop (*frightened*) Oh, my child, I'm afraid I can help
only those whom I know.

Young Woman Listen to me, listen to me, first. My heart is
bad, and doctors say that death may seize me at any
moment, and take me out of life. There's a young man who
loves me, and is going to marry me, but I want you to come
with me to see him, and make him marry me at once.

Bishop (*bewildered*) But I know nothing about you or
about him.

Young Woman You will, please, you must; you are a man
after God's own heart – you'll help a young girl whose one
chance is help at once.

Bishop (*frightened to be seen talking to the girl – looking
round him nervously*) Why do you run to the priest for
help only when you begin to feel the terrible consequences
of your shame?

Young Woman (*irritated at the Bishop's thought*) Oh, I'm
not going to have a kid, man, if that's what you mean.
Nothing like that for me yet, thank you! It's because I'd
love to have one that I came to you; – to save me from
falling into the condition that could never give me one.

Bishop But you can't discuss such things with a man and a perfect stranger, girl.

Young Woman You're neither a man nor a stranger; you are a priest of the most high God.

Bishop (*frightened and petulant*) Oh, be sensible, girl! Go and talk these things with your father and mother.

Young Woman (*bitterly*) I never knew my father, and my mother drinks, and hates me.

Bishop (*reprovingly*) You mustn't talk like that about your mother. Whatever she may be, she should be sacred to you.

Young Woman (*impatiently*) Sacred to me! A mother can be sacred only when she makes herself sacred to her children; – can't you understand that, man?

Bishop (*coldly*) I have no help to offer you, and I must ask you to go away, please.

Young Woman (*impulsively sitting down beside him*) Do listen to me, please do, Lord Bishop. I've seen you laughing and talking with common people, and it gave me heart to speak to you.

Bishop (*in his best manner; putting his hand on her knee and patting it*) Go and live with your mother, and show her you realize what a mother really is. Work steadily, cultivate thrifty habits, and in a few years' time you'll be able to face marriage far more brightly and firmly than you could possibly face it now.

Young Woman (*trembling and agitated, pushing his hand from her knee*) Oh, piping out of you the same old rot that I've heard a thousand times – mother, work, and thrift! (*Indignantly*) If you knew what a rip she was, I wonder if you'd like to live with her? I wonder, if you were a girl, and good-looking, would you bray about the happiness of work? (*Raising her voice a little*) Do you know why I had to fly out of the two last jobs I was in, had to – d'ye hear – had to fly out of them?

Bishop (*taking a book from his pocket and beginning to read – coldly*) I do not want to know the reason.

Young Woman (*vehemently*) Because I wouldn't let the manager see how I looked with nothing on. Oh, you hide behind your book when facts frighten you. There's many an old graven image has made a girl dance out of her job and chance the streets, sooner than strip herself for his benefit, with nine hours a day and three pounds a week added on to the pleasure.

Bishop (*from behind his book*) You mustn't annoy me in this way. Please leave me in peace.

Young Woman (*vehemently*) It's the truth. Can't you put your book down for a second and listen? (*She pushes the book aside.*) Come with me to the shop, and I'll bring you face to face with the man!

Bishop (*beginning to read again*) Be good enough to go away, please.

Young Woman (*imploringly*) Please listen to me! Are you afraid to find a lie in what you think to be the truth, or the truth in what you think to be a lie? Come and tell the manager you're my friend, and make him give me back the job I have had to leave. Oh, do, do, please!

The Bishop still remains behind the shelter of his book.

(*After a pause*) Won't you help me?

Bishop (*in cold and final tones*) No.

Young Woman (*with quiet bitterness*) I suppose you'd have helped me had I let you go on handling my knee.

Bishop (*in cold and tense voice*) If you don't go away at once, I'll have you handed over to the police for annoying me!

The Young Woman sits silent and shocked for a few moments, looking fixedly at the Bishop.

Young Woman (*mockingly*) Oh, hand me over to a policeman, would you? I see. Easy way of getting over a difficulty by handing it over to a policeman. (*She stands up.*) Get back, get back, please; gangway, gangway, there – policemen making a gangway for Jesus Christ! (*The Bishop stiffens himself behind his book. With intense scorn and bitterness*) You and your goodness are of no use to God! If Christ came again, He'd have to call, not the sinners, but the righteous to repentance. Go out into the sun, and pick the yellow primroses! Take your elegant and perfumed soul out of the stress, the stain, the horrid cries, the noisy laugh of life; and go out into the sun to pick the yellow primroses! When you go to where your God is throned, tell the gaping saints you never soiled a hand in Jesu's service. Tell them a pretty little lass, well on her way to hell, once tempted you to help her; but you saved yourself by the calm and cunning of a holy mind, an' went out into the sun to pick the yellow primroses, leaving her, sin-soddened, in the strain, the stain, the horrid cries, an' the noisy laugh of life. Tell them you were ever calm before the agony in other faces, an', an' the tip of your finger never touched a brow beaded with a bloody sweat!

The horrified Bishop suddenly closes his book, and rises from his seat to go away, but the Young Woman with a vigorous push from her hand, sends him sitting down in the seat again.

(*Passionately, thrusting her face close to the Bishop's*) A tired Christ would be afraid to lean on your arm. Your

Christ wears a bowler hat, carries a cane, twiddles his lavender gloves, an' sends out gilt-edged cards of thanks to callers. Out with you, you old shivering sham, an' go away into the sun to pick the yellow primroses!

As the Young Woman is speaking her last few sentences the Old Woman enters. She is pale and haggard, and vicious lines harden the look of her mouth. Her hair is white, but her black eyes are still undimmed by age. Her thin body is still upright, showing that in her youth she was slim and vigorous, and her face still shelters traces of what were once very good looks. Her boots, though polished, are old and broken, and everything about her, though old and patched and shabby, is clean and neat. Constant, quiet drinking has made her a little incoherent in her thoughts. In one hand she carries a small wreath of red poppies and laurel leaves, which has a bunch of violets where the wreath is tied together by a bow of black ribbon. She had heard the voice of the Young Woman, and comes down to where the girl is speaking, gripping her roughly by the arm as the Young Woman is about to go away from the Bishop.

Old Woman (*to the Young Woman*) Putting yourself again on the market for men, are you? Piling up money, and not a penny nor the thought of a penny for your lonely and suffering mother. (*as the Young Woman tries to free herself*) No use your trying to get away. (*She drops the wreath to the ground, and holds the girl tighter.*) I have you and I hold you till I get a little to help me on in life for a day or two!

Young Woman (*doggedly*) I haven't any money; and even if I had, I wouldn't part with a penny to you, for all you want it for is drink!

Old Woman (*furiously*) Drink! Hear that now! Is it any wonder God has given her a heart that may go phut any

minute? (*Over to the Bishop*) Hear what she says, you?
That I want the money for drink!

Young Woman (*with a frightened laugh*) Let me go, will
you? If my heart does go phut, I'll go game, see! Pass out
dancing – see?

*The Old Woman claws at the girl's hat, pulls it off, and
flings it on the ground.*

Old Woman (*wildly*) Want the money for drink, do I? I'll
tear every stitch on you into ribbons!

Young Woman (*appealing*) Please, please, Mother, don't
ruin the few little decent things I have to wear!

*The Bishop gets up from his seat, goes over to the
struggling Women, and tries to separate them.*

Bishop (*trying to restore peace*) For shame, for shame!
Mother and daughter, – for shame, for shame!

*As soon as she hears the Bishop's voice the Old Woman
releases her hold on the girl, and stares at the Bishop.
The Young Woman, excited and exhausted, sinks into a
seat a little distance away. The Bishop returns the Old
Woman's look for a moment, and then rather hastily
returns to his seat and resumes the reading of his book.
The Old Woman's eyes follow the Bishop and, after a
moment's hesitation, she comes up close to him.*

Old Woman (*looking fixedly at the Bishop –
murmuringly*) Your voice has a strange echo in it. Behind
that wizened face is hidden a look of the first young man
who conquered me on a Sunday night, after the ora pro
nobis people had pulled down their blinds and were
slinking into sleep. There under a yellow moon, among the
shadows by a grove of birch trees, on a bed of flattened
bluebells, one of the prettiest fillies that ever wore a skirt
was jockeyed into sin, and out of the rapture and the risk

came this girl who dares to fancy men more than she does her own mother. (*Suddenly*) Is your name Gilbert?

Bishop (*over the top of his book – looking very uneasy*) Go away, you wretched and forgotten creature. My name is not Gilbert!

Old Woman (*still staring at him – murmuring*) I'm not much to look at now; but the man who first got the better of me's a big jack-a-dandy in the church, for I saw him once in a holy procession, helping to sing a canticle, a purple cape hanging from his shoulders. (*Suddenly pushing the Bishop's book aside*) Eh, you, is your name Gilbert?

Bishop (*roughly*) Get away, get away, woman. My name is not Gilbert. Get away, get away, I tell you!

The Old Woman goes over to the Young Woman, limping, sitting on a seat. The Bishop leans forward with his elbows on his knees and his head in his hands.

Old Woman (*to the Young Woman – whiningly*) Why don't you try to be decent to your poor mother? She won't trouble you for long. I feel a few more months will see the end of me.

Young Woman (*savagely*) I'd dance and sing if I thought you'd die in an hour!

Old Woman (*wildly*) You'd dance and sing if I died in an hour? Hear that, now? Dance and sing? How can God listen to such a saying and not strike you dead? (*over to the Bishop*) Didja hear what she said? – dance and sing if I died in an hour? Come over and bruise her hopes with a grim curse from God.

Bishop (*his hands covering his face*) Oh, hush, hush, woman; hush and go home.

Old Woman (*wrathful at the Bishop's indifference*) Hush, hush, and go home you! Hear what she said to me, said to her mother? Dance if I died in an hour, and you take her part. You ought to be driven helter-skelter out of everything holy. Hush you, and go home, with your ora pro pugeree mugeree rigmarolum! (*Turning violently on the Young Woman*) In league with you, is he? (*She seizes hold of the Young Woman and shakes her violently*.) Dance if I was dead today, or died tomorrow, would you?

Young Woman (*terrified*) Mother, mind; don't – I didn't mean anything!

Old Woman (*shaking her more violently still*) I think of nothing but drink, do I not?

Young Woman (*hysterically*) My heart, my heart – you'll be the death of me!

The Dreamer appears on the slope above and looks on at those below.

Old Woman (*fiercely flinging her back so that the girl falls on her knees*) I'll teach you a little of the duty a daughter owes to her mother!

She raises a hand to strike the girl, but the Dreamer, who has come close, seizes her, and prevents her arm from falling. The Bishop rises, makes a step forward to interfere, but stops in hesitation.

Dreamer (*gently shaking the Old Woman*) Now then, now then – what's this?

The Young Woman pulls herself on to a seat. She is panting for breath. She reclines down on the bench, closing her eyes, while trying to regain her breath.

Young Woman (*her eyes closed – between breaths*) Get her away; send her away, for God's sake!

Dreamer (*firmly conducting the Old Woman out*) Go away; go home, old woman, better go home. Let the old pray by the fire, and leave a way for the young to live.

Old Woman (*murmuringly, as she goes out*) No pity in the young; only waiting for time to hustle us off. (*She brushes with her hand the laurel wreath she has picked up from the ground.*) The bad present, and the good absent; the shame living, and the pride buried; gone from my grasp and my sight in the flame and smoke of the war. Oh, Jesus, is there no rest to be found anywhere!

The Old Woman goes out, and the Dreamer returning to the Young Woman, sees the Bishop beckoning to him. He goes to him.

Bishop (*anxiously*) Do you think she'll be all right?

Dreamer Yes; she'll be herself again in a few minutes.

Bishop (*handing the Dreamer three pound notes*) Steal over and slip these in her handbag. Don't mention me. I've no real interest in her, you understand? Still I pity her in a way. I must go now. It's all the money I have with me. I'll return this way again, later on. (*He turns to go, wheels, and grasps the Dreamer's arm tight.*) Please don't be anyway cruel to her. She is – God's child.

Dreamer I'll watch her till she has recovered.

Bishop Thanks.

The Bishop goes up the slope. The Dreamer steals over to where the Young Woman is reclining on the bench. He takes up her handbag; sees the Bishop's back is turned; slips one of the notes into his pocket, and the other two into the handbag. When the Bishop reaches the top of the slope, he turns back to look at the Young Woman. The Dreamer waves a hand reassuringly, and

*the Bishop goes out. The Dreamer goes to the Young
Woman, and sits down beside her.*

Dreamer (*to the Young Woman*) Feeling a little better now?

Young Woman (*still panting a little*) Bit better now. It's my
heart – goes curious now when anything happens. Please
sit down beside me for a minute or two.

Dreamer For a year and a day, if you like. (*He sits beside
her and takes her hand in his and strokes it.*)

Young Woman (*bitterly*) I'll go off in one of these attacks
yet. Nice thing to have for a mother, isn't she? I love the
dear silver that shines in her hair! Feeling better, now,
anyhow. (*slyly*) Well, how do you like the hand?

Dreamer Lovely – like a blue-veined, pink-tipp'd lily.

Young Woman (*taking her hand away*) Well, let it go for a
minute, till I straighten myself up a little. (*She arranges her
hat, smoothes the folds of her skirt, gives a few touches to
her blouse, and sits down again.*) I'm a little more
presentable now.

Dreamer (*moving a hand semicircularly over her breasts*)
There's a wrinkle or two in your blouse still.

Young Woman (*taking his hand away*) Now, now! Dad's
spoken about you. Not the real Dad – never saw my real
father; don't even know who or what he was. Hard lines,
isn't it?

Dreamer It doesn't matter very much now, dear.

Young Woman My second Dad – the Atheist, you know –
calls you a poet. How do you live?

Dreamer Oh, I sell an odd article, or, maybe, a song or a
story, and so manage to live an austere life. But oughtn't
you to go home and have a rest? I'll see you safe there.

Young Woman (*slyly*) Tuck me up, and sing me to sleep with one of your songs?

Dreamer (*earnestly*) I'd love to! (*He rises and catches her by an arm.*) Come! Don't let this rosy chance be pulled to bits by prudence. Come, sweet lass, and let's transmute vague years of life into a glowing hour of love!

Young Woman (*pulling her arm free, and speaking somewhat sharply*) Not so quick, please! Men are always ready to rush a pretty woman into love, looking for joy, and behold, trouble. Supposing I go and give, what do I get?

Dreamer I'll pay your merry kindness with a song.

Young Woman (*a little scornfully*) A song! A puff of scented air! You're out on the hunt for bargains, young man. Go with a priest for a prayer and with a poet for a song! It's a poor offer, young sir.

Dreamer (*sitting beside her; earnestly – close to the Young Woman's face*) Young lady, many great queens and many grand ladies have joyfully snared themselves in the golden meshes of a poet's song!

Young Woman (*laughingly*) Well, I'm neither a great queen nor a grand lady; I'm not even a clergyman's daughter.

Dreamer To me you're a great lady and a grand queen, and it was for you I wrote the song.

Young Woman (*a little recklessly*) Well, let's see if your little song can snare the hapless heart of a pretty little maiden.

Dreamer Wait till we get to your flat, so that I can kiss you between the verses.

Young Woman Oh, you're travelling quick along your own little road, young singer. Sing it now or sing it never.

Dreamer (*resignedly*) Oh, all right, then. We'll call it by your name – what is it?

Young Woman Just Jannice.

Dreamer What a pretty name! Well, we'll call the song just 'Jannice'. (*He gives a shy little cough and sings. He is standing now, with one foot on the seat of the bench.*)

Her legs are as pliant and slim
  As fresh, golden branches of willow;
  I see lustre of love on each limb,
  Looking down from the heights of a pillow,
  Looking down from the heights of a pillow!

Tossed by a soft breeze in the spring,
  The blooms of an apple tree billow;
  And her breasts are as lovely to me,
  Looking down from the heights of a pillow,
  Looking down from the heights of a pillow!

Gay, white apple-blossoms her breast,
  Her legs golden branches of willow;
  I'd enjoy for a year and a day,
  Looking down from the heights of a pillow,
  Looking down from the heights of a pillow!

(*after a pause – expectantly*) Well?

Young Woman (*not satisfied, but pleased withal on account of the praise that is in it*) A pretty song, young singer, but its grace and meaning are hardly a fit for me. I cannot live, or even hope, on the sweet sound of a song. Have you nothing else to offer?

Dreamer (*reluctantly*) I could give you a pound.

Young Woman A pound! A small gift of gold for a grand lady or a great queen! Have you nothing more?

Dreamer (*rather wearily*) A few shillings for a meal today and a meal tomorrow.

The Young Woman lays a hand almost affectionately on his arm. He covers her hand with his.

Young Woman Keep the little you have for yourself, young singer, for your life seems uncertain as my own.

The Bishop has strolled in, and now sits on the bench opposite, apparently reading his book, but really watching the Young Woman. She gives him a hasty, scornful glance.

Dreamer (*tightening his grip on her hand*) Well, at least, let me walk across the park with you.

Young Woman (*releasing her hand, and rising*) No, no; I don't want you. Why do you keep insisting that I need you with me?

Dreamer I am thinking, not of your need, but of my own, Jannice.

The young Salvation Army Officer enters, and comes down the slope slowly. He keeps looking at the Young Woman.

Young Woman (*to Dreamer*) That is selfish. Your way, young singer, though bright with song, is dim with danger. At the end of the way, I might find myself even lower than I am. There is no peace with you. (*She indicates the Salvation Army Officer.*) Here is a real friend who offers peace as a child might offer a friend a new-blown daisy.

Dreamer His voice is not the voice of peace, but of fear.

The Young Woman goes to meet the young Salvation Army Officer.

Young Woman (*gaily*)
Good morrow, good morrow, young sir;
Let's sanction this bold, sunny weather,
By lying aside in the shade,
And cooling warm feelings together!

S.A. Officer (*seriously*) God's blessing on you, sister, though your thoughtless manner is fashioned to the woe of the world.

Young Woman (*putting her arms round the neck of the Salvation Army Officer – recklessly*) Oh, come out of the gloom for a moment, dear! Come into the sun, and kiss me with the kisses of thy mouth.

S.A. Officer (*gently removing the arms of the Young Woman*) Our ways are not your ways, sister; we have been led to turn our eyes aside from the gaudy beckoning of the world's vanities.

Young Woman (*a little abashed*) Sometimes it is very hard to choose. If I lodge where you do, can your people be my people, and your God my God?

S.A. Officer (*eagerly*) Ah, if you only will it, sister, it is so! Out of self, into Christ, into glory! It is as simple as that, sister.

Bishop (*over to the Salvation Army Officer – sharply*) The saints didn't find it quite so simple, my young friend.

S.A. Officer (*to Young Woman*) Never heed him, sister. He would hide God's countenance with a cloud of ritual. Come with me: the yoke is easy; the burden light.

Young Woman To peace?

S.A. Officer To peace that is perfect, and peace everlasting.

Young Woman I will go a little way to hear more of the

peace that seems so far away. (*She takes the arm of the Salvation Army Officer, and bows mockingly to the Bishop.*) Goodbye, old man, who, saving yourself, had no time to save others.

The Bishop does not reply, but sits sadly on the bench looking down towards the ground. The Dreamer sits sadly on the bench opposite, watching the Young Woman go with the Salvation Army Officer. The air of 'Jannice' is heard softly, either on flute or fiddle. The Salvation Army Officer and the Young Woman go slowly up the slope. When they reach the top, and are about to go off, the Young Woman turns and looks down towards the Dreamer.

Young Woman (*down to the Dreamer*) I have not quite forgotten your sweet song, young singer!

The two go out.
   The gates close.

Scene Three

The same part of the Park on an Autumn evening. The sky now is a deep rich crimson, faintly touched at the horizon with golden yellow; while the upper part has a plainly visible and sweeping border of purple and mauve. The leaves of the trees are red and yellow, the trunks a rich bronze. Now and again, one of them flutters to the ground. At the back, against the slope, are a number of tall, gaunt sunflowers, something like those shown to us by Van Gogh. The figure of the Soldier now shows a deep black against the crimson hue of the sky. Chairs having coloured cloth seats and backs, are here and there.

The Two Attendants, looking more haggard and decayed than ever, are lying, apparently asleep, on the slope.

Before the gates open, a band, somewhere in the Park, is heard playing 'Land of Hope and Glory'. The music is quite clear and definite, but when the Park is in view the music becomes fainter, as if it was being played at some distance away. The music ceases when the Young Woman and the Dreamer appear.

Older One (*suddenly rousing up and leaning on his elbow to listen*) 'Land of 'Ope en' Glory'! There's not much of the glory left, en' none of the 'ope. (*He nudges his sleeping companion.*) Eh, Godfrey, 'ear wot they're playin'?

Younger Attendant grunts sleepily.

'Land of 'Ope en' Glory'! Wot d'ye think of that?

Young One (*in a sleepy mutter*) Aw, wot they plays don't concern us.

Older One (*somewhat sharply*) 'Course it concerns us! Why aren't we part of the 'ope en' the glory? There's that Dreamer, the Atheist, the Man with the Stick, and that gay-dressed young 'eifer goin' abaht good en' proper, denyin' of Gord en' all as is His; en' 'ere we are, two God-fearin', upright men, en' wot's the misery for?

The Young Attendant takes no notice, so he pokes him.

Two God-fearin' men, Godfrey, I syes.

Young One (*drowsily*) Yeh; two God-fearin' young men, ri' enough. I wanna go asleep.

Older One (*bending over and giving him a shake – impatiently*) Not tykin' no interest in public affaires helps us dahn. Is there a Gord or ain't there? (*His head falls on his breast for a few moments, and he falls back a little in sleepiness, but jerks himself upright again.*) Wot I said before, I syes again: There'll be nothing left if we lift th' pahnd off th' gold stannard. (*He shakes the Younger Attendant again.*) I 'olds we're ruined if we go off th' gold stannard! (*He sinks slowly down on the slope, weary, and full of sleep. A pause.*)

Young One (*suddenly sitting up*) En' I syes no! Give the British pahnd a charnce in the world's market. While we keep on sterling, we lose our gold in masses. I olds we're ruined, if we don't go off the stannard. (*He sinks down.*)

Older One (*sleepily*) I 'olds we're ruined if we does!

They both apparently sink into sleep as the Young Woman and the Dreamer appear above, and come down the slope, passing the sleeping figures by. She is pale, but her eyes are asparkle, though she has the Dreamer by the arm, and leans a little on him.

Young Woman (*as she is coming down*) I shouldn't have

taken the wine, Dreamer. It has made me unsteady, inclining me to see the world fairer than I should.

Dreamer It was good wine, then. You see clearly, for wine is the mirror of the heart.

Young Woman I feel uneasy, feeling so much joy.

Dreamer (*setting her on a seat*) Wait for me here, Jannice. I must cash the cheque I got this morning. I won't be from you over half an hour.

Young Woman I wish you wouldn't go, dear Dreamer. Alone, I feel afraid of myself. (*A little roguishly*) Supposing when you are gone, Salvation's Officer comes and I go with him?

Dreamer I'm not afraid of him: there's no peace or joy for you where he is. To him, peace may bring joy; to such as you, only joy can give you peace.

Young Woman Still, stay here, Dreamer. I've two pounds I found suddenly in my bag this morning.

Dreamer Keep them. I'll go. The music of the band will keep you company till I come again. A kiss!

He kisses her, and goes, waving back from the top of the slope, while she reclines a little sleepily on the seat, as the Man wearing the Trilby comes hurriedly in, followed as quickly by the Man with the Stick; he is followed a little more slowly by the Atheist, a Man wearing a Bowler Hat, and a Man wearing a Straw Hat – commonly called 'a boater'. They come together, and form an arguing group. Each, excepting the Atheist, carries a big newspaper under an arm.

Man with Stick (*calling to Man wearing Trilby*) Eh, stand your ground! If we wants knorledge, we must ask questions.

Man wearing Trilby (*halting, and letting the rest come up to him*) Let there be an end of mockery, then.

Man wearing Bowler Yes; let's conduct the debate with decorum.

Man with Stick I wasn't mockin' enyone – I was only mockin' Genesis.

Man wearing Trilby Well, Genesis is part of me, en' I'm part of Genesis.

Man with Stick (*looking at the sky, and giving a long, impatient sigh*) Uuh!

Atheist (*gently to Man wearing Trilby*) You see, friend, your arguments for existence of a Gord can't be the cause of belief, for the reason that the belief was there before them; and this belief was born into the mind of primitive man by ignorance and fear.

Man wearing Straw Hat So you say!

Atheist (*turning to him*) And so say the most eminent anthropologists we have. (*to Man wearing Trilby*) You, my friend, are arguing for the arguments usually set forth to prove the belief, and not for the belief itself which existed before the arguments – see?

Man with Stick 'Ee don't warnt to see!

Man wearing Trilby All I syes is use your eyes, use your ears, use your brine, en' wot's the explyenation of all the wunnerful things we sees en' 'ears arahnd us – on the earth en' above us in the sky – en' I syes Gord myde them orl!

Man with Stick (*impatiently*) Ah, wot we warnt to know, man, is who myde Gord!

Man wearing Straw Hat (*pushing in truculently*) 'Ee always existed! In the beginning all things was myde by 'im, en' withaht 'im was not enything myde wot was myde!

Man with Stick (*with another look at the sky*) Aw, aw – we're back to Genesis again!

Atheist (*quietly and firmly*) There never was a beginning, friend. Nothing 'as been myde, en' everything's been evolved out of matter, energy, en' force; forms chynging, but substance remineing the syme.

Man with Stick (*tapping the ground affirmatively*) 'Course they 'as.

Man wearing Trilby (*hesitant*) Yes; in a way, yes; but even Einstein syes –

Man with Stick (*interrupting fiercely*) Aw, we're not responsible for wot Einstein syes!

Atheist (*deprecatingly – to Man with Stick*) Patience, brother.

Man wearing Trilby Wot first created this matter en' this energy en' this force you speak abaht? If it was always, 'ow was it always, en' where was it always? We gets nowhere when we syes thet wot's to come comes aht of wot is, en' wot is, is aht of wot was: it only mystifies a man; so I syes in the beginning, before enything wot is was, was Gord, en' it was 'e manipulated energy en' force to mike us wot we are.

Young Woman (*who has been listening abstractedly for some time – running a little unsteadily over to them, and pushing her way into the group*) And aren't you fellows a fine example of what we are! (*to Atheist*) No beginning? As it was in the beginning, is now, and ever shall be; world without end. Amen. See?

Man with Stick (*indignantly*) You mustn't interrupt,

young woman! Your mind isn't able to comprehend wot we're torking abaht.

Young Woman And yours is? Why, the wisdom each of you has, taken together, would fit on a spoon. (*She pushes them about a little wildly.*) Oh, go away, you little chirrupers, and leave the Park to peace. Let a quiet place enjoy the quietness it gives.

Atheist (*moving off*) The discussion's ended, gentlemen, for the present. Go and read your papers.

> *He goes off. The four men, Man with Stick, Man wearing Trilby, Man wearing Bowler, and Man wearing Straw Hat, sit down on the seats having coloured cloth seats and backs. The seats are so placed that if a line was drawn to each of them, the lines would make an X. They take the papers from under their arms, spread them out, and begin to read. Each of the newspapers on the page facing outwards has one large word only. One has Murder, another Rape, another Suicide, on the fourth Divorce. The Young Woman returns, still a little unsteady, to the bench. As the men read, the Band is heard softly playing 'London Bridge is Falling Down'. As the tune is played for the second time, the Man wearing the Straw Hat sings the words half to himself.*

Man wearing Straw Hat (*singing*)
London Bridge is falling down, falling down, falling
 down,
London Bridge is falling down, my fair lady.

Man wearing Bowler (*with complacent dignity – singing*)
Build it up with gold and silver, gold and silver, gold and
 silver,
Build it up with gold and silver, my fair lady.

Young Woman (*singing with distinct note of denial*)

Gold and silver will not do, will not do, will not do,
Gold and silver will not do, my fair lady.

Man wearing Straw Hat (*singing a little sadly*)
Gold and silver's grown a god, grown a god, grown a
    god,
Gold and silver's grown a god, my fair lady.

Young Woman (*standing up, stamping her foot, and
singing fiercely*)
Let it fall to pieces then, pieces then, pieces then,
Let it fall to pieces then, my fair lady!

Older One (*rising from slope to lean on his elbow – in a
protesting, whining snarl*) Wot's yous warnt to make such
a row when two poor men is tryin' to sleep awye the
worries of the world! (*The Older Attendant sinks down to
sleep again.*)

Young Woman (*mockingly – after watching the Readers
for a few moments*) Let every sound be hushed, for the
oblate fathers are busy reading the gospel for the day.
Furnishing their minds with holy thoughts, and storing
wisdom there. Let us pray! Oh, Lucifer, Lucifer, who has
caused all newspapers to be written for our learning –
stars of the morning and stars of the evening – grant we
may so read them that we may always find a punch in
them, hot stuff in them, and sound tips in them; so that,
outwardly in our bodies and inwardly in our souls, we
may get closer and closer to thee! (*Indignantly*) Why the
hell don't you all say Amen!

Man wearing Trilby (*to Young Woman*) Hush, woman:
we want quietness when our minds are busy.

Young Woman (*rising and moving about among the
Readers recklessly*) I've had a few drinks, but what about
it! A short life and a merry one! My heart's due to stop
beating any minute now, but what about it! (*She

contemplates the Readers.) Devoted, body and soul, to the love of learning. Listen: Jannice is going to die dancing. (*Vehemently*) Are all you damn perishers deaf and dumb?

Man wearing Bowler (*with irritation*) Oh, go away; we want to read in peace.

Young Woman (*singing softly, but a little drunkenly*)
Stirr'd by a soft breeze in the Spring,
The blooms of an apple tree billow;
And her breast is as fragrant to me,
Looking down from the height of a pillow,
Looking down from the height of a pillow!

(*She coughs, becomes a little breathless, and presses a hand to her side.*) I'm a sick woman. (*She bends her head down on her breast.*) Death has touched me, and is telling me to be ready; take your things off, and come with me. (*Defiantly*) I'll not give in, I'll not hold back. And when I go, should God's angels beckon me up or push me down, I'll go game. (*Horrified*) Jesu, Son of Mary, what'm I saying? I'll fold all the things done in this life round me like a mantle, and wait for judgement. (*She sinks down on a seat, and stares thoughtfully in front of her.*)

Man with Stick (*reading from behind the paper marked Murder*) The condemned man, who is to be hanged for cutting a woman into bits, ate a hearty breakfast, spent an edifying time with the chaplain, smoked a cigarette while being pinioned, and walked with a goose-step to the gallows.

Rest of the Readers (*in chorus*) Walked with a goose-step to the gallows.

Man with Straw Hat (*reading from behind the paper marked Suicide*) The dead man left a letter saying, I have ruined thousands and have made many mad; I have shaken hands with Dukes and Duchesses; before I put the pistol-point to my ear and scatter my brains, I kiss the pictures of my little darlings; knowing that, while all men condemn, all men will understand.

Rest of the Readers (*in chorus*) All men will understand.

Young Woman (*getting up from the bench with a half-hysterical laugh*) Never say die till you're dead! (*She looks at the Readers.*) Rape, murder, and suicide! A bit of a change from the life of the saints. (*Loudly to the Readers*) What will you fellows do when you die, and have to leave it all behind you!

Readers (*in chorus*) Go away, young woman – we want quietness.

Man wearing Bowler (*reading from behind the paper marked Divorce*) The housemaid said she climbed the ivy, got to the verandah, looked in through the window, saw the co-respondent in bed, the respondent in her camisole trotting towards the bed; then came darkness, and she would leave the judge and jury to guess the rest.

Rest of the Readers (*in chorus*) Leave the learned judge and jury to guess the rest.

While the last phrase is being chorused by the Readers, the Bishop appears on the slope above, looking down anxiously at the Young Woman.

Bishop (*from the slope above*) Jannice!

Young Woman (*up to the Bishop*) Are you following me still? (*Angrily*) Go away, go away and leave me in peace! Let me run my race in my own way. Don't be mousing after me.

Bishop (*pleadingly*) I want to help you, Jannice; let me help you!

Young Woman (*loudly*) Go away, I tell you; I want no

God's grenadier running after me. (*In a half-scream*) Go away!

> *The Bishop goes back to the Memorial, and the Young Woman again contemplates the Readers.*

What are you all seeking? You look like a silent gang of monkeys searching for fleas!

Readers (*in chorus*) Go away; we want to read our papers in peace!

Young Woman (*softly and thoughtfully*) Most important thing, too, is peace; most important. Peace most pure and peace most perfect, due to the children of the Prince of Peace. (*Recklessly*) But what have I to do with peace! When I come to the temple of peace, the veil of the temple turns to steel! Is there no one far enough from the way of the world to take an interval of rest, and have a look at me?

> *The tune of 'The Danube Waltz' has been heard for a few moments before, played softly by the Band. She begins to dance to the tune, in and out among the Readers.*

Now, you deaf and dumb perishers, have a look at a lovely pair of legs, if you're not blind as well!

> *She lifts her skirts as she dances, and makes her movements keep time with the tune. The Readers look over the tops of their papers and watch her.*

All interested now? Well, what do you think of them – saucy, eh? (*Slapping her left leg*) This one's lovely. (*Slapping the right one*) This divine!

> *She stops breathless, and scans them scornfully. The music slowly fades away.*

(*Breathless and scornful*) You bunch of high-minded toads, don't look at me long, for there's only venom for a woman in the things ye think of her. The dear joy of a sin ye turn to a sting and a bruising. (*She half sinks on a seat.*) Oh, my heart, my heart's restless again! (*She speaks in a lower tone to the Readers.*) In your looking after a woman there is no kindliness; before ye no image of loveliness, neither can ye hear the sound of a song as ye follow her, for your desire's but a venomous heat and a shame and a bruising!

She sinks down, pale, breathless, and frightened, on the seat. The Readers return to their reading; and take no more notice of her.

Man wearing Bowler (*reading from behind his paper*) The great cricketer, unbuckling his pads, said, You may take it from me that out there somewhere is a supreme, infinitely wise mind, which we call God, behind everything. God won't let the English people dahn. He'll keep our wicket up, and the bat of faith will drive the bad ball of unbelief far away over the boundary of England!

Man with Stick (*with scornful disgust*) Wot the 'ell does a cricketer know abaht them abstruse things!

Young Woman (*who has been moving uneasily on the bench*) I can't breathe, I can't breathe! (*She pulls the neck of her bodice open.*) It's on me again, but I'll go game, I'll go game. Eyes front up or down!

The Bishop begins to come down slowly towards the Young Woman.

(*In a panic of fear*) Dance, sing, and strip for the fun of the thing – that's all they want from a woman! A sigh, a sob of pain, a thought higher than their own from a woman, and they're all hurrying home. (*Turning towards the Readers*) God damn you, will none of you stir to help when you see a Christian in danger! (*She calls out in a semi-scream.*) Dreamer, Dreamer – where's the Dreamer!

She sinks down half fainting on the bench. The Bishop

comes quickly to her, now, and chafes her hands. The Readers have risen from their seats, have folded up their newspapers, and now come to where the Young Woman and the Bishop are, forming a semicircle around them.

Bishop (*gently and fervently*) Jannice, my little Jannice, I've come to help you; everything will be all right soon. (*addressing the Readers*) Don't gather round, friends. Leave the girl to me. I'll watch over her. (*As they don't stir – sharply*) Leave us alone, I say, and don't stand there, staring like apes! (*All but the Man with the Stick go silently and slowly out. To Man with the Stick*) Didn't you hear me tell you to go away, man?

Man with Stick (*indignantly*) 'Oo are you to sye come en' 'e cometh, en' go en' 'e goeth? Wot she warnts is a doctor, en' not a pryer!

Bishop (*in a burst of fury – using some of the strength of his younger days, and pushing him out roughly*) Oh, go to hell!

  He returns to the Young Woman as she recovers slightly, looking up at him without any confidence in her look.

(*Returning a little to formal speech, but softly, and with feeling*) You are ill, my child; and you are lonely. You have forgotten God for a few moments, but He sends you His help in time of trouble; and, through me, unworthy messenger, a share of His sympathy and love.

  He sits down beside her. She recovers a little, sits up, and stretches out a hand to him, which he takes in his own, and strokes gently.

Young Woman (*with a sigh of relief*) I'm glad you came. I was very lonely. My heart's beating a bit steadier now, thank God.

Bishop (*gently patting her hand*) That's good, now; that's good.

Young Woman (*regaining confidence*) A lot steadier now. I think it's more fear than anything else. I've had a hard time of it; and I get into a panic whenever my heart gives a double-time beat. I feel nearly normal again.

Bishop (*encouragingly*) That's good. Keep calm for a little while and you'll soon be all right.

Young Woman I'm waiting for the Dreamer. He'll be here shortly, and then I'll be safe again.

Bishop (*still stroking her hand – a little coldly*) My child, I shouldn't think too much of the Dreamer, or make a friend of him. The things he writes give scandal, and tend to undermine morality and overthrow tradition. He is a bad influence, my child.

Young Woman (*taking her hand out of the Bishop's – firmly*) I won't hear a word said against the Dreamer. He was the only one from whom I got courage and help. The Atheist, when he acted as my dad, was kind, too, in his own self-interested way. (*She looks innocently into the Bishop's face.*) I never saw my real father. Mother often said he had a high place in your church; but he never had the courage to come and claim his child.

Bishop (*coldly*) From what I saw of her, your mother isn't to be trusted.

Young Woman (*emphatically*) Well, the Dreamer is. He is as poor as I am, but he gaily shares with me his money and his joy. So, you see, he is more important to me than the God you praise.

Bishop (*shocked*) You mustn't say such things, my child! I am here to help you, showing how kind and gentle God can be to – er – a straying lamb seeking in devious ways to find a way back to the waiting flock.

Young Woman (*fretfully*) Oh, the flock doesn't care a

damn whether I'm in or out, man. The flock! So long as
they get their four meals a day, with a gay hour after, and
a cosy fire in the winter, they'll never stretch a neck to see
where a ram or a ewe has wandered.

Bishop (*soothingly*) Well, never mind, now, and don't let
your thoughts irritate you into any excitement, child.
What you need most, now, is rest, and a chance to live a
sober and a quiet life.

Young Woman (*more irritably than ever*) And follow the
commandments of God – always trying to crimp people
into piety. You cross, crown, and anchor boys expect the
very linnets to sing hymns in their spare time. The
Salvation Army Officer, too, has the same gloomy glimpse
of life. Miserere, miserere, all the way to heaven!

Bishop Hush. Forget everything but your own
helplessness; and don't get excited.

Young Woman (*vehemently*) I have to get a little farther
away from the devil before I try to get a little nearer to
God. I've a long way to travel yet before the white and
holy candles are lit, and the golden incense scattered.

Bishop My child, the sinner is always nearer to God than
the sinner dares to think.

Young Woman (*a little hysterically*) Amen, and let us get
to business. Make me safe and make me happy, and I'll
give sweet thanks to God. Why've you been following me
about for days? I sought you once, and you sent me empty
away. Why do you want to help me now? (*Indicating
sleeping Attendants*) Why don't you try to help those poor
sleeping devils there?

Bishop (*a little impatiently*) Oh, it would be waste of time
to think of them.

Young Woman They're still God's children, aren't they?

Bishop (*more impatiently*) We'll see about them another time. You seem to be an interesting case – young and intelligent. You don't seem to be an ordinary – eh – what shall I say?

Young Woman (*bitterly*) Oh, a whore! You may as well say it as think it.

The Bishop is shocked at the girl's bluntness. He stiffens, and stays silent.

(*Looking intently at the Bishop's face*) What was it made you light on me, I wonder? There are hundreds of girls, some of them better, some of them worse, than me, and it's curious that I should be the lucky dip.

The Bishop remains silent.

Well, go on; open up the overture, and play us something nice.

Bishop (*trying to control his impatience*) My child, your present way of life is an evil one. I wish to give you a chance to turn aside from it; so please try to be decently attentive, and listen seriously to what I am about to say.

Young Woman (*with a half-suppressed giggle*) Wine's beginning to take effect again. I had a wild time all this week with the Dreamer. He got an advance on a book that's to be published soon, and he's gone for another advance now. (*She prods the Bishop's breast.*) If he comes back before our treaty's signed, I'm off, and you won't see me again till what he gets is gone: so go ahead, and strike a light, and let us see the way we're walking.

Bishop (*with gloomy indignation*) I can't listen any longer to these frivolous remarks. You have no pity for yourself. You have gone too far away for any helping hand to reach. I will leave you alone. (*He rises from the bench to go.*) I have done my best. I will leave you alone.

Young Woman (*catching his cassock – pleadingly*) No, no; don't go away. I will listen; I will listen quietly; I promise. Be kind, and help me. I do want to try to do what is lawful and right. In God's name, be kind, dear Bishop.

Bishop (*rather sternly*) Listen, child, then, and be serious. When trying to help you, I must be careful of what others may think.

Young Woman Why have you to be careful? Can't you yourself pray, or push yourself out of the fear of what may be said about you? What does it matter how many say a man's a sinner if God thinks him a saint?

Bishop (*very annoyed*) I can't waste time going into those questions now. You said you were going to be serious. Well, then, one more flippant word and I leave you, never to turn a thought to you again.

Young Woman (*earnestly*) I will be serious; I promise. I fix my face, and am serious. I'll do anything you ask me to do.

She pulls gently at his cassock, and he slowly resumes his seat on the bench beside her.

Bishop (*with some embarrassment*) I'm about to say something now which, I fear, will sound very unpleasant to you, perhaps even harsh and ungenerous; something that will bite deeply into all that you may think to be a pleasure. (*He puts a hand gently and appealingly on her shoulder.*) God alone knows, my dear daughter, how deep is my desire to save you!

Young Woman (*with calm and innocent confidence*) Oh, with your power and position, you should be able to push me into a job that wouldn't make the change such a sad one.

Bishop (*taking his hand from her shoulder, and speaking harshly*) I wouldn't think of getting you a place till, after a year or two of trial, I felt certain you had learned how to behave yourself.

A pause and a tense silence.

Young Woman (*with a stifled sob of humiliation*) I see. (*Pause.*) How am I to live through the two years?

Bishop (*forcing himself to speak harshly*) I've arranged that a pious Sisterhood should receive you into their Hostel, where the Reverend Mother will care for you, watch over you, and help you to live with becoming circumspection. In return, when you begin to feel at home, you can make yourself useful to the good Sisters.

Young Woman (*with tightened lips*) I see.

The Policewoman enters, crosses in front of the Young Woman and the Bishop, and looks fixedly and wonderingly at the pair of them. The Young Woman looks down at her feet and the Bishop stares in front of him.

Policewoman (*speaking towards the Bishop*) Nice die, m'lud.

Bishop I beg your pardon?

Policewoman Said it was a nice die, m'lud.

Bishop (*stammeringly*) Oh yes, quite; lovely day, beautiful day; yes, indeed, a very beautiful day.

The Policewoman, watching them as long as possible, goes slowly out.

(*Appealingly*) Why do you keep silent? Take your chance, take your last chance; for God's sake take your last chance.

The Young Woman sits silent.

Do you hear me? The offer I have made is a good offer. In it is peace, and a fair hope of better things to come. Go on, girl, speak; make up your mind, make up your mind.

Young Woman (*rising with hysterical laughter that rouses the sleeping Attendants, who lean on their elbows, watching*) Wine's beginning to take effect again. Your old mind must be worn out thinking of such a wonderful plan. He lifted me up and set me down in the midst of a holy sisterhood. Refugium peccatorum, but not for me, thank you kindly. (*She bows mockingly to the Bishop.*) Chained fast to prayer and firm to fasting! (*She puts her face near the Bishop's.*) Not for me, thank you kindly!

Bishop (*with intense feeling*) What will you do when your good looks go, and you lose the means to earn your bread?

Young Woman (*with a snarling look on her face as she thrusts it close to the Bishop's*) Die, I dare say, while you heap up hopes in the books of a bank, and carry your faith about in a coffin!

> *She hurriedly opens her handbag, takes out two notes, and holds them close to the Bishop's nose. The Two Attendants are now alert, and are watching intently.*

(*Viciously*) See, old purple buttons – the last two between all I need and me! (*She rolls each into the shape of a crumpled ball, and calls to the Attendants.*) Eh, you there – up, and see what God has sent you!

> *She flings a crumpled note to each of them. They open them, smoothe them out, and put them joyously into their pockets.*

(*To the Bishop – recklessly*) I fling my wealth away! (*She points a finger at the Bishop's nose.*) Faith in God, old purple buttons, faith in God! Be merry, man, for a minute, for you'll be a long time dead!

The Bishop, full of sorrow and disappointment, mixed with shame, bends forward on the seat and rests his head in his hands. The Young Woman dances round with mock stateliness as she sings words to the tune of 'Little Brown Jug'. The Two Chair Attendants, as far as their game legs will allow, imitate her in a reckless manner, beating out time, one with his good right leg, and the other with his good left one. Singing and dancing round with mock stateliness.

Sing and dance, dance and sing,
Brief life should be a joyous thing;
The minds that are to troubles wed
Are fit to host but with the dead!
Ha ha ha, you and me, till we both have ceased to be,
Sling out woe, hug joy instead,
For we will be a long time dead!

Chair Attendants (*joining in vigorously*)
Sling aht woe, 'ug joy instead,
For we will be a long time dead!

Young Woman (*singing*)
Life is born and has its day,
Sings a song, then slinks away;
Speaks a word – the word is said,
Then hurries off to join the dead!
Ha ha ha, you and me, till we both have ceased to be,
Sling out woe, hug joy instead,
For we will be a long time dead!

Attendants (*joining in*)
Sling aht woe, 'ug joy instead,
For we will be a.long time dead!

During the singing of the second verse of the song the Atheist has made his appearance on the top of the slope, and stands there watching what is going on below. As

*the Young Woman is ending the latter verse of the song,
the drum-beat and chant of the Down-and-Out is heard
in the near distance, coming nearer and nearer. The
Chair Attendants hear it, stiffen with fear, and end the
chorus weakly. Then the Young Woman recognizes it,
and stands stiff, frightened, while she listens intently.*

(*together*) The drum-beat and chant of the Down-and-Out!

*The scene grows dark and chilly, and even the Bishop
shivers, though the Atheist seems not to notice the
change. The sky seems to turn a cold grey, and against
it, the Down-and-Out pass by. They are all grey, vague
figures of young and old men and women, hopelessness
graven on every grey face. They go by in a rather slow
shuffling march, chanting their miserere to the
monotonous tap, tap of the drum-beat. They go behind
the Atheist, but he stands there, indifferent to march or
chant. The Attendants sink down to their knees, one on
the right of the grass sward, the other to the left of it.*

Down-and-Outs (*chanting*)
   We challenge life no more, no more, with our dead faith,
      and our dead hope;
   We carry furl'd the fainting flag of a dead hope and a
      dead faith.
   Day sings no song, neither is there room for rest beside
      night in her sleeping;
   We've but a sigh for a song, and a deep sigh for a drum-
      beat.
   Oh where shall we go when the day calls?
   Oh where shall we sleep when the night falls?
   We've but a sigh for a song, and a deep sigh for a drum-
      beat!

*The Down-and-Out pass out, their song fading out in
the repetition of the line, 'We've but a sigh for a song,
and a deep sigh for a drum-beat'.*

Bishop (*pointing towards where the Down-and-Out have gone*) There go God's own aristocracy, the poor in spirit! Their slogan, Welcome be the Will of God; their life of meek obedience and resignation in that state of poverty unto which it has pleased God to call them, a testimony that God's in His heaven, all's well with the world. (*To the Attendants*) Join them, my sons. (*To Young Woman*) Join them, my daughter, in the spirit of penitence and prayer!

Atheist (*from the slope above*) Jannice, stand firm, and remember that you are the bride of the Dreamer. Tell him that the world shall be, not what his God wills, but what fighting man can make it. Tell him you have given life a dance and the Dreamer has given life a song!

Bishop (*coming close to the Young Woman, who is leaning for help on the back of a bench*) They came close, my child, they came close. They will get you some day, if you do not let me save you now.

Young Woman (*with a quivering lip*) No!

Attendants (*together*) Save us, sir; save us!

　The Bishop takes no notice of them.

Bishop (*bending over the Young Woman*) The day is fair, my daughter, the day is fair; but what of the night, when youth has faded, and the shadows fall, and the heart is lonely?

Young Woman (*tonelessly, but defiantly*) When youth has gone, when night has fallen, and when the heart is lonely, I will stand and stare steady at a God who has filled the wealthy with good things and has sent the poor empty away.

Bishop (*sorrowfully*) Don't say such things, child. Come with me, I beg of you to come with me.

Young Woman (*with tight lips*) No.

The Bishop looks sadly at her for a moment, then turns and goes slowly up the slope.

The Young Salvation Army Officer followed by other members of the Army, all in uniform, peaked caps and red jerseys, come in, and group themselves in a half-circle, near the centre, to the left of the grass sward. One of them has a trombone, another a cornet, and a third, a big drum. Beside them is raised the red and blue and yellow banner of the sect. A small, box-like stand is placed on the grass, so that a speaker may be raised a little above the crowd. Around them gather various people, among them the Man wearing a Bowler Hat, the Man wearing a Straw Hat, the Man wearing a Trilby, the Nursemaid with her Guardsman, the Attendants, and the Man with the Stick, who stands off, nearer to the Atheist, as if for protection. The young Salvation Army Officer stands out to watch the Bishop going slowly up the slope. When he reaches the top, he turns, and speaks pleadingly to the Young Woman.

Bishop (*making a quiet sign of the cross*) My poor child, I ask you, in the Name of God – come!

Young Woman (*firmly, though her lips quiver a little*) No!

The Bishop looks sadly at her for a moment, and then turns, goes by the Atheist, and passes out. The Young Woman reclines weakly back on the bench, silent and desolate-looking. The scene brightens and the birds sing once more. The Young Salvation Army Officer goes over close to the Young Woman.

S.A. Officer (*to Young Woman*) The ritualist has left you in your need, but the evangelist is here to comfort and help you – if you will. Dear sister, set your foot, by faith, on the path that leads to the land that is fairer than day; where the Father waits to prepare you a dwelling-place – a house not made with hands, eternal in the heavens.

She is silent, and stirs not. He quietly signals to the musicians, and they softly play the tune, 'There Were Ninety and Nine', the rest of the Army and some of the crowd singing the words.

Crowd
There were ninety and nine that safely lay
In the shelter of the fold,
But one was out on the hills away,
Far off from the gates of gold,
Away on the mountains wild and bare,
Away from the tender Shepherd's care;
Away from the tender Shepherd's care.

S.A. Officer (*to Young Woman*) You, sister. But the Lord was anxious, and would not be satisfied with His ninety and nine who were safe. So He set out to find His lost sheep – you, dear sister, you!

He again quietly signals the musicians, who play the air again, while the rest sing the words.

Crowd
But none of the ransomed ever knew
How deep were the waters crossed,
Nor how dark was the night that the Lord pass'd
    through,
Ere He found His sheep that was lost.
Out in the desert He heard its cry –
Sick and helpless and ready to die;
Sick and helpless and ready to die.

The Young Woman is visibly affected. She rises from the bench, and half turns towards where the Salvation Army members are grouped. The young Salvation

Army Officer, seeing this, lays a hand gently on her shoulder.

S.A. Officer (*with uplifted eyes – prayerfully*) There is a young sinner with us now who needs the pardon Christ can give. Let her come to the foot of the cross. She must struggle down to the cross before she can climb up to the crown. Brothers and sisters, let us pray that she may turn from her sin, and be saved!

As he is speaking the Dreamer appears on the top of the slope above, gets in front of the Atheist, and stands to look at what is happening.

Save this wandering lamb, O God, and bring her safely home!

Salvationists (*in chorus*) Save her, great and most merciful Redeemer!

S.A. Officer That the trumpets of the angels may have a new note in their sounding!

Salvationists (*in chorus*) Save her, great and most merciful Redeemer!

S.A. Officer That the crown of thorns on the head of the crucified one may shine as the sun in the season of summer!

Salvationists (*in chorus*) Save her, great and most merciful Redeemer!

S.A. Officer That the nails in His hands and His feet may gleam like the moon at the full in the season of harvest!

Young Woman (*in a frightened voice*) Ah, save me from the life that is never quenched, and give me peace!

Dreamer (*from the slope above*) Jannice, Jannice, the Dreamer calls!

*The air of 'Jannice' is faintly heard, as if from a
distance. The Young Woman stands listening, and the
look of fright fades from her face.*

S.A. Officer (*up to the Dreamer*) Go your wild way,
young man; for our sister has shut herself away from the
pride and vanity of your thoughtless life.

Dreamer (*to S.A. Officer*) The rose that once has opened
can never close again. (*To the Young Woman*) Jannice,
here is peace; peace unharmed by the fire of life. I have
that will give another month of gay and crowded life; of
wine and laughter; joy in our going out and our coming in;
and the dear pain from the golden flame of love. Jannice,
the Dreamer calls!

*The tune of 'Jannice' is heard much more clearly now.
The Young Woman has retreated away from the
Salvationist group; now the Young Salvation Army
Officer holds out his arms to her, but she backs away
from him and half turns towards the Dreamer.*

S.A. Officer (*sadly*) Let us all pray silently and together
against the power trying to draw our young sister from the
offer of redemption.

*The Attendants fall on their knees, and with outspread
fingers cover their faces. The Men Salvationists remove
their caps and bend their heads in an attitude of prayer.
The Women Salvationists do the same, but do not
remove their bonnets. The Young Salvation Army
Officer takes off his cap, and covers his face with one
hand. The tune of 'Jannice' is heard clearly.*

Dreamer (*taking a step down the slope*) Jannice, the
Dreamer calls you to the deep kiss and clutch of love; to
sing our song with the song that is sung by a thousand
stars of the evening!

*The Young Woman moves slowly away from the
praying group, gradually quickens her movement, till
finally she runs to be clasped in the arms of the
Dreamer; while the Atheist looks down on the
Salvationists with a slight twist of mockery disarranging
his lips.*

*The Young Salvation Army Officer glances up, and
sees that the Young Woman is about to go with the
Dreamer. He bends his head on his breast – a picture of
disappointment, and, maybe, of vanity cheated of its
due. The Musicians, replacing their caps on their heads,
play the tune of 'Ninety and Nine' very softly, and the
rest sing the words as softly, too, for the tune of
'Jannice' has faded away as the Young Woman goes
into the arms of the Dreamer, as the Dreamer and the
Young Woman pass out on their way together.*

Chorus

Oh, sad is the fate of the lamb who strays
Far off from her Shepherd's care,
Leaving fair fields where the sunlight plays
For the gloom of the mountains bare;
Oh, sad is the Shepherd seeking his sheep,
To find that his lov'd one is nowhere there;
To find that his lov'd one is nowhere there!

The gates close.

Scene Four

A Winter's night in the Park. The colour of the sky is a deep black, brightening from the centre to the horizon to a rich violet, deepening to a full purple hue. To the right, where the purple sky begins to sink into the darkness, is a group of stars; one red, the other golden, and a third, silver. The trees are quite bare of leaves, and their branches form a pattern against the purple parts of the sky.

Light from an electric lamp behind the War Memorial shines on the head and shoulders of the figure, making them glow like burnished aluminium; and the bent head appears to be looking down at the life going on below it. A Group of Men is standing to the right, looking as if they were directly under the stars. They are the Man wearing a Trilby, the Man wearing a Bowler Hat, the Man who wore a Straw One, but now is wearing a Tweed Cap, the Man with the Stick, and some others. They are all wearing topcoats or mackintoshes, and their collars are pulled up as high as they can go around their throats. The Man with the Stick now carries an Umbrella. As the scene is opening, the latter part of the bugle-call, The Last Post, *is heard sounding in the far distance.*

Man wearing Cap (*to the others*) Wot's that, now?

Man wearing Bowler Sounds like *The Last Past.*

Man wearing Trilby It is *The Last Post.*

Man wearing Cap Wunner where's it from?

Man wearing Trilby From the barracks up Kensington

way. You can 'ear any sound pline on a still, clear night like this one.

Man wearing Bowler Creepy sound, 'asn't it? Alwyes mikes me think of grives when I 'ears it.

Man with Umbrella En' wot if it does? A grive's as common as a crydle, man, en' we've no caurse to be afride of either.

Man wearing Cap It's easy to talk, but a grive's a grive; en' with winter 'ere, en' the Park nearly desolyte, the sahnd of *The Last Post* 'as en eerie effect on me.

Man wearing Trilby (*suddenly*) 'Ere 'e is agine! Like 'Amlet's ghost. Wot interest 'as 'e in the girl, I wunner?

Man with Umbrella Up to no good, I bet. No Bishop ever is. Keep back in the gloom so as 'e won't see.

They retire a little. The Bishop comes down the slope, looking from right to left, then stopping to look behind him. His face is grey, and a deep look of worry lines it. He is followed by his Sister, who looks stern and appears to be annoyed.

Bishop's Sister (*with suppressed anger*) Gilbert, for goodness' sake, have sense. Why do you trouble yourself like this for a trollop?

Bishop (*angrily*) Don't call her by that name; I won't have it, I won't have it!

Bishop's Sister You're a fool, Gilbert! She never was your child; and even if she ever had a claim, she ceased to be your child when we put her into the Institution.

Bishop Even if she ceased to be my child, she, nevertheless, remains a child of God; she still has her claim to the Kingdom of Heaven. I must not forget that now; I must never forget that again!

Bishop's Sister If you go on like this much longer, Gilbert, you'll find yourself becoming ridiculous to respectable and important opinion.

Bishop (*vehemently*) That has been my besetting sin all along – fear of the respectable opinion of others. I renounce it now! She herself has said, What does it matter how many think a man to be a sinner if God believes him to be a saint. That's what she said – to my very face.

Bishop's Sister Just like the impudent and semi-blasphemous thing such as she would say!

Bishop (*impatiently*) Don't waste time talking, woman. (*catching her arm*) Look at that figure out there in the shadows. (*He points with his finger.*) Can you see? Is it she?

Bishop's Sister (*freeing her arm*) I refuse to look! What has happened to you, Gilbert, after all these years of forgetfulness? Why do you suddenly so concern yourself with such a trivial thing.

Bishop A human soul is not a trivial thing.

Bishop's Sister Some souls are, and well you know it, and she is one of them. I tell you this fancy solicitude of yours is just a sentimental fear of something done years ago in a foolish moment. I tell you, such a soul is a trivial thing to be a torment to you.

Bishop (*sadly*) Not hers, but our souls, I'm afraid, are the trivial things in the sight of God, and in the minds of brave men. (*Fiercely*) But mine's going to be trivial no longer! I go to seek her, and don't follow me.

Bishop's Sister (*doggedly*) I will follow you! You're not sensible enough to be left alone.

Bishop (*angrily*) Go home, woman. Being too sensible has

been my curse all along. By trying to save my honoured
soul, I am losing it. Go home, woman, and let me find a
way to my girl and my God!

*He hurries away among the trees to the left, and, after a
moment's hesitation, his Sister follows him. The Man
with the Umbrella comes out from the group, and peers
after them. The others, too, come out of the gloom and
join the Man with the Umbrella in staring towards the
direction in which the Bishop and his Sister have gone.
As they stare, the Guardsman and the Nursemaid, arm-
in-arm, enter from the opposite direction, and, seeing
the men staring, are interested, so they join the group of
peerers.*

Man with Umbrella (*pointing with his umbrella*) There
they go, one after the other – foller my leader like. Thet
sister of 'is'll 'ave to keep a close eye on 'er brother. At 'is
age too, runnin' after a girl as might 'ave been 'is
daughter!

Guardsman (*wonderingly*) 'Oo?

Man wearing Trilby Now, now; the gentleman 'as no evil
aims in 'is afollowing 'er. I 'eard 'im sye 'e warnted to save
'is soul en' 'ers.

Guardsman (*wonderingly*) 'Oo's soul, wot soul?

Man with Umbrella (*contemptuously*) Soul! There ain't
no soul. Wot you 'ave in your mind is mind; the mind wot
conquers time, spice, en' material conditions.

Man wearing Trilby En' when did mind begin, en' 'oo
myde it?

Man with Umbrella Nothing begins, man; things like
mind simply appear, sudden like; when, 'ow, or where, we
don't know.

Guardsman (*impatiently*) But what was it arunning after the girl?

Man with Umbrella That clergyman fella 'oo's been runnin' rahnd tryin' to mike free with ordinary people.

Guardsman (*indignantly*) 'Im, is it? Th' bloke wot tried to interfere once with me en' my girl. Why didn't some of you tell 'im orf?

Nursemaid (*chucking his arm*) Aw, come on, Harry.

Guardsman (*impatiently to Nursemaid*) Wyte a minute, carn't you! (*To the Group*) Wot prevented you from atellin' 'im orf? I'd ha' done it. Our company sergeant-major's a fire terror, 'e is. Gives you a feelin' 'e 'ites everyone, 'e does, en' wishes you was dead. But whenever 'e gets me on the rawr, I tells 'im orf, I do, s'elp me!

Man with Umbrella (*with amused scorn*) You does, does you?

Guardsman (*getting warm to his subject*) T'other dye, Guardsman Odgerson, 'e syes, wot's th' meanin' of your bed not bein' properly folded? Git your poor mind movin' 'e roars, fer Gord's syke, en' sye wye your bed's not properly folded, 'e syes.

Nursemaid 'E's en' ign'rant barstid, 'e is; we all knows 'im.

Guardsman (*mimicking how he did it*) I gits 'old of a byenet en' chises 'im rahnd the barrack square till I was caught up by the picket!

Man wearing Trilby A serious thing to do in the Awmy.

Guardsman When I was on the carpet before the Myjor, 'e did look fierce. Serious breach of discipline, 'e syes. But, 'e syes, considering the provocytion, 'e syes, admonished, 'e syes, I think will meet the cyse. Agoin' aht, 'e syes to me, private, served 'im right, Guardsman Odgerson; pity you didn't give 'im a jeb, 'e syes – I know th' bugger!

Nursemaid A real torf, the myjor, 'e is; a proper torf. Come on, Harry.

Guardsman Wyte a minute, carn't you.

Man wearing Trilby Well, I won't wyte no longer for the Atheist to come en' amuse us with his relativity ideas. I knew 'e wouldn't fyce us aht, for everyone knows spice is one thing en' time is another.

Man with Umbrella It's not 'im's afryde to come; it's you're afryde to stye. Spice-time gives a noo meanin' to th' universe. Spice is relative to time, en' time is relative to spice – there's nothin' easier to understand.

Man wearing Trilby (*dubiously*) Yes, quite; I gets thet, but –

Man with Umbrella (*interrupting impatiently*) Wyte, 'old on a second. Don't question me, yet. Listen carefully; let your mind foller wot I sye, en' you'll get th' idear.

Guardsman Listen cautiously to wot th' gentleman's asyein' – 'e knows wot 'e's torking abaht.

Nursemaid (*tugging at the Guardsman's sleeve*) Aw, c'm on, Harry; you knows I 'as to be back by ten.

The Guardsman takes no notice.

Man with Umbrella (*pompously*) Now try to remember that all th' old idears of the cosmos – Greek for all things th' 'uman mind knows of – are buried with Copernicus, Kepler, Newton, en' all that crew.

Guardsman (*emphatically*) 'Course they is, en' deep too.

Man with Umbrella Now we all know that the clock created time, en' the measuring-rod created spice, so that there is really neither spice nor time; but there is such a thing as spice-time. See? Get that?

Man wearing Trilby (*with confidence*) Quite; that much is perfectly clear.

Man with Umbrella Right. Now, suppose that one night, when we all slept, th' universe we knows sank down to the size of a football, en' all the clocks began to move a thousand times quicker, – no, slower – it wouldn't mike the slightest difference to us, for we wouldn't realize that any difference 'ad tyken plice, though each of us would live a thousand times longer, en' man couldn't be seen, even under a microscope.

Guardsman (*jocularly*) Could a woman be seen under a microscope?

Man wearing Cap (*to Guardsman*) Levity's outa plice, friend, when men are trying to think out th' truth of things.

Guardsman But 'ow could th' world sink dahn to th' size of a football? Doesn't seem a sife thing to me.

Man with Umbrella (*with cold dignity*) I said *if* it did, friend.

Guardsman (*trying to find a way out*) Yes; but if a man couldn't be seen under a microscope, wot abaht 'is kids?

Man with Umbrella I simply styted a hypothenuse, friend.

Man wearing Cap (*to Guardsman*) It's only en hypothenuse, you understand? (*To Man with Umbrella*) But it's en impossible one, I think. D'ye mean that under your hypothenuse, en hour of the clock would stretch aht into ten years of time?

Man with Umbrella Exactly that in spice-time; en 'undred years if you like.

Man wearing Cap Wot? Then in your spice-time, a man doin' eight hours would be workin' for eight 'undred years!

Guardsman (*to Man with Umbrella*) You're barmy, man! Wot abaht th' bloke doin penal servitude fer life? When is 'e agoin' to get aht? You're barmy, man!

Nursemaid (*to Guardsman – chucking his arm*) Are you comin' Harry? If you don't 'urry, I'll 'ave to go, en' you'll 'ave to go withaht even a firewell squeeze.

Man with Umbrella (*annoyed – to Guardsman*) Look, friend, if I was you, I'd go with the girl; for it's pline your mind 'asn't been educyted yet to grasp the complicyted functions of wot we know as spice-time problems.

Guardsman (*with heat*) 'Oo 'asn't a mind? 'Oo're you to sye I 'asn't a mind? I 'asn't a mind as would warnt to tern th' world into a football. It's a punch on the jawr you warnts for thinkin' people warnts the world to be a football. Wye's there different thoughts in every mind, en' different rules in every country? Becorse people like you 'as th' world turned upside dahn! Wot do I mean when I syes th' world is upside dahn? Why, I means th' whole world is upside dahn, en' ennyone as 'as a mind'll unnerstend me!

Man with Umbrella (*to Guardsman*) Wite a minute, wite a minute – you've got it all wrong.

Nursemaid (*anxiously – pulling Guardsman's arm*) Come awye, do! They'll get you with their tork right on the carpet, in front of the colonel; so mind yourself, for I warn you, en' everyone knows as 'ow it ain't never allowed by the War Office to tork politics – soldiers is above them things.

Guardsman (*freeing himself – stormily*) I won't let no blighter sye as 'ow I ain't got no eddicytion to tork of things! (*To the Group*) Where would you muckers be if it warnt for us swaddies, eh? Poor swaddies rovin' the world, pickin' up fevers, to keep you sife at 'ome, en' 'appy. 'Oo is it does it, I asks? (*He strikes his chest.*) We blighters, us blokes!

Man with Trilby Tike it easy, soldier; tike it easy.

Guardsman (*more stormily still*) 'Oo was it, en' 'oo is it is holdin' dahn Africar en' Indiar, en' teachin' 'em 'ow to behive theirselves proper, eh? (*He strikes his breast.*) We blighters, us poor blokes!

Nursemaid (*butting in hotly*) Yes, en' we done a thing or two for the Chinks of China, too!

Guardsman Too true, we did!

Nursemaid (*dragging the Guardsman away*) Come on, come aht – we're wastin' our time torkin' to these silly old cacklers!

Guardsman (*as he is being pulled out*) If it warn't my dooty to see my gal 'ome sife, I'd mike you muckers do a right-about-wheel en' quick march off the field; I would, en' proper, too, blimey; if I was to spend a month in clink for it, s'help me, I would!

He and the Nursemaid pass out of view.

Man with Umbrella There's an example, a fine example of militarism for us!

Man wearing Bowler (*deprecatingly*) He wasn't altogether to blime. It was en unfortunate hypothenuse to set before ignorent minds; en', to me, wholly ahtside respect to things unknowable, which should be left with 'Im 'oo mide things comprehensible en' incomprehensible. Introducin' the universe as a football was a regrettable en' might become a dinegerous conception, even as a mere hypothenuse, as you might sye.

*While the Man wearing the Bowler Hat has been
speaking, the Old Woman comes in slowly and wearily,
and now and again gives an unsteady step, as if she had
a little drink taken. She plods along till she is beside the
Group of Men. She stops and looks rather vacantly at
them. She carries a laurel wreath tied with red ribbon.*

Old Woman (*tonelessly*) Anyone here see a young girl
pass? My daughter; a poor one; yes, indeed, regardless of
her poor mother. A scarlet crescent on the hip of a black
dress; a black one on the side of a scarlet hat. My dearest
daughter. A good mother I've been; some say too good;
but she doesn't care, never thinks of me. (*to the Group*)
Did she pass you by?

Man wearing Bowler I shouldn't worry, ma'am; she'll
soon be in good hands – the Bishop is seeking for her.

Old Woman (*cocking an ear*) The Bishop? That villain!
He took her part against me – against her own mother.
What does he want with her?

Man wearing Bowler Don't know, ma'am; he seemed to
be anxious to find her.

Old Woman (*musingly*) My first husband is now a man
like him. Somewhere he stands before an altar jewelled
with candlelight, wearing a crimson cassock and a golden
cope. And a mean heart is hiding under them. He left me
alone. Somewhere he's powerful and pompous; in some
place or other he's brightly hidden away where I can't
reach. (*She sighs.*) Everything golden is going into the
bellies of the worms.

Man wearing Cap Maybe the Bishop could help you,
ma'am.

Old Woman Him? He'd help no one. God can, though. I
never have to raise my voice, for God can hear a whisper

better than a thunderclap. Yet a little while, and He'll level down to nothing the stir that still remains around us; for everything golden is going into the bellies of the worms.

Man wearing Trilby If I was you, ma'am, I'd go home and have a rest.

Old Woman There can be no rest nor work nor play where there is no life, and the golden infancy of England's life is tarnishing now in the bellies of the worms. But God can save us, maybe, even at this late hour.

Man with Umbrella (*mockingly*) Gord's a poor prop for enny one to lean on, ma'am.

Old Woman (*awake and lively at once*) Who said that about God? (*To Man with Umbrella – fiercely*) You did, you, you worm! Is it any wonder we're all as we are, and I'm as I am? Provoking God to hide His goodness and His mercy. Go away you – (*She raises an arm as if to strike him. He stretches out the hand holding the umbrella to guard himself, and she, with an unexpected jerk, snatches it from him and flings it from her.*) Ah, you'd strike an old woman, would you; and with a weapon, too? (*with bitterness*) And to think that all our hero soldiers died that such as you might live! (*She catches sight of the wreath she is carrying.*) May this little token ease the anger of the dead. (*She wanders over till she is facing the base of the War Memorial. She remains silent before it for a few moments with head bent; then speaks tonelessly and sadly.*) A few more moments of time, and Spring'll be dancing among us again; dancing in gold and purple pavilions of laburnum an' lilac; the birds'll be busy at building small worlds of their own in the safe an' snug breast of the hedges; the girls will go rambling round, each big with the thought of the life in the loins of the young men; but those who are gone shall sink into stillness, deep under the stillness that shelters the dead!

Man wearing Trilby (*removing his hat*) May they all rest in peace!

Man wearing Bowler (*removing his hat*) Amen!

The Old Woman lifts the wreath she is carrying, high above her head, much in the same way a priest elevates the Host. Man with Umbrella has picked it up.

Old Woman (*lifting her head till she faces the Memorial Figure*) O soldier in bronze, cold guard of remembrance for those who rode out on swift horses to battle, and fell, I lay at thy feet this circle of green and ribbon of red as a signal of shame unto those who've forgotten the dead. (*She bends down and lays the wreath at the foot of the Memorial. Then she sings softly and quietly, without moving.*)

(*singing*)
When souls are lin'd out on th' cold Judgement Day,
To stand shaking and sad in sin's wild disarray;
When pardon is lost, and all hopes lie in ruin,
May God give a thought to an Irish Dragoon!

Voices (*singing*)
May God give a thought to an Irish Dragoon!

Old Woman (*singing*)
Who fought on hills high and who fought in lands low,
Till a blustering bullet came swift from a foe,
And left me alone, though I'll follow full soon
The path blaz'd to death by an Irish Dragoon!

Voices (*singing*)
The path blaz'd to death by her Irish Dragoon!

She turns down and slowly comes towards the Group of Men, singing as she goes.

Old Woman (*singing*)
Though God makes the brightest of mornings look sad,

Though He's taken from me all the joys I once had;
Though He deny all, let Him grant me one boon,
To sleep when I die with my Irish Dragoon!

Voices (*singing*)
To sleep when she dies with her Irish Dragoon!

*As she crosses while singing the last line, the Bishop,
followed by his Sister, comes in from the opposite side,
his face full of anxiety and dejection. He and the Old
Woman meet when they reach the Group of Men.*

Old Woman (*lifting her head, and seeing the Bishop*) Ah,
his reverence, the Bishop! Looking for my daughter, too.
And what may you want with her, your reverence?

Bishop's Sister (*getting in front of the Bishop – to Old
Woman*) Get away, woman! He isn't looking for your
daughter. She would be the last person he would wish to
meet!

Old Woman Aha, are you another of the night-strollers
seeking lightsome contacts in the gloomier parts of the
Park?

Bishop's Sister (*furiously*) How dare you say such a thing!
How dare you even hint at such a desire in me, you
tumble-down, wicked woman! I do not tread the ways of
sin like you or your daughter!

Old Woman Indeed you don't; but you could, you know,
without a risk. No harm could ever come to you.

Bishop's Sister I am what you never were, never can be – a
good woman!

Old Woman Your misfortune, madam; but there's some
compensation in being a stony monument to good conduct
and virtue.

Bishop (*coming forward in front of his Sister*) Go away, you wretched woman, and cease from annoying a Bishop's sister!

Old Woman (*a little confusedly*) Oh, yes, a bishop; I forgot. Tell me, do you, at festivals, wear a crimson cassock and a golden cope?

Bishop What I wear concerns you not; so go away.

Old Woman You've been looking for a girl, haven't you? The one with a red crescent on the hip of a black dress, and a black one on the side of a scarlet hat? She's my daughter.

Bishop (*somewhat sharply*) I wasn't seeking any girl, woman. No girl at all. I once tried to help your daughter, but it was useless. So I washed my hands of her completely and for ever.

Man wearing Trilby (*coming forward*) You've forgotten, I think, sir. Remember you asked me if I saw her, some little time ago?

Bishop (*hesitantly*) No, no; I did not.

Bishop's Sister (*quickly*) If he asked for anyone, it must have been I he was looking for.

Man wearing Trilby (*embarrassed and confused*) Yes, of course, ma'am; my mistake. (*He retires again.*)

Old Woman (*meditatively – to the Bishop*) There's a hidden hum in your old voice that carries a wisp of remembrance to me. (*Suddenly*) Is your name Gilbert?

Bishop (*hastily*) No, no; it is not. Nothing like it either.

Bishop's Sister (*quickly*) His name is not Gilbert! (*To the world at large*) What are the police doing that undesirable persons are allowed to annoy and molest people in this way!

Bishop (*to Old Woman*) Go away from us, woman. If our politics were what they should be, you wouldn't be permitted to wander about interfering with people enjoying the innocent pleasures of the Park!

Old Woman (*scornfully*) Pleasures and politics! Your politics are husks that only swine will eat; your power shelters behind a battlement of hunger; your religion's as holy as a coloured garter round a whore's leg: truth's bent in two, and hope is broken. (*Mournfully*) O Jesus! is there no wisdom to be found anywhere! All gone with the golden life of England into the bellies of the worms! (*While she has been saying the last few sentences, she has been going out slowly, with tired steps, and now passes from view.*)

Bishop (*turning towards the Group of Men, and trying to appear in no way affected by his scene with the Old Woman*) Shocking example, friends, of what a woman can become! Under the influence of drink, I'm afraid. But go on with your discussion, gentlemen – it is a fine thing to see working men trying to elevate and develop their minds.

Man wearing Cap We've finished it, sir. We have had enough of argument for one dye. We were about to go home when the Old Woman made her appearance.

Bishop's Sister (*to the Men*) We were going homewards, too, gentlemen, when, as you saw, the half-insane creature interfered with us. Good night to you all. Come along, Gilbert.

Bishop (*suddenly catching his Sister by the arm, and pointing away from himself – agitatedly*) Look! That girl going down the path there! Is that she? She'll be passing through the light from a lamp in a second, and my old eyes are too dim to be sure. (*Short pause.*) Now! Quick, quick, look, can't you!

Bishop's Sister (*angrily*) I won't, I won't look. Think of what you're trying to do, Gilbert: help and kindness are but tortures to girls of her kind and class. Please be sensible and come home!

He shakes off a hand she has placed on his arm, and hurries out in the direction of where he thinks he had seen the girl. His Sister remains motionless where she is for a few moments, and then, distractedly, follows him out.

Man wearing Trilby See, we were right after all: his name is Gilbert, en' 'e is looking for the girl. There's something curious in it all.

Man with Umbrella May be something curious in it, but nothing strynge – you don't know bishops as well as I do.

Man wearing Bowler Odd how, after denying it, she called him Gilbert; en' 'e, forgetting wot 'e said a second before, called aht to 'er to tell 'im if the passing figure was the girl 'e sought.

Man wearing Cap Aware of nothing save wot was in their minds – like a man not feeling or hearing ennything when he's unconscious.

Man with Umbrella Nonsense, man; 'course you can feel en' 'ear when you're unconscious. You're unconscious when you're asleep, but you still 'ave the faculty of 'earin' en' feeling.

Man wearing Cap No, sir, no; all the so-called senses are dormant in a styte of unconsciousness.

Man with Umbrella Wot abaht en alawm clock agoing off first thing in the mawning?

Man wearing Cap You 'ear it only when you become conscious of its striking.

Man in Bowler 'Ow does it wyeken you up, then?

Man wearing Cap It doesn't wyeken you up, it can't wyeken you up till you become conscious of its sahnd. You understand thet, surely?

Man wearing Bowler I understand, but I don't agree. Wot I sye is, while I'm asleep, which is a styte of unconsciousness, I 'ear.

Man with Umbrella 'Course 'e 'ears!

Man wearing Cap The styte of unconsciousness implies a condition unaccompanied by conscious experience. We experience something when we 'ear; 'ow then can we, when we're unconscious, pass into the experience of 'earing?

Man with Umbrella You're confusing the issue: let's decide first wot is 'earing: now wot do we mean when we say we 'ear?

Man wearing Cap The sense of 'earing exists simply as the sense of feeling exists, manifested, for instance, in pleasure or pine, though we know thet pine is non-existent, strictly speaking.

Man wearing Bowler (*scornfully*) Pine non-existent? Oh, don't be silly, man!

Man with Umbrella (*with disgust*) Aw, 'e's a giving us Christian Science now!

Man wearing Bowler Mean to sye you carn't feel the jeb of a pin or the sting of a wasp?

Man wearing Cap You can, if you want to feel them.

Man with Umbrella Can if you – but no one warnts to feel them. Aw! We're back again at where we sterted.

Man wearing Bowler (*to the Man with Umbrella*) Wite a minute, wite a minute; impatience 'll never get at the truth of things. (*To the Man wearing Cap*) Suppose you cut your finger, wouldn't you feel pine?

Man wearing Cap I'm not going to suppose ennything of the kind. As mind willed pine into existence, so mind c'n will pine awye again.

Man with Umbrella (*with impatience*) Aw!

Man wearing Bowler (*to the Man with Umbrella*) Wite a minute, wite a minute. (*To the Man wearing Cap*) You said thet if you cut your finger you wouldn't feel pine?

Man wearing Cap I never said ennything of the kind.

Man with Umbrella Never said ennything of the kind? But we 'eard you syeing it just now, man!

Man wearing Cap I argued in a general wye, en' I refuse to be refuted by a trivial particular, the genesis of which I deny: immaterially speaking, you carn't cut your finger.

Man with Umbrella (*with consternation*) Immaterially speaking – carn't cut your finger – oh, mister, mister!

Man wearing Bowler (*suddenly interrupting*) Hush, hush; look – she's coming; the girl the Bishop warnted; coming with the Dreamer!

> *They all cease talking, and look towards the point indicated by the Man wearing the Bowler Hat.*
>
> *After a moment or two the Young Woman enters with the Dreamer. She is leaning heavily on his arm. Her breathing is quick; her face is very pale, and in her eyes is a fixed look of fear. The lie of her clothing shows that she has dressed hastily. She is dressed as before, in black, slashed with crimson.*
>
> *The Dreamer wears a vivid orange scarf thrown carelessly round his neck and shoulders. He leads the Young Woman to a bench opposite to where the Group*

of Men is standing, and gently helps her to sit down on it. There is a hushed pause for a few moments.

Young Woman (*tremulously*) I'm bad, Dreamer; please go and find the Bishop for me. (*She mechanically arranges her dress.*) My clothes seem to be on me every way and any way. (*With a wan smile*) You hurried me into them, Dreamer, as quick as you hurried me out of them! Things are twisting before my eyes. (*Frightened*) Get the Bishop, go for the Bishop!

Dreamer Aren't you safer in the arms of the Dreamer than you are at the Bishop's feet?

Young Woman (*tonelessly*) While I had life – yes; but I feel close to death now, and I have a lot to answer for, Dreamer.

Dreamer (*vehemently*) Not you, fair lass; not you! A few smiles bestowed on the unworthy is all that you have to answer for. It is those who disordered your life with their damned whims; those who have left a lovely thing lonely and insecure; who have neglected to nurture the rare; it is we, dear lass, who will have to answer for all these things!

Young Woman You were always kind, Dreamer, and, at least, you led me to where I heard a song. Be kind to me still, and bring the Bishop here.

The Dreamer goes over to the Group of Men who are watching him and the Young Woman.

Dreamer (*to the Men*) Have any of you seen the Bishop lately?

Man wearing Trilby 'E was 'ere a short time ago. (*He points at the Young Woman.*) En' 'e was looking for 'er.

Dreamer If any of you see him, send him here – the spot where the Memorial is, near the Bird Sanctuary – please.

Man wearing Bowler As we go 'ome, if we see 'im, we'll send 'im along.

*They go out by different ways, and the Dreamer goes
back to the Young Woman.*

Dreamer On their way home, if they see him, the men will send the Bishop here.

Young Woman (*agitated*) You go, too, Dreamer – none of them might meet the Bishop. Oh, please do!

Dreamer I don't like to leave you alone, Jannice.

Young Woman (*with a faint smile*) You will soon have to leave me alone, whether you like it or no. I will be quite safe here. No one will bother me now.

Dreamer Don't stir then till I come back.

*He takes her hand in his, gently kisses it, and goes up
the slope, and out.*
   *The Young Woman sits on the bench, staring straight
before her, looking lonely and unhappy. She remains
alone in the scene for a few moments; then the Bishop's
Sister comes on to the top of the slope, looking from
side to side, as if in search of someone. As she appears
above, the Old Woman comes in from the shadows on
the left below. She is greatly bent, and walks with slow
and dragging feet. She shivers as she looks about and
catches sight of the lonely figure sitting on the bench.
She shuffles over to it.*

Old Woman (*peering at the figure*) Have you seen a Bishop strolling about anywhere here recently? He's a friend of mine. I am in sore straits, having no home now, and he may be willing to help me. (*She pauses for an answer, but gets none.*) A man, a comfortable man wearing a cassock adorned with purple buttons, with a scarlet cap on his head. Why don't you answer? (*She peers* *more closely at the figure, and recognizes the Young Woman.*) Oh, it's you, is it? So here you are, looking very pale, and as if you were settling down for death. Remember now the way you treated your poor mother! No fancy dreams in front of you now – only the last things staring you in the face!

> *The Bishop's Sister has heard the Old Woman talking, has watched her while she spoke, and now comes down the slope towards them.*

Young Woman (*doggedly – with a vicious look at the Old Woman*) Anyhow, if I go, I'll go game, and die dancing!

Old Woman (*with some exultation in her voice*) Looks as if it would be me who would be dancing over your grave, my merry lady!

> *The Young Woman rises from the bench, and walks unsteadily away from the Old Woman, meeting the Bishop's Sister, who has come down the slope. The Young Woman retreats a few steps from her, so that she is between them both, where she stands shivering.*

Bishop's Sister (*to the Young Woman*) So I've found you just before the Bishop could come to you. Waiting for his help and pity, are you? Be off out of the Park, and hide yourself, you shameless thing, or I'll send the police to take you out!

Old Woman (*getting in front of the Young Woman, and bowing low in mockery before the Bishop's Sister*) Salaam, mem pukka memsahib, salaam, and pardon her and pardon me and pardon us all for getting in the way of thy greatness; and grant us grace to have faith in thy dignity and importance, per benedicite pax hugger muggery ora pro puggery rigmarolum!

Bishop's Sister (*venomously*) The pair of you ought to be stretched out naked on the ground so that decent women could trample the life out of you!

Old Woman (*confidently*) Gallant men would lift us up on to our feet again.

Bishop's Sister (*violently*) Sympathy for such as you would be a sin. The soft and gentle hand of pity must be changed to the punishing hand of bronze!

Old Woman (*remonstrating*) Oh, sister, sister!

Bishop's Sister (*furiously*) How dare you call me sister!

Old Woman (*reflectively*) How savage women can be when God has been unkind and made us plain, so that no man can find a vision in our face.

> *In the distance is heard the beat of the drum and the faint murmur of the Down-and-Out chant. The Three Women become rigid, and listen intently.*
>
>   *Down the slope come the tottering Attendants, followed by the Two Evangelists, bent, and with unsteady legs. All their faces are full of fear. They come into the centre, an Evangelist and an Attendant going behind the Bishop's Sister, and an Evangelist and an Attendant behind the Young Woman.*

Evangelists and Attendants (*in chorus, as they come down the slope*) With drum-beat and chant the Down-and-Out are close upon us!

Bishop's Sister (*with merry rancour*) Soon they will encompass you round about; and there will be no way of escape, even for the lady of the good looks!

> *The Bishop appears on the slope above. He stands so that the light from a lamp falls on him, a sad and dignified figure in his cassock with its purple buttons, and the scarlet biretta on his head. He stretches out an*

arm over those below, extending two fingers of a hand in blessing, and speaks in sad and low tones, almost intoning the words.

Bishop Benedicti vos a Domino, qui fecit coelum et terram.

He comes slowly down the slope, backed by the chant, louder now, of the Down-and-Outs, and the Young Woman rushes over to him, and falls on her knees.

Young Woman (*imploringly*) Bless me, even me, oh! my father!

With a shiver and a quivering lip, the Bishop stretches an arm over her, extends his fingers to bless her, but his arm falls slowly to his side again, and he remains silent.

The Dreamer now appears on the slope, and stands in the light where the Bishop had stood before, looking at those below him. The Bishop walks away from the kneeling Young Woman, and stands in the centre, with a group on his right and another on his left.

1st Evangelist We have danced no dance, neither have we sought the beauty of any woman; we have sung no songs, nor have we ever made merry in our hearts.

2nd Evangelist We have honoured pain; bound up joy with sighing; and multiplied sorrows that men might know Thy mercy and Thy kindness.

Bishop Grant them pardon, O Lord, and bring them peace!

Dreamer Let them sink into the grave, O Lord, and never let their like appear on the face of the earth again.

1st Evangelist Stricken, we struck not back; we blessed them that cursed us; and prayed for them that took no note of our misery and want.

Bishop Grant them pardon, O Lord, and bring them peace!

Dreamer Let brambles, O Lord, grow thick where they are buried deep; let the fox and the vixen guard their cubs in the midst of the brambles; and let children sing and laugh and play where these have moaned in their misery!

The Down-and-Outs are here now, spreading over the slope above, and making to come down; but the Dreamer with outstretched arms bars the way. On their way, and just before coming in on to the slope, they are heard singing.

Down-and-Outs (*chanting*)
Life has pass'd us by to the loud roll of her drum,
With her waving flags of yellow and green held high,
All starr'd with the golden, flaming names of her most
    mighty children.

Oh, where shall we go when the day calls?
Oh, where shall we sleep when the night falls?
We've but a sigh for a song, and a deep sigh for a drum-
    beat!

Their chant changes into a menacing hum, like that of a swarm of wasps, to the tune of the chant, as the rest speak to each other. The Young Woman goes unsteadily over to the Bishop.

Young Woman (*imploring*) Let me not mingle my last moments with this marching misery!

Bishop (*to Young Woman – slow, but with decision*) You must go where they go, and their sighing shall be your song!

Down-and-Outs (*chanting*)
She must be merry no more; she must walk in the midst
    of the mournful;

196

Who've but a sigh for a song, and a deep sigh for a
drum-beat!

*The Young Woman has stiffened with resentment as she
has listened, and now stands facing the Dreamer,
looking at him for encouragement.*

Dreamer (*to Young Woman*) Turn your back swift on the
poor, purple-button'd dead-man, whose name is absent
from the book of life. Offer not as incense to God the dust
of your sighing, but dance to His glory, and come before
His presence with a song!

Young Woman (*with reckless defiance*) I'll go the last few
steps of the way rejoicing; I'll go, go game, and I'll die
dancing!

Dreamer (*exultantly*) Sing them silent, dance them still,
and laugh them into an open shame!

*Faintly, as if the tune was heard only in the minds of
the Dreamer and the Young Woman, the notes of a
dance tune are heard, coming from the subdued playing
of a flute and other instruments. The Young Woman
and the Dreamer dance to the melody, she a little
unsteadily. They dance for about a minute, then the
movements of the Young Woman become a little
uncertain; she staggers, recovers herself, dances again,
but with faltering steps. The music of the dance
becomes fainter.*

Young Woman (*frightened*) Dreamer, Dreamer, I'm
fainting – I think I'm going to die.

Dreamer (*fiercely*) Sing them silent; dance them still; laugh
them into an open shame!

Down-and-Outs (*chanting and coming down a little by
the centre*)

She must be merry no more; she must be set in the midst
    of the mournful,
Who've but a sigh for a song, and a deep sigh for a
    drum-beat!

Dreamer (*fiercely, with his face close to the Young
Woman's*) Sing them silent; dance them still; laugh them
into an open shame!

Bishop (*prayerfully as they dance*) O Lord, who taketh
pleasure in thy people, let this dance be unto thee as a
merry prayer offered by an innocent and excited child!

*The tune of the dance is now mournful, and the
Dreamer is almost carrying the Young Woman in his
arms. They dance in this way for a few moments, then
the head of the Young Woman falls limp, and the
Dreamer lifts her in his arms, carries her to a soft spot
on the green sward, and lays her down there.*

Young Woman (*almost in a whisper*) I die, Dreamer, I die,
and there is fear in my heart.

Dreamer (*tenderly*) Fear nothing: courage in the hearts of
men and women is what God needs most; and He will
find room for one scarlet blossom among a thousand
white lilies!

*The Bishop goes unsteadily to where the Young Woman
is lying. He kneels beside her, and takes one of her
hands in his.*

Young Woman (*to the Bishop*) Guide the hand you hold
into making the sign of the cross, that I may whisper my
trust in the golden mercy of God!

*The Bishop guides her hand as she makes the sign of the
cross. She lies still and silent. The Down-and-Out come
down the rest of the way, changing the waspish hum of
their voices to the dolorous chant of their miserere.*

They spread out, enveloping the Evangelists, the Attendants and the Old Woman.

Down-and-Outs (*chanting*)

We challenge life no more, no more, with our dead faith and our dead hope;
We carry furl'd the fainting flags of a dead hope and a dead faith.
Day sings no song, neither is there room for rest beside night in her sleeping:
We've but a sigh for a song, and a deep sigh for a drum-beat!

They force the Dreamer back a few paces at first; but exerting his strength, he forces a way through them, scattering them to right and left, as he chants his vigorous song of defiance and resolution.

Dreamer

Way for the strong and the swift and the fearless:
Life that is stirr'd with the fear of its life, let it die;
Let it sink down, let it die, and pass from our vision for ever.
Sorrow and pain we shall have, and struggle unending:
We shall weave courage with pain, and fight through the struggle unending.
Way for the strong and the swift and the fearless:
Life that is stirr'd with the fear of its life, let it die;
Let it sink down, let it die, and pass from our vision for ever!

The Dreamer goes up the slope. When he reaches the top, he turns, looks down at the still form of the Young Woman. The Bishop's Sister stands apart, and watches the Bishop kneeling beside the form of the Young Woman. She goes over, after a moment's pause, and gently touches the Bishop's shoulder.

Bishop (*looking up at his Sister*) Go home, go home, for Christ's sake, woman, and ask God's mercy on us all!

She looks at the kneeling figure for a moment, then, turning, she goes out without a word.

(*In low and grief-stricken tones*) She died making the sign of the cross!

Dreamer (*looking down to where the Young Woman is lying*) You fought the good fight, Jannice; and you kept the faith: Hail and farewell, sweetheart; for ever and for ever, hail and farewell!

The Dreamer turns, and begins to go out slowly. The sky's purple and black changes to a bright grey, pierced with golden segments, as if the sun was rising, and a new day about to begin. The music, sounding low, of the song he sang to her, is heard; in the middle of the melody the gates begin to close slowly, coming together on the last few notes of the tune.

The gates close.

Music to *Within the Gates*

Composed and adapted by   Herbert Hughes

SPRING CHORUS

Founded on "Haste to the Wedding"   SCENE I

SUMMER CHORUS

1. Ye who are hag-gard and gid-dy with care bu-sy
2. Ye who are twist-ing a pray'r from your thoughts in the
3. Ye who in sen-ates and par-lia-ments talk, Talk

count-ing your pro-fit and loss-es Show-ing the might of your
dim - ness and gloom of the church-es Light-ing your can-dle pe-'
on—through the day— and the night - time Talk and still talk and—

name un-to God in the gay col-our'd page of a
-ti - tions a - - way to—— chalk col-our'd vir - gins and
still talk— on through the hun - dreds of cen - tur - ies

cheque book Stor - ing the best—— of your life in a
mar - tyrs Rack - ing your life—— for the hope of a
pass - ing Till the wide— ear of the wide— world is

draw'r of your desk at the of - fice——
co - sy— cor - ner in hea - ven
deaf - - en'd with— wis - dom

Bel-low good-

bye—— to the beg-gar-in' lot 'n come out to

bow down the head 'n bend down the knee to the bee 'n the bird 'n the

blos - som.——

Bann - 'ring the breast of the earth with a

won - - der-ful beau-ty.——

JANNICE

Founded on an Irish tune

SING AND DANCE
Air: "Little Brown Jug" *by R. A. Eastburn*

THE NINETY AND NINE

Elizabeth C. Clephane

Ira D. Sankey

SONG OF THE DOWN AND OUT

Air: "The FoggyDew"

Quasi Marcia Funebre di Chopin   SCENE IV

Life has pass'd us by to the
We__ chal - lenge life no__

loud roll of her drum With her wav-ing flags of yel - low and
more, no__ more With__ our__ dead__ faith__ and__

green held high All__ starr'd with her gold - en flam-ing_names of__
our dead hope. We car-ry furl'd the__ faint-ing__ flags of a

her__ most migh - ty__ chil - dren! Oh where shall we go when the
dead___ hope and a dead faith. Day sings no song, nei -ther

day____ calls? Oh__ where shall we go__ when the
is there room for rest be - - side____ night__ in her

night falls? We've but a sigh____ for a song and a
sleep - ing; For we've but a sigh____ for a song and a

(DOWN & OUTS)
(TWO EVANGELISTS etc.)

deep____ sigh_ for a drum - beat.____ She must be
deep____ sigh_ for a drum - beat.____ She who was

mer - ry no more; she must walk in the midst of the mourn - ful
mer - - - ry shall now walk in the midst of the mourn - ful

Who've but a sigh_____ for a song and a
Who've but a sigh_____ for a song and a

deep_____ sigh— for a drum - beat.
deep_____ sigh— for a drum - beat.

WAY FOR THE STRONG!

The Dreamer intones

Way for the strong and the swift and the fear - less

Life that is stirr'd with the fear of its life let____ it die

Let it sink down, let it die, and pass from our vi - sion for ev - er

Sorrow and pain we shall have and strug - gle un - end - ing

We shall have courage with pain and fight through the strug - gle un - end - ing

Way for the strong and the swift and the fear - less

Life that is stirr'd with the fear of its life let____ it die

Let it sink down, let it die, and pass from our vi - sion for ev - er.

WITHIN THE GATES

GARDENER'S SONG

Air: "Moll Roone"

Andante

A fig for the blos-soms th' big-gest vase can hold, Th'— flow'rs that face the world— shy the ones that face it bold; Men may praise them and wor-ship them as some-thing fine and rare, Loung-ing through their gor-geous per-fume so—— deft-ly hid-den there. But I'll—— nev-er won-der though some in glee dis-close The white of whit-est li-ly the red of red-dest rose,— For I'll fold in my arms a girl as bright as she is gay, And to-night the prim-rose path of love will be a won-der way!

THE IRISH DRAGOON

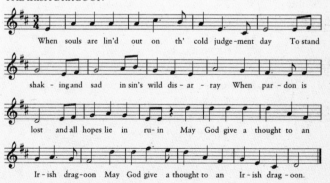

When souls are lin'd out on th' cold judge-ment day To stand shak-ing and sad in sin's wild dis-ar-ray When par-don is lost and all hopes lie in ru-in May God give a thought to an Ir-ish drag-oon May God give a thought to an Ir-ish drag-oon.

RED ROSES FOR ME

A PLAY IN FOUR ACTS

To Dr J. D. Cummins
In memory of the grand chats
around his surgery fire

*My thanks to Bridgid Edwards
for setting down the airs to
the songs*

Characters

Mrs Breydon
Ayamonn Breydon, her son
Eeada
Dympna } Mrs Breydon's neighbours in the house
Finnoola
Sheila Moorneen, Ayamonn's sweetheart
Brennan o' the Moor, owner of a few oul' houses
A Singer, a young man with a good voice
Roory O'Balacaun, a zealous Irish Irelander
Mullcanny, a mocker of sacred things
Rev. E. Clinton, Rector of St Burnupus
Samuel, verger to the church
Inspector Finglas, of the Mounted Police, and the
    Rector's churchwarden
1st Man
2nd Man } neighbours in the next house to Breydons'
3rd Man
Dowzard } members of St Burnupus' Select Vestry
Foster
A Lamplighter
1st Railwayman
2nd Railwayman

TIME – A little while ago.

Act One

*The front one of two rather dilapidated rooms in a poor
working-class locality. The walls, whitewashed, are
dwindling into a rusty yellowish tinge. The main door,
leading to the hall, is at the back, a little towards the right.
The fireplace is in the right-hand wall, and a brilliant fire is
burning in the large, old-fashioned grate. In the centre of
the room is an old ebony-hued table on which stands a one-
wick oil-lamp, its chimney a little smoky from the bad oil in
the reservoir. Some books lie on the table, some paper,
coloured chalks, a pen, and a small bottle of ink. In the left
wall, up towards the back, is the door leading to the second
room. Below this door is a horsehair sofa showing signs of
old age. On it, to the head, is a neatly folded bundle of
sheets and blankets, showing that it is used as a bed during
the night. To the left of the main door at back is a large
basket used by actors when on tour. On the other side of
this door is an ordinary kitchen dresser on which some of
the crockery is on the ledge, for the upper shelf is filled with
a row of books, by the look of them second-hand. Over the
basket, on the wall, is tacked a childlike brightly coloured
pastel of what is meant to be a copy of one of Fra
Angelico's angels blowing a curved and golden trumpet;
and beside it is a small coloured reproduction of
Constable's Cornfield. In the same wall, towards the back,
is a large, tall window, nearly reaching the ceiling, and,
when one is in front of it, the top of a railway signal, with
transverse arms, showing green and red lights, can be seen.
Under this window, on a roughly made bench, stand three
biscuit tins. In the first grows a geranium, in the second,
musk, and in the third, a fuchsia. The disks of the geranium*

are extremely large and glowing; the tubular blooms of the golden musk, broad, gay, and rich; and the purple bells of the fuchsia, surrounded by their long white waxy sepals, seem to be as big as arum lilies. These crimson, gold, and purple flowers give a regal tint to the poor room. Occasionally in the distance can be heard the whistle of an engine, followed by its strenuous puffing as it pulls at a heavy rake of goods wagons. A chair or two stand about the room.

It is towards the evening of a mid-spring day, and the hour would make it dusk, but it is darker than that, for the sky is cloudy and rain is falling heavily over the city.

Ayamonn and his mother are in the room when the scene shows itself. He is tall, well built, twenty-two or so, with deep brown eyes, fair hair, rather bushy, but tidily kept, and his face would remind an interested observer of a rather handsome, firm-minded, thoughtful, and good-humoured bulldog. His mother is coming up to fifty, her face brownish, dark eyes with a fine glint in them, and she bears on her cheeks and brow the marks of struggle and hard work. She is dressed in a black jacket, fitting close, marred by several patches, done very neatly, dark-blue skirt, a little faded, and rather heavily soled boots. At the moment this is all covered with a rich blue velvet cloak, broidered with silver lace, and she is sitting on a kitchen chair covered with a dark-red, rather ragged cloth.

Ayamonn wears a bright green silk doublet over which is a crimson velvet armless cloak bordered with white fur. The back part of the cloak is padded so as to form a big hump between his shoulders. Across his chest is a dark green baldric from which hangs a scabbard. A cross-hilted sword is in his hand. On his head he has a black felt hat with narrow turned-up rims. A black band goes round the hat, and a crimson feather sticks up from it. His legs are in heavy, black, working corduroy trousers, and he wears heavy hobnailed boots. She and he are in an intensely listening attitude.

Mrs Breydon (*whispering over to Ayamonn*) She's gone; wanted to borra something else, I suppose. They're feverish with borrowing in this blessed house!

Ayamonn Damn her for a troublesome fool! Where's this I was when the knock came?

Mrs Breydon I was just goin' to say
   Ay, an' for much more slaughter after this,
   O God! forgive my sins, and pardon thee!

Ayamonn (*looking at the floor*) Oh yes! (*He recites.*)
   What, will th' aspiring blood of Lancaster
   Sink to the ground? I thought it would have mounted.
   (*He holds the sword aloft, and stares at it.*)
   See how my sword weeps for the poor king's death!
   O, may such purple tears be always shed
   For those that wish the downfall of our house!
   If any spark of life be yet remaining, (*He stabs at the floor.*)
   Down, down to hell; and say I sent thee hither!

   A knuckle-knock is heard at the door. Ayamonn and Mrs Breydon stiffen into a silent listening attitude. A fine baritone voice, husky with age, is heard speaking outside.

Voice Is anyone in or out or what?

   Louder raps are given as Ayamonn steals over, and places his back to the door.

Eh, in there – is there anyone movin', or is the oul' shack empty?

Mrs Breydon (*in a whisper*) Oul' Brennan on the Moor. He was here before, today. He's got his rent for his oul' houses, an' he wants to be told again that the Bank of Ireland's a safe place to put it.

Ayamonn (*warningly*) Ssshush!

Voice No answer, eh? An' me afther seein' a light in th' window. Maybe they are out. For their own sakes, I hope they are; for it's hardly an honourable thing to gainsay a neighbour's knock.

> *The sound of feet shuffling away is heard outside, and then there is silence for a few moments.*

Mrs Breydon He's gone. He's always a bit lively the day he gets his rents. How a man, with his money, can go on livin' in two rooms in a house an' sthreet only a narrow way betther than this, I don't know. What was he but an oul' painter an' paperhanger, starvin' to save, an' usin' his cunnin' to buy up a few oul' houses, give them a lick o' paint, and charge the highest rent for th' inconvenience of livin' in them!

Ayamonn I wish he'd keep himself and his throubles far away from me now. I've higher things to think of and greater things to do than to be attached to the agony of an old fool for ever afraid a fistful of money'll be snatched away from him. Still, he isn't a miser, for he gives kids toys at Christmas, and never puts less than half a crown on the plate in church on Sundays.

Mrs Breydon So well he may!

Ayamonn What was he sayin' when he was here before?

Mrs Breydon Oh, th' usual question of askin' me what I thought about the Bank of Ireland; mutterin' about somebody not payin' the rent; and that his birthday's due tomorrow.

Ayamonn (*looking at the chair*) I'll have to get a loan of a chair with arms on, and someway make them golden to do the thing proper in the Temperance Hall; and I'll paint for the back of it, one thin cardboard, a cunning design of the

House of Lancaster, the red rose, so that it'll look like a kingly seat.

Mrs Breydon Th' killin' o' th' king be th' Duke o' Gloster should go down well, an' th' whole thing should look sumptuous.

Ayamonn So it will. It's only that they're afraid of Shakespeare out of all that's been said of him. They think he's beyond them, while all the time he's part of the kingdom of heaven in the nature of everyman. Before I'm done, I'll have him drinking in th' pubs with them!

Mrs Breydon I don't know that he'll go well with a Minstrel Show.

Ayamonn He'll have to go well. If only King Henry doesn't rant too much, saw the air with his hands, and tear his passion to tatthers. The old fool saw someone do it that way, and thinks it must be right. (*With a sigh*) I daren't attempt to recite my part now, for Oul' Brennan on the Moor's waitin' and listenin' somewhere down below; so I'll just get it off by heart. How old does he say he'll be tomorrow?

Mrs Breydon Only seventy-six, he says, an' feelin' as if he was lookin' forward to his twenty-first birthday.

Ayamonn Well, he won't have long to wait.

Mrs Breydon (*slyly*) He was muttherin', too, about some air or other on the oul' piano he has at home.

Ayamonn (*springing up from where he has been sitting*) It's one o' mine he's put an air to! (*He rushes from the room and returns in a few moments.*) He's not there; gone home, I suppose. (*Irritably*) I wish you'd told me that at first.

Mrs Breydon I'd thry to rest a little, Ayamonn, before you

219

go to work. You're overdoing it. Less than two hours'
sleep today, and a long night's work before you. Sketchin',
readin', makin' songs, an' learnin' Shakespeare: if you had
a piano, you'd be thryin' to learn music. Why don't you
stick at one thing, an' leave the others alone?

Ayamonn They are all lovely, and my life needs them all.

Mrs Breydon I managed to get on well enough without
them. (*Pause. She goes over to the window and tenderly
touches the fuchsia.*) There's this sorryful sthrike, too,
about to come down on top of us.

Ayamonn (*sitting in the red-covered chair and reading
Shakespeare – quietly and confidently*) There'll be no
strike. The bosses won't fight. They'll grant the extra
shilling a week demanded.

Mrs Breydon (*now fingering the musk*) I thought this
Minstrel Show was being run to gather funds together?

Ayamonn (*impatiently*) So it is, so it is; but only in case
the strike may have to take place. I haven't much to do
with it, anyway. I'm with the men, spoke at a meeting in
favour of the demand, and that's all.

Mrs Breydon You'll undhermine your health with all
you're doin', tearin' away what's left of your time be
runnin' afther – (*She checks herself, and becomes silent.*)

Ayamonn (*lowering his book to his lap – angrily*) Go on –
finish what you started to say: runnin' afther who?

Mrs Breydon Nobody, nobody.

Ayamonn Runnin' afther Sheila Moorneen – that's what
was in your mind to say, wasn't it?

Mrs Breydon If it was aself; is there a new law out that a
body's not to think of her own thoughts.

Ayamonn (*sharply*) What have you got against the girl?

Mrs Breydon Nothing. As a girl, I'd say she's a fine coloured silken shawl among a crowd of cotton ones. A girl I'd say could step away from the shadowy hedges where others slink along, tiltin' her head as she takes the centre of the road for the entherprisin' light o' day to show her off to everyone. Still – (*She stops speaking again.*)

Ayamonn Ay, but still what? You've a maddenin' way of never finishing some of your sentences.

Mrs Breydon (*braving it out*) She's a Roman Catholic; steeped in it, too, the way she'd never forgive a one for venturin' to test the Pope's pronouncement.

Ayamonn And who wants to test the Pope's pronouncement? Life and all her vital changes'll go on testing everything, even to the Pope's pronouncement. D'ye think I've laboured as I have, and am labourin' now, to furnish myself with some of the greatness of the mighty minds of the past, just to sink down into passive acceptance of the Pope's pronouncement? Let the girl believe what she may, reverence what she can: it's her own use of her own mind. That she is fair to look upon, charming to talk with, and a dear companion, is well and away enough for me, were she even a believer in Mumbo Jumbo, and had a totem pole in her front garden.

Mrs Breydon There's worse still than that in it.

Ayamonn Worse, is there? An' what may that be?

Mrs Breydon She's th' child of a sergeant in the Royal Irish Constabulary, isn't she?

Ayamonn Well, she can't help it, can she?

Mrs Breydon I know that; but many have murmured

again' a son of mine goin' with the child of a man crouchin' close to their enemy.

Ayamonn Everything, it seems, is against her, save herself. I like herself, and not her faith; I want herself, and not her father.

Mrs Breydon The bigger half of Ireland would say that a man's way with a maid must be regulated by his faith an' hers, an' the other half by the way her father makes his livin'.

Ayamonn And let the whole world join them! Fair she is, and her little ear's open to hear all that I thry to say, so, were she the child of darkness aself, I'd catch her hand and lead her out and show her off to all men.

Mrs Breydon She wouldn't be a lot to look at afther she'd wended her way through poverty with you for a year an' a day.

Ayamonn She gives no honour to gold; neither does her warm heart pine for silks and satins from China and Japan, or the spicy isles of Easthern Asia. A sober black shawl on her shoulders, a simple petticoat, and naked feet would fail to find her craving finer things that envious women love.

Mrs Breydon Ah, go on with you, Ayamonn, for a kingly fool. I'm tellin' you th' hearts of all proper girls glow with the dhream of fine things; an' I'm tellin' you, too, that the sword jinglin' on th' hip of Inspector Finglas, the red plume hangin' from his menacin' helmet, an' th' frosty silver sparklin' on his uniform, are a dazzle o' light between her tantalized eyes an' whatever she may happen to see in you.

Ayamonn Tell me something else to add to my hope.

Mrs Breydon Go on readin', an' don't bother to listen to your mother.

Ayamonn (*going over and gently putting his hands on her shoulders*) I do listen, but I am drifting away from you, Mother, a dim shape now, in a gold canoe, dipping over a far horizon.

Mrs Breydon (*with a catch in her voice*) I did an' dared a lot for you, Ayamonn, my son, in my time, when jeerin' death hurried your father off to Heaven.

Ayamonn It's I who know that well; when it was dark, you always carried the sun in your hand for me; when you suffered me to starve rather than thrive towards death in an Institution, you gave me life to play with as a richer child is given a coloured ball. (*He gently lifts up her face by putting a hand under her chin.*) The face, the dear face that once was smooth is wrinkled now; the eyes, brown still, that once were bright, have now been dimmed by a sthrained stare into the future; the sturdy back that stood so straight, is bending. A well-tried leaf, bronzed with beauty, waiting for a far-off winter wind to shake it from the tree.

Mrs Breydon (*gently removing his hand from her chin*) I have a tight hold still. My back can still bear many a heavy burden; and my eyes, dimmer now than once they were, can still see far enough. Well, I betther take this fancy robe from off me, lest it give me gorgeous notions.

She takes off her robe, and leaves it carefully folded on the basket, then goes over and arranges the fire. Ayamonn looks thoughtfully out of the window, then takes off cloak, sword, and hat, leaving them carefully on the basket.

Ayamonn (*musingly*) He'll hardly come tonight in this rain. If he does, I'll get him to read the King's part, and do mine over again.

Mrs Breydon Who's to come tonight?

Ayamonn Mullcanny: he's searching Dublin for a book he wants to give me; and, if he got it, he was to bring it tonight – *The Riddle of the Universe.*

Mrs Breydon That's another one I wouldn't see too much of, for he has the whole neighbourhood up in arms against his reckless disregard of God, an' his mockery of everything solemn, set down as sacred.

Ayamonn Oh, Tim is all right. The people are sensible enough to take all he says in good part; and a black flame stands out in a brightly coloured world.

Mrs Breydon You don't know them, if you say that; he'll meet with a mishap, some day, if he doesn't keep his mouth shut.

Ayamonn Nonsense.

She has quietly slipped a shawl around her, and is moving to the door so silently as to seem to want to prevent Ayamonn from noticing her movements, when the door opens and Eeada, Dympna, Finnoola, and several men, appear there. The three women come a little way into the room; the men stay around the door. All their faces are stiff and mask-like, holding tight an expression of dumb resignation; and are traversed with seams of poverty and a hard life. The face of Eeada is that of an old woman; that of Dympna, one coming up to middle age; and that of Finnoola, one of a young girl. Each shows the difference of age by more or less furrows, but each has the same expressionless stare out on life.

   Dympna is carrying a statue of the Blessed Virgin, more than two feet high, in her arms. The figure was once a glory of purest white, sparkling blue, and luscious gilding; but the colours have faded, the gilt is gone, save for a spot or two of dull gold still lingering on the crown. She is wearing a crown that, instead of being domed, is castellated like a city's tower, resembling those of Dublin; and the pale face of the Virgin is sadly soiled by the grime of the house. The men are dressed in drab brown, the women in a chill grey, each suit or dress having a patch of faded blue, red, green, or purple somewhere about them.

Eeada (*to Mrs Breydon*) Could you spare a pinch or two of your Hudson's soap, Mrs Breydon, dear, to give the Blessed Virgin a bit of a wash? (*To all in general*) Though I've often said it's th' washin' that's done away with the bonnie blue of th' robe an' th' braver gold of its bordhers an' th' most o' th' royalty outa th' crown. Little Ursula below's savin' up her odd pennies to bring Her where She'll find a new blue robe, an' where they'll make the royalty of th' gilt glow again; though whenever she's a shillin' up, it's needed for food an' firin'; but we never yet found Our Lady of Eblana averse to sellin' Her crown an' Her blue robe to provide for Her people's need.

Mrs Breydon gives half a packet of soap powder.

(*Gratefully*) Thank you, ma'am, an' though y'are of a different persuasion, Our Blessed Lady of Eblana's poor'll bless you an' your fine son for this little tribute to Her honour and circumspect appearance before the world.

The Rest (*murmuring*) Ay will She, an' that's a sure thing.

They open a way for Eeada to pass out, with Dympna carrying the statue, following in a kind of simple procession. Mrs Breydon is moving slowly after them.

Ayamonn (*who has noticed her under his eyes*) You're not going out again, surely – on a night like this, too?

Mrs Breydon Not really; only down the road to Mrs

Cashmore's. She's not too well; I promised I'd dhrop in, and see to a hot dhrink or something for her before she wandhered off to sleep.

Ayamonn (*irritably*) You think more of other homes than you do of your own! Every night for the past week you've been going out on one silly mission or another like an imitation sisther of charity.

Mrs Breydon I couldn't sit quiet knowin' the poor woman needed me. I'd hear her voice all through the night complainin' I never came to give her a hot dhrink, settle her bed soft, an' make her safe for th' lonely hours of th' slow-movin' night.

Ayamonn A lot they'd do for you if you happened to need help from them.

Mrs Breydon Ah, we don't know. A body shouldn't think of that, for such a belief would dismay an' dismantle everything done outside of our own advantage. No harm to use an idle hour to help another in need.

Ayamonn An' wear yourself out in the process?

Mrs Breydon (*with a sigh*) I'll wear out, anyway, sometime, an' a tired ould body can, at least, go to its long rest without any excuse.

> *As she opens the door to go out, Sheila appears on the threshold. She is a girl of about twenty-three, fairly tall, a fine figure, carrying herself with a sturdiness never ceasing to be graceful. She has large, sympathetic brown eyes that dim, now and again, with a cloud of timidity. Her mouth is rather large but sweetly made; her hair is brown and long, though now it is gathered up into a thick coil that rests on the nape of her neck. She is dressed in a tailor-made suit of rich brown tweed, golden-brown blouse, and a bright-blue hat. These are*

now covered with a fawn-coloured mackintosh,
darkened with heavy rain, and a hastily folded umbrella
is dripping on to the floor. She comes in shyly, evidently
conscious of Mrs Breydon's presence; but fighting her
timidity with a breezy and jovial demeanour. Mrs
Breydon tries, but can't keep a little stiffness out of her
greeting.

Sheila Oh! good evening, Mrs Breydon. What a night! I'm
nearly blown to bits; and the rain – oh, the wind and the
weather!

Mrs Breydon You must be perished. Take off your mac,
and come over to the fire. Get Ayamonn to make you a
cup o' tea, and bring you back to life again.

Sheila No, really; I'm burning – the battle with the wind
and the rain has made me warm and lively.

Ayamonn Hey ho, the wind and the rain, for the rain it
raineth every day. Sit down and take the weight off your
legs.

Sheila Not worth while, for I can't stop long. (*To Mrs*
Breydon) Going out on a night like this, Mrs Breydon?

Ayamonn (*hastily*) She has to go: got an urgent call from a
poor sick neighbour.

Sheila (*hesitatingly*) What is it? Could . . . could I do it for
you?

Ayamonn (*decidedly*) No, no, you couldn't. The woman
knows my mother. It's only to see her safe and warm in
bed for the night; Mother won't be long.

Mrs Breydon Good night, Miss Sheila; perhaps you'll be
here when I come back.

Sheila I don't think so. I must go almost at once.

Mrs Breydon Well, good night, then.

She goes out, and Ayamonn goes over to Sheila, kisses her, and helps her off with the mac.

Sheila You shouldn't let your mother go out on a night like this – she's no longer a young woman.

Ayamonn I don't like to interfere with her need to give help to a neighbour. She likes it, and it does her good.

Sheila But the rain's coming down in sheets, and she's got but a thin shawl round her shoulders.

Ayamonn (*impatiently*) Oh, she hasn't very far to go. Let's think of greater things than the pouring rain and an old woman on her way to smooth pillows on a sick bed. Look! – (*He feels her skirt.*) – the hem's wringing. Better dry it at the fire. Turn round and I'll unfasten it for you.

Sheila (*forcing his hand away*) It's nothing – you are thinking now of your own pleasure. You weren't so eager to see me when I was knocking at the door a while ago.

Ayamonn You! But it was Old Brennan o' the Moor that was there.

Sheila Before him, I was there. He hammered at the door too.

Ayamonn (*angry with himself*) And I thinking that the rapping was that of a pestering neighbour! I might have guessed it wasn't, it was so gentle.

Sheila After trying to slip in unnoticed, there I was left with the whole house knowing I was at the door, and when I ran down, I heard them yelling that the stylish-dressed pusher was trying to get into Breydon's again! A nice time I'll have with my people when they hear it.

Ayamonn I was doing my Shakespeare part, and didn't

want disturbance, so there I was, standing stiff and breathless like a heron in a pond, keeping my dear one away from me! (*Going over and taking her in his arms*) Well, it's all over now, and here you are in my arms, safe and sure and lovely.

Sheila (*struggling away from him*) No, it's not all over; and don't press me so hard; don't ruffle me tonight, for I feel a little tired.

Ayamonn (*peevishly*) Tired again? Well, so am I, more than a little tired; but never too tired to put a sparkle into a welcome for a loved one.

Sheila Oh, Ayamonn, I do want you to be serious for one night.

Ayamonn Very well, very well, Sheila. (*He moves away from her, and stands at the other side of the fire.*) Let us plan, then, of how we can spin joy into every moment of tomorrow's day.

Sheila That's why I hurried here to see you – I can't be with you tomorrow.

There is a long pause.

Ayamonn Why can't you be with me tomorrow?

Sheila The Daughters of St Frigid begin a retreat tomorrow, to give the Saint a warm devotion, and Mother insists I go.

Ayamonn And I insist that you go with me. Is the St Frigid more to you than the sinner Ayamonn? Would you rather go to the meeting than come to see me? (*Pause.*) Would you, would you, Sheila?

Sheila (*in a hesitant whisper*) God forgive me, I'd rather come to see you.

Ayamonn Come then; God will be sure to forgive you.

Sheila I daren't. My mother would be at me for ever if I failed to go. I've told you how she hates me to be near you. She chatters red-lined warnings and black-bordered appeals into my ears night and day, and when they dwindle for lack of breath, my father shakes them out of their drowsiness and sends them dancing round more lively still, dressed richly up in deadly black and gleaming scarlet.

Ayamonn Sheila, Sheila, on the one day of the month when I'm free, you must be with me. I wouldn't go to a workers' meeting so that I might be with you.

Sheila There's another thing, Ayamonn – the threatened strike. Oh, why do you meddle with those sort of things!

Ayamonn Oh, never mind that, now. Don't be like a timid little girl ensconced in a clear space in a thicket of thorns – safe from a scratch if she doesn't stir, but unable to get to the green grass or the open road unless she risks the tears the thorns can give.

Sheila Oh, Ayamonn, for my sake, if you love me, do try to be serious.

Ayamonn (*a little wildly*) Oh, Sheila, our time is not yet come to be serious in the way of our elders. Soon enough to browse with wisdom when Time's grey finger puts a warning speck on the crimson rose of youth. Let no damned frosty prayer chill the sunny sighs that dread the joy of love.

Sheila (*wildly*) I won't listen, Ayamonn, I won't listen! We must look well ahead on the road to the future. You lead your life through too many paths instead of treading the one way of making it possible for us to live together.

Ayamonn We live together now; live in the light of the

burning bush. I tell you life is not one thing, but many things, a wide branching flame, grand and good to see and feel, dazzling to the eye of no one loving it. I am not one to carry fear about with me as a priest carries the Host. Let the timid tiptoe through the way where the paler blossoms grow; my feet shall be where the redder roses grow, though they bear long thorns, sharp and piercing, thick among them!

Sheila (*rising from the chair – vehemently*) I'll listen no more; I'll go. You want to make me a spark in a mere illusion. I'll go!

Ayamonn Rather a spark from the althar of God, me girl; a spark that flames on a new path for a bubbling moment of life, or burns a song into the heart of a poet.

Sheila I came here as a last chance to talk things quiet with you, but you won't let me; so I'll go.

As he seizes her in his arms.

Let me go! (*pleadingly*) Please, Ayamonn, let me go!

Ayamonn I tell you it is a gay sight for God to see joy shine for a moment on the faces of His much-troubled children.

Sheila (*fearfully*) Oh, don't bring God's name into this, for it will mean trouble to the pair of us. And your love for me lasts only while I'm here. When I'm gone, you think more of your poor painting, your poor oul' Ireland, your songs, and your workers' union than you think of Sheila.

Ayamonn You're part of them all, in them all, and through them all; joyous, graceful, and a dearer vision; a bonnie rose, delectable and red. (*He draws her to him, presses her hard, lifts her on to his lap, and kisses her.*) Sheila, darling, you couldn't set aside the joy that makes the moon a golden berry in a hidden tree. You cannot close your ear to the sweet sound of the silver bell that strikes but once and never strikes again!

The door opens, and the head of Brennan o' the Moor looks into the room. It is a bald one, the dome highly polished; the face is wrinkled a lot, but the eyes are bright and peering. A long white beard gives him a faraway likeness to St Jerome. He is dressed in a shabby-genteel way, and wears a long rain-soaked mackintosh. A faded bowler hat is on his head.

Brennan Oh, dear, dear, dear me!

He comes into the room showing that his back is well bent, though he still has a sturdy look about him. A strap around his body holds a melodeon on his back. Sheila and Ayamonn separate; he rises to meet the old man, while she stares, embarrassed, into the fire.

Ayamonn Now what th' hell do you want?

Brennan (*taking no notice of Ayamonn's remark – taking off his hat in a sweeping bow*). Ah, me two sweet, snowy-breasted Dublin doves! Me woe it is to come ramblin' in through marjoram moments scentin' the serious hilarity of a genuine courtin' couple. I'm askin' now what's the dear one's name, if that isn't thresspassin' on others who are in a firmer condition of friendship? Though, be rights, it's a fair an' showy nosegay I should be throwin' through a shyly opened window into the adorable lady's lap.

Sheila (*shyly*) Me name is Sheila.

Brennan Sheila is it? Ay, an' a Sheila are you. Ay, an' a suitable one too, for there's a gentle nature in the two soft sounds, an' a silver note in the echo, describin' grandly the pretty slendher lass me two ould eyes are now beholdin'.

Ayamonn (*going over and catching him by an arm to guide him out*) I can't see you now, old friend, for the pair

of us are heavily harnessed to a question that must be
answered before either of us is a day older.

Brennan Sure I know. An' isn't it only natural, too, that
young people should have questions to ask and answers to
give to the dewy problems that get in th' way of their
dancin' feet?

Ayamonn (*impatiently*) Come again, old friend, when time
has halted us for an hour of rest.

Brennan It isn't me, I'm sayin', that would be dense
enough to circumvent your longin' to be deep down in the
silent consequence of regardin' each other without let or
hindrance. (*He goes towards Sheila, eagerly, pulling
Ayamonn after him.*) It's easy seen, sweet lady, that you're
well within the compass of your young man's knowledge,
an' unaware of nothin', so I may speak as man to lady, so
with cunnin' confidence, tell me what you think of the
Bank of Ireland?

Ayamonn Oh, for goodness' sake, old man. Sheila's no
intherest in the Bank of Ireland. She cares nothing for
money, or for anything money can buy.

Brennan (*staring at Ayamonn for a moment as if he had
received a shock*) Eh? Arra, don't be talkin' nonsense,
man! Who is it daren't think of what money can buy? (*He
crosses to the door in a trot on his toes, opens it, looks
out, and closes it softly again. Then he tiptoes back to
Sheila, bends down towards her, hands on knees, and
whispers hoarsely.*) I've just a little consideration of stocks
and bonds nestin' in the Bank of Ireland, at four per cent –
just enough to guard a poor man from ill, eh? Safe an'
sound there, isn't it, eh? (*To Ayamonn*) Now, let the fair
one speak out on her own. (*Twisting his head back to
Sheila*) Safe there as if St Pether himself had the key of
where the bonds are stationed, eh?

Sheila I'm sure they must be, sir.

Brennan (*with chuckling emphasis*) Yehess! Aren't you the sensible young lady; sure I knew you'd say that, without fear or favour. (*turning towards Ayamonn*) What do you say? You're a man, now, of tellin' judgement.

Ayamonn Oh, the State would have to totther before you'd lose a coin.

Brennan (*gleefully*) Go bang, absolutely bang! Eh?

Ayamonn Go bang!

Brennan Bang! (*to Sheila*) Hear that, now, from a man climbin' up to scholarship? Yehess! Stony walls, steely doors, locks an' keys, bolts an' bars, an' all th' bonds warm an' dhry, an' shinin' safe behind them.

Sheila Safe behind them.

Brennan (*gleefully*) Ay, so. An' none of it sthrollin' into Peter's Pence. (*chuckling*) Wouldn't the Pope be mad if he knew what he was missin'! Safe an' sound. (*To Ayamonn*) You think so, too, eh?

Ayamonn Yes, yes.

Brennan (*soberly*) Ay, of course you do. (*To Sheila – indicating Ayamonn*) A good breed, me sweet an' fair one, brought up proper to see things in their right light.

Ayamonn (*catching him impatiently by the arm*) And now, old friend, we have to get you to go.

Brennan Eh?

Ayamonn To go; Sheila and I have things to talk about.

Brennan (*suddenly*) An' what about the song, then?

Ayamonn Song?

Brennan Th' one for the Show. Isn't that what brought me up? At long last, afther hard sthrainin', me an' Sammy have got the tune down in tested clefs, crotchets, an' quavers, fair set down to be sung be anyone in thrue time. An' Sammy's below, in his gay suit for the Show, waitin' to be called up to let yous hear th' song sung as only Sammy can sing it.

Ayamonn Bring him up, bring him up – why in hell didn't you tell me all this before?

Brennan (*stormily*) Wasn't I thryin' all the time an' you wouldn't let a man get a word in edgeways. (*Gesturing towards Sheila*) He'll jib at singin' in front of her. (*He whispers hoarsely towards Sheila.*) He's as shy as a kid in his first pair o' pants, dear lady.

Ayamonn (*impatiently pushing him out of the room*) Oh, go on, go on, man, and bring him up.

Brennan goes out.

Sheila (*earnestly*) Wait till I'm gone, Ayamonn; I can't stop long, and I want to talk to you so much.

Ayamonn (*a little excited*) Oh, you must hear the song, Sheila; they've been working to get the air down for a week, and it won't take a minute.

Sheila (*angrily*) I've waited too long already! Aren't you more interested in what I want to say than to be listening to some vain fool singing a song?

Ayamonn (*a little taken aback*) Oh, Sheila, what's wrong with you tonight? The young carpenter who'll sing it, so far from being vain, is as shy as a field-mouse, and you'll see, when he starts to sing, he'll edge his face away from us. You do want to hear it, Sheila, don't you?

Sheila (*appealingly*) Let it wait over, Ayamonn; I can come to hear it some other time. I do want to say something, very serious, to you about our future meetings.

Ayamonn (*hastily*) All right then; I'll hurry them off the minute the song's sung. Here they are, so sit down, do, just for one minute more.

> *But she goes towards the door, and reaches it just as Old Brennan returns, shoving in before him a young man of twenty-three, shy, and loth to come in. He is tall, but his face is pale and mask-like in its expression of resignation to the world and all around him. Even when he shows he's shy, the mask-like features do not alter. He is dressed in a white cut-away coat, shaped like a tailed evening dress, black waistcoat over a rather soiled shirt-front, frilled, and green trousers. He carries a sheet of manuscript music in his hand. Brennan unslings his melodeon from his back, fusses the young Singer forward; bumping against Sheila, who has moved towards the door, he pushes her back with a shove of his backside; and puts Ayamonn to the other end of the room with a push on the shoulder.*

Brennan (*as he pushes Sheila*) Outa th' way, there! Stem your eagerness for a second, will yous? All in good time. Give the man a chance to get himself easy. (*As he pushes Ayamonn.*) Farther back, there, farther back! Give the performer a chance to dispose himself. Isn't he a swell, wha'? The centre group's to be dhressed the same way, while th' corner men'll be in reverse colours – green coats, black trousers, an' white vest, see? Th' whole assembly'll look famous. Benjamin's lendin' all the set o' twelve suits for five bob, 'cause o' th' reason we're runnin' th' Show for. (*To Sheila – in a hoarse whisper*) You stare at the fire as if he wasn't here. He's extravagant in shyness, an' sinks away into confusion at the stare of an eye – understand?

> *Sheila slowly, and a little sullenly, sits down to stare into*

*the fire. The door is opened, and in comes Roory
O'Balacaun with a small roll of Irish magazines under
an arm. He is a stout middle-aged man, dressed in rough
homespun coat, cap, and knee-breeches, wearing over
all a trench coat.*

Roory Here y'are, Ayamonn, me son, avic's th' Irish
magazines I got me friend to pinch for you. (*He looks at
the Singer.*) Hello, what kind of a circus is it's goin' on
here?

Ayamonn Mr Brennan Moore here's organizing the
singers for the Minsthrel show to help get funds in case we
have to go on sthrike, Roory.

Roory I'm one o' th' men meself, but I don't stand for a
foreign Minsthrel Show bein' held, an' the Sword of Light
gettin' lifted up in th' land. We want no coon or Kaffir
industry in our country.

Brennan (*indignantly*) Doesn't matter what you stand for
before you came here, you'll sit down now. Thry to regard
yourself as a civilised member of the community, man, an'
hold your peace for th' present. (*To the Singer*) Now, Sam,
me son o' gold, excavate the shyness out of your system
an' sing as if you were performin' before a Royal
Command!

Roory (*with a growl*) There's no royal commands wanted
here.

Brennan (*with a gesture of disgusted annoyance*) Will you
for goodness' sake not be puttin' th' singer out? I used the
term only as an allegory, man.

Roory Allegory man, or allegory woman, there's goin' to
be no royal inthrusions where the Sword o' Light is
shinin'.

Ayamonn Aw, for Christ's sake, Roory, let's hear the song!

Brennan (*to the Singer, who has been coughing shyly and turning sideways from his audience*) Now, Sam, remember you're not in your working clothes, an' are a different man, entirely. Chin up and chest out. (*He gives a note or two on the melodeon.*) Now!

Singer (*singing*)
A sober black shawl hides her body entirely,
Touch'd by th' sun and th' salt spray of the sea;
But down in th' darkness a slim hand, so lovely
Carries a rich bunch of red roses for me. (*He turns away a little more from his audience, and coughs shyly.*)

Brennan (*enthusiastically*) Sam, you're excellin' yourself! On again, me oul' son!

Singer (*singing*)
Her petticoat's simple, her feet are but bare,
An' all that she has is but neat an' scantie;
But stars in th' deeps of her eyes are exclaiming
I carry a rich bunch of red roses for thee!

Brennan (*after giving a few curling notes on the melodeon*) A second Count McCormack in th' makin'! An' whenever he sung 'Mother Mo Chree', wasn't there a fewroory in Heaven with the rush that was made to lean over an hear him singin' it!

While Brennan has been speaking, the door has opened, and Mullcanny now stands there gaping into the room. He is young, lusty, and restless. He is wearing fine tweeds that don't fit too well; and his tweed cap is set rakishly on his head. He, too, wears a mackintosh.

Mullcanny Is this a home-sweet-away-from-home hippodhrome, or what?

Brennan (*clicking his tongue in annoyance*) Dtchdtchdtch!

Mullcanny An' did I hear someone pratin' about Heaven, an' I coming in? (*to Brennan – tapping him on the shoulder*) Haven't you heard, old man, that God is dead?

Brennan Well, keep your grand discovery to yourself for a minute or two more, please. (*To the Singer*) Now, Sam, apologizin' for th' other's rudeness, the last verse, please.

Singer (*singing*)
    No arrogant gem sits enthron'd on her forehead,
    Or swings from a white ear for all men to see;
    But jewel'd desire in a bosom, most pearly,
    Carries a rich bunch of red roses for me!

Brennan (*after another curl of notes on the melodeon*) Well, fair damsel and gentlemen all, what do you think of the song and the singer?

Ayamonn The song was good, and the singer was splendid.

Mullcanny What I heard of it wasn't bad.

Singer (*shyly*) I'm glad I pleased yous all.

Roory (*dubiously*) D'ye not think th' song is a trifle indecent?

Mullcanny (*mockingly*) Indecent! And what may your eminence's specification of indecency be? (*Angrily*) Are you catalogued, too, with the Catholic Young Men going about with noses long as a snipe's bill, sthripping the gayest rose of its petals in search of a beetle, and sniffing a taint in the freshest breeze blowing in from the sea?

Brennan (*warningly*) Lady present, lady present, boys!

Roory It ill becomes a thrue Gael to stand unruffled when either song or story thries to introduce colour to the sabler nature of yearnin's in untuthored minds.

Brennan (*more loudly*) Lady present, boys!

Sheila (*rising out of the chair and going towards the door*)
The lady's going now, thank you all for the entertainment.
(*To Ayamonn*) I won't stay any longer to disturb the
important dispute of your friends.

Ayamonn (*going over to her*) Don't be foolish, Sheila,
dear; but if you must go, you must. We'll see each other
again tomorrow evening.

Sheila (*firmly*) No, not tomorrow, nor the next night
either.

Ayamonn (*while Brennan plays softly on the melodeon to
hide embarrassment*) When then?

Sheila I can't tell. I'll write. Never maybe. (*Bitterly*) I
warned you this night might be the last chance of a talk
for some time, and you didn't try to make use of it!

Ayamonn (*catching her arm*) I made as much use of it as
you'd let me. Tomorrow night, in the old place, near the
bridge, the bridge of vision where we first saw Aengus and
his coloured birds of passion passing.

Sheila (*wildly*) I can't; I won't, so there – oh, let me go!
(*She breaks away from him, runs out, and a silence falls
on the room for a few moments.*)

Roory (*breaking the silence*) Women is strange things!
Elegant animals, not knowin' their own minds a minute.

Brennan (*consolingly*) She'll come back, she'll come back.

Ayamonn (*trying to appear unconcerned*) Aw, to hell with
her!

Singer (*faintly*) Can I go now?

Brennan Wait, an' I'll be with you in a second.

Mullcanny (*to Ayamonn*) I just dropped in to say, Ayamonn, that I'll be getting Haeckel's *Riddle of the Universe* tomorrow, afther long searching, and I'll let you have it the minute it comes into my hand.

> *The door is suddenly flung open, and Eeada, followed by Dympna and Finnoola, with others, mingled with men behind them, rushes into the room in a very excited state. She comes forward, with her two companions a little behind, while the rest group themselves by the door.*

Eeada (*distractedly*) It's gone She is, an' left us lonesome; vanished She is like a fairy mist of an early summer mornin'; stolen She is be some pagan Protestan' hand, envious of the love we had for our sweet Lady of Eblana's poor!

Chorus Our Lady of Eblana's gone!

Ayamonn Nonsense; no Protestant hand touched Her. Where was She?

Dympna Safe in Her niche in th' hall She was, afther Her washin', lookin' down on the comin's an' goin's of Her strugglin' children: an' then we missed Her, an' th' niche was empty!

Chorus Our Lady of Eblana's gone!

Single Voice An' dear knows what woe'll fall on our poor house now.

Brennan An' a good job, too. (*Passionately*) Inflamin' yourselves with idols that have eyes an' see not; ears, an' hear not; an' have hands that handle not; like th' chosen people settin' moon-images an' sun-images, cuttin' away the thrue and homely connection between the Christian an' his God! Here, let me and me singer out of this unholy place!

He pushes his way through the people, followed by the Singer, and goes out.

Eeada (*nodding her head, to Ayamonn*) All bark, but no bite! We know him of old: a decent oul' blatherer. Sure, doesn't he often buy violets and snowdhrops, even, for little Ursula, below, tellin' her she mustn't put them before a graven image, knowin' full well that that was th' first thing she'd hurry home to do. An' she's breakin' her young heart below, now, because her dear Lady has left her. (*Suspiciously*) If oul' Brennan had a hand in Her removal, woe betide him.

Mullcanny (*mocking*) Couldn't you all do betther than wasting your time making gods afther your own ignorant images?

Ayamonn (*silencing him with a gesture*) That's enough, Paudhrig. (*To Eeada*) Tell little Ursula not to worry. Her Lady'll come back. If your Lady of Eblana hasn't returned by tonight, I'll surrender my sleep afther my night's work to search for Her, and bring Her back safe to Her niche in the hall. No one in this house touched Her.

Eeada An' you'll see She'll pay you back for your kindness, Ayamonn – (*Looking at Mullcanny*) – though it's little surprised I'd be if, of Her own accord, She came down indignant, an' slipped off from us, hearin' the horrid talk that's allowed to float around this house lately.

Mullcanny (*mocking*) Afraid of me, She was. Well, Ayamonn, I've some lessons to get ready, so I'll be off. I'll bring you the book tomorrow. (*To the crowd – mocking*) I hope the poor Lady of Eblana's poor'll find Her way home again. (*He goes out through a surly-faced crowd.*)

Ayamonn (*to Eeada*) Don't mind Mullcanny. Good night, now; and don't worry about your dear statue. If She doesn't come back, we'll find another as bright and good to take Her place.

Eeada (*growling*) The fella that's gone'll have a rough end, jeerin' things sacred to our feelin'.

> *They all go out, and Ayamonn is left alone with Roory. Ayamonn takes off his doublet, folds it up, and puts it back in the basket. He goes into the other room and comes back with oilskin coat and thigh-high leggings. He puts the leggings on over his trousers.*

Ayamonn (*putting on the leggings*) Th' shunting-yard'll be a nice place to be tonight. D'ye hear it? (*He listens to the falling rain, now heavier than ever.*)

Roory Fallin' fast. That Mullcanny'll get into throuble yet.

Ayamonn Not he. He's really a good fellow. Gave up his job rather than his beliefs – more'n many would do.

Roory An' how does he manage now?

Ayamonn Hammering knowledge into deluded minds wishing to be civil servants, bank clerks, an' constables who hope to take the last sacraments as sergeants in the Royal Irish Constabulary or the Metropolitan Police.

Roory By God, he's his work cut out for him with the last lot!

> *The door is again opened and Eeada sticks her head into the room.*

Eeada Your mother's just sent word that the woman she's mindin's bad, an' she'll have to stay th' night. I'm just runnin' round meself to make your mother a cup o' tea.

Ayamonn (*irritably*) Dtch dtch – she'll knock herself up before she's done! When I lock up, I'll leave the key with you for her, Eeada. (*He lights a shunter's lantern and puts out the lamp.*)

Eeada Right y'are. (*She goes.*)

Roory What kid was it sketched th' angel on th' wall?

Ayamonn Oh, I did that. I'd give anything to be a painter.

Roory What, like Oul' Brennan o' th' Moor?

Ayamonn No, no; like Angelico or Constable.

Roory (*indifferently*) Never heard of them.

Ayamonn (*musingly*) To throw a whole world in colour on a canvas though it be but a man's fine face, a woman's shape asthride of a cushioned couch, or a three-bordered house on a hill, done with a glory; even delaying God, busy forgin' a new world, to stay awhile an' look upon their loveliness.

Roory Aw, Ayamonn, Ayamonn, man, put out your hand an' see if you're awake! (*He fiddles with the books on the table.*) What oul' book are you readin' now?

Ayamonn (*dressed now in oilskin leggings and coat, with an oilskin sou'wester on his head, comes over to look at the book in Roory's hand, and shines the lantern on it*) Oh, that's Ruskin's *Crown of Wild Olive* – a grand book – I'll lend it to you.

Roory What for? What would I be doin' with it? I've no time to waste on books. Ruskin. Curious name; not Irish, is it?

Ayamonn No, a Scotsman who wrote splendidly about a lot of things. Listen to this, spoken before a gathering of business men about to build an Exchange in their town.

Roory Aw, Ayamonn – an Exchange! What have we got to do with an Exchange?

Ayamonn (*impatiently*) Listen a second, man! Ruskin, speakin' to the business men, says: 'Your ideal of life is a pleasant and undulating world, with iron and coal everywhere beneath it. On each pleasant bank of this world is to be a beautiful mansion; stables, and coach-houses; a park and hot-houses; carriage-drives and shrubberies; and here are to live the votaries of the Goddess of Getting-on – the English gentleman –'

Roory (*interrupting*) There you are, you see, Ayamonn – th' *English* gentleman.

Ayamonn Wait a second – Irish or English – a gentleman's th' same.

Roory 'Tisn't. I'm tellin' you it's different. What's in this Ruskin of yours but another oul' cod with a gift of the gab? Right enough for th' English, pinin' afther little things, ever rakin' cindhers for th' glint of gold. We're different – we have th' light.

Ayamonn You mean th' Catholic Faith?

Roory (*impatiently*) No, no; that's there, too; I mean th' light of freedom; th' tall white candle tipped with its golden spear of flame. The light we thought we'd lost; but it burns again, sthrengthenin' into a sword of light. Like in th' song we sung together th' other night. (*He sings softly.*)

Our courage so many have thought to be agein',
Now flames like a brilliant new star in th' sky;
And Danger is proud to be call'd a good brother,
For Freedom has buckled her sword on her thigh.

Ayamonn (*joining in*)
Then out to th' place where th' battle is bravest,
Where th' noblest an' meanest fight fierce in th' fray,
Republican banners shall mock at th' foemen,
An' Fenians shall turn a dark night into day!

A pause as the two of them stand silent, each clasping the other's hand. Ayamonn opens the door to pass out.

Roory (*in a tense whisper*) Th' Fenians are in force again, Ayamonn; th' Sword o' Light is shinin'!

They go out, and Ayamonn closes the door as the curtain falls.

Act Two

The same as in Act One.

It is about ten o'clock at night. The rain has stopped, and there is a fine moon sailing through the sky. Some of its rays come in through the window at the side.

Ayamonn, in his shirt-sleeves, is sitting at the table. He has an ordinary tin money-box in his hand, and a small pile of coppers, mixed with a few sixpences, are on the table beside him. He is just taking the last coin from the slit in the box with the aid of a knife-blade. His mother is by the dresser piling up the few pieces of crockery used for a recent meal. The old one-wick lamp is alight, and stands on the table near to Ayamonn. Several books lie open there, too.

Ayamonn There's th' last one out, now. It's quite a job getting them out with a knife.

Mrs Breydon Why don't you put them in a box with a simple lid on?

Ayamonn The harder it is to get at, the less chance of me spending it on something more necessary than what I seek. (*He counts the money on the table.*) One bob – two – three – an' sixpence – an' nine – three an' ninepence; one an' threepence to get yet – a long way to go.

Mrs Breydon Maybe, now, th' bookseller would give you it for what you have till you can give him th' rest.

Ayamonn (*in agony*) Aw, woman, if you can't say sense, say nothing! Constable's reproductions are five shillings second-hand, an' he that's selling is the bastard that nearly

247

got me jailed for running off with his Shakespeare. It's touch an' go if he'll let me have it for the five bob.

Mrs Breydon (*philosophically*) Well, seein' you done without it so long, you can go without it longer.

Ayamonn (*with firm conviction*) I'll have it the first week we get the extra shilling the men are demandin'.

Mrs Breydon I shouldn't count your chickens before they're hatched.

Ayamonn (*joking a little bitterly*) Perhaps our blessed Lady of Eblana's poor will work a miracle for me.

Mrs Breydon (*a little anxiously*) Hush, don't say that! Jokin' or serious, Ayamonn, I wouldn't say that. We don't believe in any of their Blessed Ladies, but as it's somethin' sacred, it's best not mentioned. (*She shuffles into her shawl.*) Though it's a queer thing, Her goin' off out of Her niche without a one in th' house knowin' why. They're all out huntin' for Her still.

> *The door opens, and Brennan comes in slowly, with a cute grin on his face. He has a large package, covered with paper, under his arm.*

Brennan Out huntin' still for Her they are, are they? Well, let them hunt; She's here! A prisoner under me arm!

Mrs Breydon (*indignantly*) Well, Mr Brennan Moore, it's ashamed of yourself you should be yokin' th' poor people to throubled anxiety over their treasure; and little Ursula breakin' her heart into th' bargain.

Ayamonn It's god-damned mean of you, Brennan! What good d'ye think you'll do by this rowdy love of your own opinions – forcing tumult into the minds of ignorant, anxious people?

Brennan (*calmly*) Wait till yous see, wait till yous see,

248

before yous are sorry for sayin' more. (*He removes the paper and shows the lost image transfigured into a figure looking as if it had come straight from the shop: the white dress is spotless, the blue robe radiant, and the gold along its border and on the crown is gleaming. He holds it up for admiration. Triumphantly*) There, what d'ye think of Her now? Fair as th' first grand tinge of th' dawn, She is, an' bright as th' star of the evenin'.

Mrs Breydon Glory be to God, isn't She lovely! But hurry Her off, Brennan, for She's not a thing for Protestant eyes to favour.

Ayamonn (*a little testily*) Put it back, Brennan, put it back, and don't touch it again.

Brennan Isn't that what I'm going to do? Oh, boy alive, won't they get th' shock o' their lives when they see Her shinin' in th' oul' spot. (*He becomes serious.*) Though, mind you, me thrue mind misgives me for decoratin' what's a charm to the people of Judah in th' worship of idols; but th' two of you is witness I did it for the sake of the little one, and not in any tilt towards honour to a graven image.

Mrs Breydon (*resignedly*) It's done now, God forgive us both, an' me for sayin' She's lovely. Touchin' a thing forbidden with a startled stir of praise!

Ayamonn Put it back, put it back, man, and leave it quiet where you got it first.

Brennan goes out, looking intently out, and listening, before he does so.

Mrs Breydon He meant well, poor man, but he's done a dangerous thing. I'll be back before you start for work. (*With a heavy sigh*) It won't take us long to tend her for the last time. The white sheets have come, th' tall candles wait to be lit, an' th' coffin's ordhered, an' th' room'll look sacred with the bunch of violets near her head. (*She goes out slowly. As she goes.*) Dear knows what'll happen to th' three children.

> *Ayamonn sits silent for a few moments, reading a book, his elbows resting on the table.*

Ayamonn (*with a deep sigh – murmuringly*) Sheila, Sheila, my heart cries out for you! (*After a moment's pause, he reads.*)

> But I am pigeon-livered, an' lack gall
> To make oppression bitther; or, ere this,
> I should have fatted all th' region kites
> With this slave's offal: Bloody, bawdy villain!

Oh, Will, you were a boyo; a brave boyo, though, and a beautiful one!

> *The door opens and Old Brennan comes in, showing by his half-suppressed chuckles that he is enjoying himself. He wanders over the room to stand by the fire.*

Brennan (*chuckling*) In Her old place she is, now, in Her new coronation robe; and funny it is to think it's the last place they'll look for Her.

Ayamonn I'm busy, now.

Brennan (*sitting down by the fire*) Ay, so you are; so I see; busy readin'. Read away, for I won't disturb you; only have a few quiet puffs at th' oul' pipe. (*Pause.*) Ah, then, don't I wish I was young enough to bury meself in th' joy of readin' all th' great books of th' world. Ah! but when I was young, I had to work hard.

Ayamonn I work hard, too.

Brennan 'Course you do! Isn't that what I'm sayin'? An' all th' more credit, too, though it must be thryin' to have

thoughtless people comin' in an' intherferin' with the
golden movements of your thoughts.

Ayamonn It's often a damned nuisance!

Brennan 'Course it is. Isn't that what I'm sayin'? (*As the
door opens.*) An' here's another o' th' boobies entherin'
now.

  Roory comes in, and shuts the door rather noisily.

Eh, go easy, there – can't you see Ayamonn's busy
studyin'?

Roory (*coming and bending over Ayamonn*) Are you still
lettin' oul' Ruskin tease you?

Ayamonn (*angrily*) No, no; Shakespeare, Shakespeare, this
time! (*Springing from his chair*) Damn it, can't you let a
man alone a minute? What th' hell d'ye want now?

Brennan (*warningly*) I told you he was busy.

Roory (*apologetically*) Aw, I only came with the tickets
you asked me to bring you for the comin' National
Anniversary of Terence Bellew MacManus.

Ayamonn All right, all right; let's have them.

Roory How many d'ye want? How many can you sell?

Ayamonn Give me twelve sixpennies; if the sthrike doesn't
come off I'll easily sell that number.

Roory (*counting out the tickets which Ayamonn gathers
up and puts into his pocket*) I met that Mullcanny on the
way with a book for you; but he stopped to tell a couple of
railwaymen that the Story of Adam an' Eve was all a cod.

Brennan (*indignantly*) He has a lot o' the people here in a
state o' steamin' anger, goin' about with his bitther belief
that the patthern of a man's hand is nearly at one with a

monkey's paw, a horse's foot, th' flipper of a seal, or th' wing of a bat!

Ayamonn Well, each of them is as wonderful as the hand of a man.

Roory No, Ayamonn, not from the Christian point of view. D'ye know what they're callin' him round here? Th' New Broom, because he's always sayin' he'll sweep th' idea of God clean outa th' mind o' man.

Brennan (*excited*) There'll be dire damage done to him yet! He was goin' to be flattened out be a docker th' other day for tellin' him that a man first formin' showed an undoubted sign of a tail.

Ayamonn Ay, and when he's fully formed, if he doesn't show the tail, he shows most signs of all that goes along with it.

Roory But isn't that a nice dignity to put on th' sacredness of a man's conception!

Brennan (*whisperingly*) An' a lot o' them are sayin', Ayamonn, that your encouragement of him should come to an end.

Ayamonn Indeed? Well, let them. I'll stand by any honest man seekin' th' truth, though his way isn't my way. (*to Brennan*) You, yourself, go about deriding many things beloved by your Catholic neighbours.

Brennan I contest only dangerous deceits specified be the Council o' Thrent, that are nowhere scheduled in th' pages of the Holy Scriptures.

Roory Yes, Ayamonn, it's altogether different; he just goes about blatherin' in his ignorant Protestant way.

Brennan (*highly indignant*) Ignorant, am I? An' where would a body find an ignorance lustier than your own, eh?

If your Council o' Thrent's ordher for prayers for the dead
who are past help, your dismal veneration of Saints an'
Angels, your images of wood an' stone, carved an'
coloured, have given you the image an' superscription of a
tail, th' pure milk of the gospel has made a man of me,
God-fearin', but stately, with a mind garlanded to th'
steady an' eternal thruth!

> *While they have been arguing, Mullcanny has peeped*
> *round the door, and now comes into the room, eyeing*
> *the two disputants with a lot of amusement and a little*
> *scorn. They take no notice of him.*

Roory Sure, man, you have the neighbourhood hectored
with your animosity against Catholic custom an' Catholic
thought, never hesitatin' to give th' Pope even a deleterious
name.

Brennan (*lapsing, in his excitement, into a semi-Ulster
dialect*) We dud ut tae yeh in Durry, on' sent your bravest
floatin' down dud in th' wathers of th' Boyne, like th'
hosts of Pharaoh tumblin' in the rush of th' Rud Sea! Thut
was a slup in th' puss tae your Pope!

Mullcanny You pair of damned fools, don't you know
that the Pope wanted King Billy to win, and that the
Vatican was ablaze with lights of joy afther King James's
defeat over the wathers of the Boyne?

Roory You're a liar, he didn't!

Brennan You're a liar, it wasn't!

> *They turn from Mullcanny to continue the row with*
> *themselves.*

Brennan Looksee, if I believed in the ministhration of
Saints on' Angels, I'd say thut th' good Protestant St
Puthrick was at the hud of what fell out at Durry,
Aughrim, on' th' Boyne.

Roory (*stunned with the thought of St Patrick as a Protestant*) Protestant St Pathrick? Is me hearin' sound, or what? What name did you mention?

Brennan I said St Puthrick – th' evangelical founder of our thrue Church.

Roory Is it dhreamin' I am? Is somethin' happenin' to me, or is it happenin' to you? Oh, man, it's mixin' mirth with madness you are at thinkin' St Pathrick ever looped his neck in an orange sash, or tapped out a tune on a Protestant dhrum!

Brennan (*contemptuously*) I refuse to argue with a one who's no' a broad-minded mon. Abuse is no equivalent for lugic – so I say God save th' King, an' tae hull with th' Pope!

Roory (*indignantly*) You damned bigot – to hell with th' King, an' God save th' Pope!

Mullcanny (*to Ayamonn*) You see how they live in bittherness, the one with the other. Envy, strife, and malice crawl from the coloured slime of the fairy-tales that go to make what is called religion. (*Taking a book from his pocket*) Here's something can bear a thousand tests, showing neatly how the world and all it bears upon it came into slow existence over millions of years, doing away for ever with the funny wonders of the seven days' creation set out in the fairy book of the Bible.

Ayamonn (*taking the book from Mullcanny*) Thanks, Pether, oul' son; I'm bound to have a good time reading it.

Mullcanny It'll give you the true and scientific history of man as he was before Adam.

Brennan (*in a woeful voice*) It's a darkened mind that thries tae lower us to what we were before th' great an' good God fashioned us. What does ony sensible person

want to know what we were like before the creation of th'
first man?

Ayamonn (*murmuringly*) To know the truth, to seek the
truth, is good, though it lead to th' danger of eternal
death.

Roory (*horror-stricken – crossing himself*) Th' Lord
between us an' all harm!

Brennan (*whispering prayerfully*) Lord, I believe, help
Thou mine unbelief.

Mullcanny (*pointing out a picture in the book*) See? The
human form unborn. The tail – look; the os coccyx
sticking a mile out; there's no getting away from it!

Brennan (*shaking his head woefully*) An' this is holy
Ireland!

Roory (*lifting his eyes to the ceiling – woefully*) Poor St
Pathrick!

Mullcanny (*mockingly*) He's going to be a lonely man
soon, eh? (*To Ayamonn*) Keep it safe for me, Ayamonn.
When you've read it, you'll be a different man. (*He goes to
the door.*) Well, health with the whole o' you, and
goodbye for the present. (*He goes out.*)

Roory Have nothin' to do with that book, Ayamonn, for
that fellow gone out would rip up the floor of Heaven to
see what was beneath it. It's clapped in jail he ought to be!

Brennan An' th' book banned!

Ayamonn Roory, Roory, is that th' sort o' freedom you'd
bring to Ireland with a crowd of green branches an' th' joy
of shouting? If we give no room to men of our time to
question many things, all things, ay, life itself, then
freedom's but a paper flower, a star of tinsel, a dead lass
with gay ribbons at her breast an' a gold comb in her hair.

Let us bring freedom here, not with sounding brass an'
tinklin' cymbal, but with silver trumpets blowing, with a
song all men can sing, with a palm branch in our hand,
rather than with a whip at our belt, and a headsman's axe
on our shoulders.

*There is a gentle knock at the door, and the voice of
Sheila is heard speaking.*

Sheila (*outside*) Ayamonn, are you there? Are you in?

Brennan (*whispering*) The little lass; I knew she'd come
back.

Ayamonn I don't want her to see you here. Go into the
other room – quick. (*He pushes them towards it.*) An' keep
still.

Roory (*to Brennan*) An' don't you go mockin' our Pope,
see?

Brennan (*to Roory*) Nor you go singlin' out King Billy for
a jeer.

Ayamonn In with yous, quick!

Brennan I prophesied she'd come back, didn't I,
Ayamonn? That she'd come back, didn't I?

Ayamonn Yes, yes; in you go.

*He puts them in the other room and shuts the door.
Then he crosses the room and opens the door to admit
Sheila. She comes in, and he and Sheila stand silently for
some moments, she trying to look at him, and finding it
hard.*

Sheila (*at last*) Well, haven't you anything to say to me?

Ayamonn (*slowly and coldly*) I waited for you at the
bridge today; but you didn't come.

Sheila I couldn't come; I told you why.

Ayamonn I was very lonely.

Sheila (*softly*) So was I, Ayamonn, lonely even in front of God's holy face.

Ayamonn Sheila, we've gone a long way in a gold canoe over many waters, bright and surly, sometimes sending bitter spray asplash on our faces. But you were ever listening for the beat from the wings of the angel of fear. So you got out to walk safe on a crowded road.

Sheila This is a cold and cheerless welcome, Ayamonn.

Ayamonn Change, if you want to, the burning kiss falling on the upturned, begging mouth for the chill caress of a bony, bearded Saint. (*Loudly*) Go with th' yelling crowd, and keep them brave, and yell along with them!

Sheila Won't you listen, then, to the few words I have to say?

Ayamonn (*sitting down near the fire, and looking into it, though he leaves her standing*) Go ahead; I won't fail to hear you.

Sheila God knows I don't mean to hurt you, but you must know that we couldn't begin to live on what you're earning now – could we? (*He keeps silent.*) Oh, Ayamonn, why do you waste your time on doing foolish things?

Ayamonn What foolish things?

A hubbub is heard in the street outside; voices saying loudly 'Give him one in the bake' or 'Down him with a one in th' belly'; then the sound of running footsteps, and silence.

Sheila (*when she hears the voices – nervously*) What's that?

Ayamonn (*without taking his gaze from the fire.*) Some drunken row or other.

They listen silently for a few moments.

Well, what foolish things?

Sheila (*timid and hesitating*) You know yourself, Ayamonn: trying to paint, going mad about Shakespeare, and consorting with a kind of people that can only do you harm.

Ayamonn (*mockingly prayerful – raising his eyes to the ceiling*) O Lord, let me forsake the foolish, and live; and go in the way of Sheila's understanding!

Sheila (*going over nearer to him*) Listen, Ayamonn, my love; you know what I say is only for our own good, that we may come together all the sooner. (*Trying to speak jokingly*) Now, really, isn't it comical I'd look if I were to go about in a scanty petticoat, covered in a sober black shawl, and my poor feet bare! (*mocking*) Wouldn't I look well that way!

Ayamonn (*quietly*) With red roses in your hand, you'd look beautiful.

Sheila (*desperately*) Oh, for goodness' sake, Ayamonn, be sensible! I'm getting a little tired of all this. I can't bear the strain the way we're going on much longer. (*A short pause.*) You will either have to make good, or – (*She pauses.*)

Ayamonn (*quietly*) Or what?

Sheila (*with a little catch in her voice*) Or lose me; and you wouldn't like that to happen.

Ayamonn I shouldn't like that to happen; but I could bear the sthrain.

Sheila I risked a big row tonight to come to tell you good news: I've been told that the strike is bound to take place; there is bound to be trouble; and, if you divide yourself from the foolish men, and stick to your job, you'll soon be a foreman of some kind or other.

Ayamonn (*rising from his seat and facing her for the first time*) Who told you all this? The Inspector?

Sheila Never mind who; if he did, wasn't it decent of him?

Ayamonn D'ye know what you're asking me to do, woman? To be a blackleg; to blast with th' black frost of desertion the gay hopes of my comrades. Whatever you may think them to be, they are my comrades. Whatever they may say or do, they remain my brothers and sisters. Go to hell, girl, I have a soul to save as well as you. (*With a catch in his voice*) Oh, Sheila, you shouldn't have asked me to do this thing!

Sheila (*trying to come close, but he pushes her back*) Oh, Ayamonn, it is a chance; take it, do, for my sake!

Rapid footsteps are heard outside. The door flies open and Mullcanny comes in, pale, frightened, his clothes dishevelled, and a slight smear of blood on his forehead. His bowler hat is crushed down on his head, his coat is torn, and his waistcoat unbuttoned, showing his tie pulled out of its place. He sinks into a chair.

Ayamonn What's happened? Who did that to you?

Mullcanny Give's a drink, someone, will you?

Ayamonn gets him a drink from a jug on the dresser.

Mullcanny A gang of bowseys made for me, and I talking to a man. Barely escaped with my life. Only for some brave oul' one, they'd have laid me out completely. She saved me from worse.

Ayamonn How th' hell did you bring all that on you?

Mullcanny (*plaintively*) Just trying to show a fellow the foolishness of faith in a hereafter, when something struck me on the head, and I was surrounded by feet making kicks at me!

A crash of breaking glass is heard from the other room, and Brennan and Roory come running out of it.

Roory A stone has done for th' window! (*He sees Mullcanny.*) Oh, that's how th' land lies, is it? Haven't I often said that if you go round leerin' at God an' His holy assistants, one day He's bound to have a rap at you!

Brennan Keep away from that window, there, in case another one comes sailin' in.

Immediately he has spoken, a stone smashes in through the window. Brennan lies down flat on the floor; Mullcanny slides from the chair and crouches on the ground; Roory gets down on his hands and knees, keeping his head as low as possible, so that he resembles a Mohammedan at his devotions; Sheila stands stiff in a corner, near the door; and Ayamonn, seizing up a hurley lying against the dresser, makes for the door to go out.

I guessed this was comin'.

Ayamonn (*angrily*) I'll show them!

Sheila (*to Ayamonn*) Stop where you are, you fool!

But Ayamonn pays no attention to the advice and hurries out of the door.

Roory (*plaintively and with dignity – to Mullcanny*) This is what you bring down on innocent people with your obstinate association of man with th' lower animals.

Mullcanny (*truculently*) Only created impudence it is that strives to set yourselves above the ape's formation, genetically present in every person's body.

Brennan (*indignantly*) String out life to where it started, an' you'll find no sign, let alone a proof, of the dignity, wisdom, an' civility of man ever having been associated with th' manners of a monkey.

Mullcanny And why do children like to climb trees, eh? Answer me that?

Roory (*fiercely*) They love it more where you come from than they do here.

Sheila (*from her corner*) It's surely to be pitied you are, young man, lettin' yourself be bullied by ignorant books into believing that things are naught but what poor men are inclined to call them, blind to the glorious and eternal facts that shine behind them.

Mullcanny (*pityingly*) Bullied be books – eternal facts – aw! Yous are all scared stiff at the manifestation of a truth or two. D'ye know that the contraction of catharrah, apoplexy, consumption, and cataract of the eye is common to the monkeys? Knowledge you have now that you hadn't before; and a lot of them even like beer.

Roory Well, that's something sensible, at last.

Brennan (*fiercely*) Did they get their likin' for beer from us, or did we get our likin' of beer from them? Answer me that, you, now; answer me that!

Roory Answer him that. We're not Terra Del Fooaygeeans, but sensible, sane, an' civilised souls.

Mullcanny (*gleefully*) Time's promoted reptiles – that's all; yous can't do away with the os coccyges!

Brennan Ladies present, ladies present.

Roory (*creeping over rapidly till his face is close to that of Mullcanny's – fiercely*) We stand on the earth, firm, upright, heads cocked, lookin' all men in th' face, afraid o' nothin'; men o' goodwill we are, abloom with th' blessin' o' charity, showin' in th' dust we're made of, th' diamond-core of an everlastin' divinity!

Sheila (*excitedly*) Hung as high as Gilderoy he ought to be, an' he deep in the evil of his rich illusions, spouting insults at war with th' mysteries an' facts of our holy faith!

Brennan (*to Sheila*) Hush, pretty lady, hush. (*To the others*) Boys, boys, take example from a poor oul' Protestant here, never lettin' himself be offended be a quiver of anger in any peaceable or terrified discussion. Now, let that last word finish it; finis – the end, see?

Roory (*angrily – to Brennan*) Finis yousself, you blurry-eyed, wither-skinned oul' greybeard, singin' songs in th' public streets for odd coppers, with all th' boys in th' Bank of Ireland workin' overtime countin' all you've got in their front room! Finis you!

Brennan (*indignantly*) An office-boy, in a hurry, wouldn't stop to pick up from th' path before him the few coins I have. An' as for being withered, soople as you I am, hands that can tinkle a thremblin' tune out of an oul' melodeon, legs that can carry me ten miles an' more, an' eyes that can still see without hardship a red berry shinin' from a distant bush!

> *The door opens and Ayamonn and his mother come in. She runs over to the blossoms at the window, tenderly examining the plants growing there – the musk, the geranium, and the fuchsia.*

Mrs Breydon (*joyfully*) Unharmed, th' whole of them. Th' stone passed them by, touchin' none o' them – thank God for that mercy!

Ayamonn What th' hell are you doin' on your knees? Get up, get up.

They rise from the floor shamefacedly.

Th' rioters all dispersed. (*To Mullcanny*) Mother was th' oul' one who saved you from a sudden an' unprovided death. An' th' Blessed Image has come back again, all aglow in garments new. Listen!

A murmur of song has been heard while Ayamonn was speaking, and now Eeada, Dympna, Finnoola, and the Men appear at the door – now wide open – half backing into the room singing part of a hymn softly, their pale faces still wearing the frozen look of resignation; staring at the Image shining bright and gorgeous as Brennan has made it for them, standing in a niche in the wall, directly opposite the door.

Eeada, Dympna, Finnoola and the Men (*singing softly*)
Oh! Queen of Eblana's poor children,
Bear swiftly our woe away;
An' give us a chance to live lightly
An hour of our life's dark day!
Lift up th' poor heads ever bending,
An' light a lone star in th' sky,
To show thro' th' darkness, descending,
A cheerier way to die.

Eeada (*coming forward a little*) She came back to Her poor again, in raiment rich. She came back; of Her own accord. She came to abide with Her people.

Dympna From her window, little Ursula looked, and saw Her come in; in th' moonlight, along the street She came, stately. Blinded be the coloured light that shone around about Her, the child fell back, in a swoon she fell full on the floor beneath her.

1st Man My eyes caught a glimpse of Her too, glidin'
back to where She came from. Regal an' proud She was,
an' wondrous, so that me eyes failed; me knees thrembled
an' bent low, an' me heart whispered a silent prayer to
itself as th' vision passed me by, an' I fancied I saw a smile
on Her holy face.

Eeada Many have lived to see a strange thing this
favoured night, an' blessin' will flow from it to all
tempered into a lively belief; and maybe, too, to some who
happen to be out of step with the many marchin' in the
mode o' thruth.

> *She comes a little closer to Mrs Breydon. The others,
> backs turned towards the room, stand, most of them
> outside the door, a few just across the threshold, in a
> semicircle, heads bent as if praying, facing towards the
> Image.*

Th' hand of a black stranger it was who sent the stones
flyin' through your windows; but ere tomorrow's sun is
seen, they will be back again as shelther from th' elements.
A blessin' generous on yous all – (*Pause.*) – except th' evil
thing that stands, all stiff-necked, underneath th' roof!

Mullcanny (*mockingly*) Me!

Sheila (*fiercely*) Ay, you, that shouldn't find a smile or an
unclenched hand in a decent man's house!

Mullcanny I'll go; there's too many here to deal with – I'll
leave you with your miracle.

Ayamonn You can stay if you wish, for whatever surety of
shelther's here, it's open to th' spirit seeking to add another
colour to whatever thruth we know already. Thought that
has run from a blow will find a roof under its courage
here, an' a fire to sit by, as long as I live an' th' oul' rooms
last!

Sheila (*with quiet bitterness*) Well, shelter him, then, that by right should be lost in the night, a black night, an' bitterly lonely, without a dim ray from a half-hidden star to give him a far-away companionship; ay, an' a desolate rest under a thorny and dripping thicket of lean and twisted whins, too tired to thry to live longer against th' hate of the black wind and th' grey rain. Let him lie there, let him live there, forsaken, forgotten by all who live under a kindly roof and close to a cosy fire!

Mullcanny (*with pretended alarm*) Good God, I'm done, now! I'm off before worse befall me. Good night, Ayamonn.

Ayamonn Good night, my friend.

Mullcanny goes out.

Brennan We're keepin' decent people out of their beds – so long, all.

Roory I'll be with you some o' th' way, an' we can finish that argument we had. Good night all.

He and Brennan go out together, closing the door after them. Sheila stands where she was, sullen and silent.

Mrs Breydon Shame on you, Sheila, for such a smoky flame to come from such a golden lamp!

Sheila stays silent.

Tired out I am, an' frightened be th' scene o' death I saw today. Dodge about how we may, we come to th' same end.

Ayamonn (*gently leading her towards the other room*) Go an' lie down, lady; you're worn out. Time's a perjured jade, an' ever he moans a man must die. Who through every inch of life weaves a patthern of vigour an' elation can never taste death, but goes to sleep among th' stars, his

266

withered arms outstretched to greet th' echo of his own
shout. It will be for them left behind to sigh for an hour,
an' then to sing their own odd songs, an' do their own odd
dances, to give a lonely God a little company, till they, too,
pass by on their bare way out. When a true man dies, he is
buried in th' birth of a thousand worlds.

> *Mrs Breydon goes into the other room, and Ayamonn*
> *closes the door softly behind her. He comes back and*
> *stands pensive near the fire.*

(*After a pause*) Don't you think you should go too?

Sheila (*a little brokenly*) Let me have a few more words
with you, Ayamonn, before we hurry to our separation.

Ayamonn (*quietly*) There is nothing more to be said.

Sheila There's a lot to be said, but hasty time won't stretch
an hour a little out to let the words be spoken. Goodbye.

Ayamonn (*without turning his head*) Goodbye.

> *Sheila is going slowly to the door when it partly opens,*
> *and half the head of Eeada peers around it, amid an*
> *indistinct murmur as of praying outside.*

Eeada (*in half a whisper*) Th' Protestan' Rector to see Mr
Breydon. (*The half of her head disappears, but her voice is*
heard a little more loudly.) This way, sir; shure you know
th' way well, anyhow.

> *The door opening a little more, the Rector comes in. He*
> *is a handsome man of forty. His rather pale face wears a*
> *grave scholarly look, but there is kindness in his grey*
> *eyes, and humorous lines round his mouth, though these*
> *are almost hidden by a short, brown, pointed beard,*
> *here and there about to turn grey. His black clothes are*
> *covered by a warm black topcoat, the blackness*
> *brightened a little by a vivid green scarf he is wearing*

*round his neck, the fringed ends falling over his
shoulders. He carries a black, broad-brimmed, soft
clerical hat and a walking-stick in his left hand. He
hastens towards Ayamonn, smiling genially, hand
outstretched in greeting.*

Rector My dear Ayamonn.

They shake hands.

Ayamonn (*indicating Sheila*) A friend of mine, sir – Sheila
Moorneen. (*Moving a chair*) Sit down, sir.

*The Rector bows to Sheila; she returns it quietly, and
the Rector sits down.*

Rector I've hurried from home in a cab, Ayamonn, to see
you before the night was spent. (*His face forming grave
lines*) I've a message for you – and a warning.

*The door again is partly opened, and again the half
head of Eeada appears, mid the murmurs outside,
unheard the moment the door closes.*

Eeada Two railwaymen to see you, Ayamonn; full house
tonight you're havin', eh?

*The half head goes, the door opens wider, and the two
railwaymen come into the room. They are dressed
drably as the other men are, but their peaked railway
uniform caps (which they keep on their heads) have
vivid scarlet bands around them. Their faces, too, are
like the others, and stonily stare in front of them. They
stand stock still when they see the Rector.*

1st Railwayman (*after a pause*) 'Scuse us. Didn' know th'
Protestan' Minister was here. We'll wait outside till he
goes, Ayamonn.

Ayamonn Th' Rector's a dear friend of mine, Bill; say
what you want, without fear – he's a friend.

1st Railwayman (*a little dubiously*) Glad to hear it. You know th' sthrike starts tomorrow?

Ayamonn I know it now.

2nd Railwayman Wouldn' give's th' extra shillin'. Offered us thruppence instead – th' lowsers! (*Hastily – to Rector*) 'Scuse me, sir.

1st Railwayman (*taking a document from his breast pocket*) An' th' meetin's proclaimed.

Rector (*to Ayamonn*) That's part of what I came to tell you.

1st Railwayman (*handing document to Ayamonn*) They handed that to our Committee this evening, a warrant of warning.

Rector (*earnestly – to Ayamonn*) I was advised to warn you, Ayamonn, that the Authorities are prepared to use all the force they have to prevent the meeting.

Ayamonn Who advised you, sir – th' Inspector?

Rector My churchwarden, Ayamonn. Come, even he has good in him.

Ayamonn I daresay he has, sir; I've no grudge against him.

Rector (*convinced*) I know that, Ayamonn.

Ayamonn (*indicating document – to 1st Railwayman*) What are th' Committee going to do with this?

1st Railwayman What would you do with it, Ayamonn?

Ayamonn (*setting it alight at the fire and waiting till it falls to ashes*) That!

2nd Railwayman (*gleefully*) Exactly what we said you'd do!

Sheila (*haughtily*) It's not what any sensible body would think he'd do.

1st Railwayman (*ignoring her*) Further still, Ayamonn, me son, we want you to be one of the speakers on the platform at the meeting.

Sheila (*bursting forward and confronting the railwaymen*) He'll do nothing of the kind – hear me? Nothing of the kind. Cinder-tongued moaners, who's to make any bones about what you suffer, or how you die? Ayamonn's his reading and his painting to do, and his mother to mind, more than lipping your complaints in front of gun muzzles, ready to sing a short and sudden death-song!

1st Railwayman (*a little awed*) To see Ayamonn we came, an' not you, Miss.

2nd Railwayman (*roughly*) Let th' man speak for himself.

Ayamonn (*catching Sheila's arm and drawing her back*) It's my answer they're seeking. (*To railwaymen*) Tell the Committee, Bill, I'll be there; and that they honour me when they set me in front of my brothers. The Minstrel Show must be forgotten.

Sheila (*vehemently – to the Rector*) You talk to him; you're his friend. You can influence him. Get him to stay away, man!

Rector It's right for me to warn you, Ayamonn, and you, men, that the Authorities are determined to prevent the meeting; and that you run a grave risk in defying them.

2nd Railwayman (*growling*) We'll chance it. We've barked long enough, sir; it's time to bite a bit now.

Sheila (*to Rector*) Warning's no good; that's not enough – forbid him to go. Show him God's against it!

Rector (*standing up*) Who am I to say that God's against it? You are too young by a thousand years to know the mind of God. If they be his brothers, he does well among them.

Sheila (*wildly*) I'll get his mother to bar his way. She'll do more than murmur grand excuses. (*She runs to the door of the other room, opens it, and goes in. After a few moments, she comes out slowly, goes to the chair left idle by the Rector, sits down on it, leans her arms on the table, and lets her head rest on them.*)

Ayamonn Well?

Sheila (*brokenly*) She's stretched out, worn and wan, fast asleep, and I hadn't the heart to awaken her.

Rector (*holding out a hand to Ayamonn*) Come to see me before you go, Ayamonn. Be sure, wherever you may be, whatever you may do, a blessing deep from my breast is all around you. Goodbye. (*To the railwaymen*) Goodbye, my friends.

Railwaymen Goodbye, sir.

> *The Rector glances at Sheila, decides to say nothing, and goes towards the door; Ayamonn opens it for him, and he goes out through the semicircle of men and women, still softly singing before the Statue of the Queen of Eblana's poor. Sheila's quiet crying is heard as a minor note through the singing.*

Chorus
    Oh, Queen of Eblana's poor children,
    Bear swiftly our woe away,
    An' give us a chance to live lightly
    An hour of our life's dark day!

Curtain.

Act Three

A part of Dublin City flowering into a street and a bridge across the River Liffey. The parapets are seen to the right and left so that the bridge fills most of the scene before the onlooker. The distant end of the bridge leads to a street flowing on to a point in the far distance; and to the right and left of this street are tall gaunt houses, mottled with dubious activities, with crowds of all sorts of men and women burrowing in them in a pathetic search for a home. These houses stand along another street running parallel with the river. In the distance, where the street, leading from the bridge, ends in a point of space, to the right, soars the tapering silver spire of a church; and to the left, Nelson's Pillar, a deep red, pierces the sky, with Nelson, a deep black, on its top, looking over everything that goes on around him. A gloomy grey sky is over all, so that the colours of the scene are made up of the dark houses, the brown parapets of the bridge, the grey sky, the silver spire, the red pillar, and Nelson's black figure.

On one of the bridge parapets a number of the men seen in the previous scenes are gathered together, their expressionless faces hidden by being bent down towards their breasts. Some sit on the parapets, some lounge against the gaunt houses at the corner of the street leading from the bridge, and, in one corner, a man stands wearily against the parapet, head bent, an unlit pipe dropping from his mouth, apparently forgotten. The sun shines on pillar and church spire, but there is no sign of sun where these people are.

On the pavement, opposite to where the men sit, nearer to this end of the bridge, sit Eeada, Dympna, and

*Finnoola, dressed so in black that they appear to be
enveloped in the blackness of a dark night. In front of
Eeada is a drab-coloured basket in which cakes and apples
are spending an idle and uneasy time. Dympna has a
shallower basket holding decadent blossoms, and a
drooping bunch of violets hangs from a listless hand.*

Eeada (*drowsily*) This spongy leaden sky's Dublin; those
tomby houses is Dublin too – Dublin's scurvy body; an'
we're Dublin's silver soul. (*She spits vigorously into the
street.*) An' that's what Eeada thinks of th' city's soul an'
body!

Dympna You're more than right, Eeada, but I wouldn't
be too harsh. (*Calling out in a sing-song way*) Violets,
here, on'y tuppence a bunch; tuppence a bunch, th' fresh
violets!

Eeada (*calling out in a sing-song voice*) Apples an' cakes,
on'y tuppence a head here for th' cakes; ripe apples a
penny apiece!

Dympna Th' sun is always at a distance, an' th' chill grey
is always here.

Finnoola Half-mournin' skies for ever over us, frownin'
out any chance of merriment that came staggerin' to us for
a little support.

Eeada That's Dublin, Finnoola, an' th' sky over it.
Sorrow's a slush under our feet, up to our ankles, an' th'
deep drip of it constant overhead.

Dympna A graveyard where th' dead are all above th'
ground.

Eeada Without a blessed blink of rest to give them hope.
An' she cockin' herself up that she stands among other
cities as a queen o' counsel, laden with knowledge, afire
with th' song of great men, enough to overawe all livin'

beyond th' salty sea, undher another sun be day, an'
undher a different moon be night.

They drowse, with heads bent lower.

1st Man (*leaning wearily against the parapet*) Golden
Gander'll do it, if I'm e'er a thrue prophet. (*Raising his
voice a little*) He'll flash past th' winnin' post like an arra
from th' bow, in the five hundhred guinea West's Awake
Steeplechase Championship.

2nd Man (*drowsily contradicting*) In me neck he will!
He'd have a chance if it was a ramble. Copper Goose'll
leave him standin', if I'm e'er a thrue prophet.

Eeada (*waking up slightly*) Prophets? Do me ears deceive
me, or am I afther hearin' somebody say prophets?

Dympna You heard a murmur of it, Eeada, an' it's a bad
word to hear, remindin' us of our low estate at th' present
juncture. Th' prophets we once had are well hidden behind
God be now, an' no wondher, for we put small pass on
them, an' God in His generous anger's showin' us what it
is to be saddled with Johnnies-come-marchin'-home, all
song an' shirt an' no surety.

Finnoola (*shaking her head sadly*) A gold-speckled candle,
white as snow, was Dublin once; yellowish now, leanin'
sideways, an' guttherin' down to a last shaky glimmer in
th' wind o' life.

Eeada Well, we've got Guinness's Brewery still, givin' us a
needy glimpse of a betther life an hour or so on a Saturday
night, though I hold me hand at praisin' th' puttin' of
Brian Boru's golden harp on every black porther bottle,
destined to give outsiders a false impression of our pride in
th' tendher an' dauntless memories of th' past.

*The Rector and the Inspector appear at the farther end
of the bridge, and come over it towards where the men*

*and women are. The Rector is dressed in immaculate
black, wears a glossy tall hat, and carries a walking-
stick. He has shed his topcoat, but wears his green scarf
round his neck. The Inspector is clad in a blue uniform,
slashed with silver epaulettes on the shoulders, and
silver braid on collar and cuffs. He wears a big blue
helmet, back and front peaks silver-bordered, and from
a long silver spike on the top flows a graceful plume of
crimson hair. On the front is a great silver crown
throned on a circle of red velvet. A sword, in a silver
scabbard, hangs by his side. He is wearing highly
polished top-boots. They both pause on the bridge, the
Rector looking pensively down over the parapet at the
flowing river.*

Inspector It was a great wedding, sir. A beautiful bride
and an elegant bridegroom; a distinguished congregation,
and the Primate in his fine sermon did justice to the grand
occasion, sir. Fittingly ended, too, by the organ with 'The
Voice that Breathed o'er Eden'.

Rector (*apparently not very interested*) Oh yes, yes; quite.

Inspector Historic disthrict, this, round here: headquarters
of a Volunteer Corp in Grattan's time – not, of course, that
I agree with Grattan. A great-great-grandfather of mine
was one of the officers.

Rector Oh yes; was he?

Inspector Yes. Strange uniform he wore: richly black, with
sky-blue facings, a yellow breast-piece, ribbed with red
braid, and, capping all, a huge silver helmet having a
yellow plume soaring over it from the right-hand side.

Rector (*smiling*) Your own's not too bad, Mr
Churchwarden.

Inspector Smart; but a bit too sombre, I think, sir.

Eeada (*whining towards them*) On'y a penny each, th' rosy apples, lovely for th' chiselurs – Jasus! what am I sayin'? Lovely for th' little masters an' little misthresses, stately, in their chandeliered an' carpeted dwellin'-houses; or a cake – on'y tuppence a piece – daintily spiced, an' tastin' splendid.

Dympna (*whining towards them*) Tuppence, here, th' bunch o' violets, fit for to go with th' white an' spotless cashmere gown of our radiant Lady o' Fair Dealin'.

Eeada (*deprecatingly*) What are you sayin', woman? That's a Protestan' ministher, indeed, gentleman, Dympna!

Dympna Me mind slipped for a poor minute; but it's pity he'll have on us, an' regulate our lives with what'll bring a sudden cup o' tea within fair reach of our hands.

Eeada Apples, here, penny each, rosy apples, picked hardly an hour ago from a laden three; cakes tuppence on'y, baked over scented turf as th' dawn stepped over th' blue-gowned backs o' th' Dublin Mountains.

Dympna Tuppence a bunch, th' violets, shy an' dhrunk with th' dew o' th' mornin'; fain to lie in the white bosom of a high-born lady, or fit into th' lapel of a genuine gentleman's Sunday courtin' coat.

> *The Rector takes a few coins from his pocket and throws them to the women, who pick them up and sink into silence again.*

Inspector Swift, too, must have walked about here with the thorny crown of madness pressing ever deeper into his brain.

Rector (*indicating the men and women*) Who are these?

Inspector (*indifferent*) Those? Oh, flotsam and jetsam. A few of them dangerous at night, maybe; but harmless during the day.

Rector I've read that tens of thousands of such as those followed Swift to the grave.

Inspector Indeed, sir? A queer man, the poor demented Dean; a right queer man.

A sleepy lounger suddenly gives a cough, gives his throat a hawk, and sends a big spit on to one of the Inspector's polished boots, then sinks back into sleep again.

(*Springing back with an angry exclamation*) What th' hell are you after doing, you rotten lizard! Looka what you've done, you mangy rat! (*He takes hold of the lounger and shakes him sharply.*)

2nd Man (*sleepily resentful*) Eh, there! Wha' th' hell?

Inspector (*furiously*) You spat on my boots, you tousled toad – my boots, boots, boots!

2nd Man (*frightened and bewildered*) Boots, sir? Is it me, sir? Not me, sir. Musta been someone else, sir.

Inspector (*shaking him furiously*) You, you, you!

2nd Man Me, sir? Never spit in public in me life, sir. Makin' a mistake, sir. Musta been someone else.

Rector Inspector Finglas! Remember you wear the King's uniform! Quiet, quiet, man!

Inspector (*subsiding*) Pardon me. I lost my temper. I'm more used to a blow from a stone than a dirty spit on my boot.

Rector (*shuddering a little*) Let us go from here. Things here frighten me, for they seem to look with wonder on our ease and comfort.

Inspector Frighten you? Nonsense – and with me!

Rector Things here are of a substance I dare not think about, much less see and handle. Here, I can hardly bear to look upon the same thing twice.

Inspector There you are, and as I've said so often, Breydon's but a neat slab of a similar slime.

Rector You wrong yourself to say so: Ayamonn Breydon has within him the Kingdom of Heaven. (*He pauses.*) And so, indeed, may these sad things we turn away from.

They pass out.

Eeada (*thinking of the coins given*) Two tiny sixpences – fourpence a head. Oh, well, beggars can't be choosers. But isn't it a hard life to be grindin' our poor bums to powder, for ever squattin' on the heartless pavements of th' Dublin streets!

Dympna Ah, what is it all to us but a deep-written testament o' gloom: grey sky over our heads, brown an' dusty streets undher our feet, with th' black an' bitther Liffey flowin' through it all.

Eeada (*mournfully*) We've dhrifted down to where there's nothin'. Younger I was when every quiet-clad evenin' carried a jaunty jewel in her bosom. Tormented with joy I was then as to whether I'd parade th' thronged sthreets on th' arm of a 16th Lancer, his black-breasted crimson coat a sight to see, an' a black plume droopin' from his haughty helmet; or lay claim to a red-breasted Prince o' Wales's Own, th' red plume in his hat a flame over his head.

Dympna It was a 15th King's Own Hussar for me, Eeada, with his rich blue coat an' its fairyland o' yellow braid, two yellow sthripes down his trousers, an' a red badg' an' plume dancin' on his busby.

Eeada Lancers for me, Dympna.

Dympna Hussars for me, Eeada.

Eeada An' what for you, Finnoola?

Finnoola What would a girl, born in a wild Cork valley, among the mountains, brought up to sing the songs of her fathers, what would she choose but the patched coat, shaky shoes, an' white hungry face of th' Irish rebel? But their shabbiness was threaded with th' colours from the garments of Finn Mac Cool of th' golden hair, Goll Mac Morna of th' big blows, Caoilte of th' flyin' feet, an' Oscar of th' invincible spear.

Eeada (*nudging Dympna*) That was some time ago, if y'ask me.

> *Brennan comes slowly over the bridge from the far side. His melodeon is hanging on his back. He looks around for a likely place to play. He leans against a parapet, some distance off, and unslings his melodeon from his back.*

Eeada Here's that oul' miser creepin' after coppers, an' some bank bulgin' with what he has in it already.

2nd Man (*waking suddenly, spitting out vigorously, and speaking venomously*) Rowlin' in th' coin o' th' realm – bastard! (*He sinks into a coma again.*)

Brennan (*giving himself confidence*) Evenin', ladies an' gentlemen. Good thing to be alive when th' sun's kind.

> *They take no heed of what he says. Brennan sighs; then plays a few preliminary notes on the melodeon to make sure it is in tune. He begins to sing in a voice that was once a mellow baritone, but now is a little husky with age, now and again quavering a little on the higher notes in the song.*

(*singing*)
> I stroll'd with a fine maid far out in th' counthry,
> Th' blossoms around us all cryin' for dew;
> On a violet-clad bench, sure, I sat down beside her,
> An' tuck'd up my sleeves for to tie up her shoe.
> An' what's that to anyone whether or no
> If I came to th' fore when she gave me th' cue?
> She clos'd her eyes tight as she murmur'd full low,
> Be good enough, dear, for to tie up my shoe.

Eeada (*with muttered indignation*) Isn't that outrageous, now; on a day like this, too, an' in a sober mood!

Dympna In front o' decent women as well!

1st Man (*waking up suddenly*) Disturbin' me dhreams of Golden Gandher gallopin' home to win in a canther!

Brennan (*singing*)
> Th' hawthorn shook all her perfume upon us,
> Red poppies saluted, wherever they grew,
> Th' joyous exertion that flaunted before me,
> When I tuck'd up my sleeves for to fasten her shoe.
> An' what's it to anyone, whether or no
> I learn'd in that moment far more than I knew,
> As she lifted her petticoat, shyly an' slow,
> An' I tuck'd up my sleeves for to fasten her shoe?

> The heathery hills were all dancin' around us,
> False things in th' world turn'd out to be thrue,
> When she put her arms round me, an' kiss'd me an'
>   murmur'd,
> You've neatly an' tenderly tied up my shoe.
> An' what's that to anyone whether or no,
> I ventur'd quite gamely to see th' thing through,
> When she lifted her petticoat, silent an' slow,
> An' I tuck'd up my sleeves for to tie up her shoe?

Some pennies have been thrown from the windows of

*the houses. Brennan picks them up, and taking off a
shabby, wide-brimmed hat, bestows a sweeping bow on
the houses. During the singing of the last verse of the
song, Ayamonn and Roory have strolled in, and have
listened to the old man singing while they leant against
the balustrade of the bridge. The scene has grown
darker as the old man is singing his song, for the sun is
setting.*

2nd Man (*waking up suddenly*) Off with you, old man,
thinkin' to turn our thoughts aside from th' way we are,
an' th' worn-out hope in front of us.

1st Man (*waking up – wrathfully*) Get to hell outa that,
with your sootherin' songs o' gaudy idleness!

Eeada Makin' his soul, at his age, he ought to be, instead
o' chantin' ditties th' way you'd fear what would come
upon you in th' darkness o' th' night, an' ne'er a sword be
your side either.

3rd Man Away with you an' your heathen songs to parts
renowned for ignorance an' shame!

Finnoola Away to where light women are plenty, an' free
to open purple purses to throw you glitterin' coins!

*Brennan slings his melodeon on to his back, puts his hat
back on his head, and wends his way across the bridge.*

Roory (*as he passes*) Isn't it a wondher, now, you
wouldn't sing an Irish song, free o' blemish, instead o' one
thickly speckled with th' lure of foreign enthertainment?

*Brennan heeds him not, but crosses the bridge and goes
out. The men and women begin to sink into drowsiness
again.*

Ayamonn Let him be, man; he sang a merry song well,
and should have got a fairer greeting.

Roory (*taking no notice of Ayamonn's remark – to the men and women*) Why didn't yous stop him before he began? 'Pearl of th' White Breasts', now, or 'Battle Song o' Munster' that would pour into yous Conn's battle-fire of th' hundhred fights. Watchman o' Tara he was, his arm reachin' over deep rivers an' high hills, to dhrag out a host o' sthrong enemies shiverin' in shelthers. Leadher of Magh Femon's Host he was, Guardian of Moinmoy, an' Vetheran of our river Liffey, flowin' through a city whose dhrinkin' goblets once were made of gold, ere wise men carried it with frankincense an' myrrh to star-lit Bethlehem.

Eeada (*full of sleep – murmuring low*) Away you, too, with your spangled memories of battle-mad warriors buried too deep for words to find them. Penny, here, each, th' ripe apples.

Dympna (*sleepily – in a low murmur*) Away, an' leave us to saunter in sleep, an' crave out a crust in the grey kingdom of quietness. Tuppence a bunch the fresh violets.

Finnoola (*sleepily*) Run away, son, to where bright eyes can see no fear, an' white hands, idle, are willin' to buckle a sword on a young man's thigh.

1st Man (*with a sleepy growl*) Get to hell where gay life has room to move, an' hours to waste, an' white praise is sung to coloured shadows. Time is precious here.

2nd and 3rd Men (*together – murmuringly*) Time is precious here.

Ayamonn Rouse yourselves; we hold a city in our hands!

Eeada (*in a very low, but bitter voice*) It's a bitther city.

Dympna (*murmuring the same way*) It's a black an' bitther city.

Finnoola (*speaking the same way*) It's a bleak, black, an' bitther city.

1st Man Like a batthered, tatthered whore, bullied by too long a life.

2nd Man An' her three gates are castles of poverty, penance, an' pain.

Ayamonn She's what our hands have made her. We pray too much and work too little. Meanness, spite, and common patterns are woven thick through all her glory; but her glory's there for open eyes to see.

Eeada (*bitterly – in a low voice*) Take your fill of her glory, then; for it won't last long with your headin' against them who hold the kingdom an' who wield th' power.

Dympna (*reprovingly*) He means well, Eeada, an' he knows things hid from us; an' we know his poor oul' mother's poor feet has worn out a pathway to most of our tumbling doorways, seekin' out ways o' comfort for us she sadly needs herself.

Eeada (*in a slightly livelier manner*) Don't I know that well! A shabby sisther of ceaseless help she is, blind to herself for seein' so far into th' needs of others. May th' Lord be restless when He loses sight of her!

Finnoola For all her tired look an' wrinkled face, a pure white candle she is, blessed this minute by St Colmkille of th' gentle manner, or be Aidan, steeped in th' lore o' Heaven, or be Lausereena of th' silver voice an' snowy vestments – th' blue cloak o' Brigid be a banner over her head for ever!

The Other Two Women (*together*) Amen.

Roory (*impatiently*) We waste our time here – come on!

Ayamonn Be still, man; it was dark when th' spirit of God first moved on th' face of th' waters.

Roory There's nothin' movin' here but misery. Gun peal an' slogan cry are th' only things to startle them. We're useless here. I'm off, if you're not.

Ayamonn Wait a moment, Roory. No-one knows what a word may bring forth. Th' leaves an' blossoms have fallen, but th' three isn't dead.

Roory (*hotly*) An' d'ye think talkin' to these tatthered second-hand ghosts'll bring back Heaven's grace an' Heaven's beauty to Kaithleen ni Houlihan?

Ayamonn Roory, Roory, your Kaithleen ni Houlihan has th' bent back of an oul' woman as well as th' walk of a queen. We love th' ideal Kaithleen ni Houlihan, not because she is false, but because she is beautiful; we hate th' real Kaithleen ni Houlihan, not because she is true, but because she is ugly.

Roory (*disgusted*) Aw, for God's sake, man! (*He hurries off angrily.*)

Eeada (*calling scornfully after him*) God speed you, scut!

Ayamonn (*placing a hand softly on Eeada's head*) Forget him, an' remember ourselves, and think of what we can do to pull down th' banner from dusty bygones, an' fix it up in th' needs an' desires of today.

> *The scene has now become so dark that things are but dimly seen, save the silver spire and the crimson pillar in the distance; and Ayamonn's head set in a streak of sunlight, looking like the severed head of Dunn-Bo speaking out of the darkness.*

Finnoola Songs of Osheen and Sword of Oscar could do nothing to tire this city of its shame.

Ayamonn Friend, we would that you should live a greater life; we will that all of us shall live a greater life. Our sthrike is yours. A step ahead for us today; another one for you tomorrow. We who have known, and know, the emptiness of life shall know its fullness. All men and women quick with life are fain to venture forward. (*To Eeada*) The apple grows for you to eat. (*To Dympna*) The violet grows for you to wear. (*To Finnoola*) Young maiden, another world is in your womb.

Eeada (*still a little gloomily*) Th' soldiers will be chasin' us with gunfire; th' polis hoppin' batons off our heads; our sons an' husbands hurried off to prison, to sigh away th' time in gloomier places than those they live in now.

Ayamonn Don't flinch in th' first flare of a fight. (*He looks away from them and gazes meditatively down the river.*) Take heart of grace from your city's hidden splendour. (*He points with an outstretched hand.*) Oh, look! Look there! Th' sky has thrown a gleaming green mantle over her bare shoulders, bordhered with crimson, an' with a hood of gentle magenta over her handsome head – look!

> *The scene has brightened, and bright and lovely colours are being brought to them by the caress of the setting sun. The houses on the far side of the river now bow to the visible world, decked in mauve and burnished bronze; and the men that have been lounging against them now stand stalwart, looking like fine bronze statues, slashed with scarlet.*

Ayamonn Look! Th' vans an' lorries rattling down th' quays, turned to bronze an' purple by th' sun, look like chariots forging forward to th' battle-front.

> *Eeada, rising into the light, now shows a fresh and virile face, and she is garbed in a dark green robe, with a silvery mantle over her shoulders.*

Eeada (*gazing intently before her*) Shy an' lovely, as well as battle-minded!

*Dympna rises now to look where Ayamonn is pointing.
She is dressed like Eeada, and her face is aglow. The
men have slid from the parapets of the bridge, turning,
too, to look where Ayamonn is pointing. Their faces are
aglow, like the women's, and they look like bronze
statues, slashed with a vivid green. Finnoola rises, last,
and stands a little behind the others, to look at the city
showing her melody of colours. Finnoola is dressed in a
skirt of a brighter green than the other two women, a
white bodice slashed with black, and a flowing silvery
scarf is round her waist.*

Finnoola She's glowin' like a song sung be Osheen
himself, with th' golden melody of his own harp helpin'!

1st Man (*puzzled*) Something funny musta happened, for,
'clare to God, I never noticed her shinin' that way before.

2nd Man Looka the loungers opposite have changed to
sturdy men of bronze, and th' houses themselves are gay in
purple an' silver!

3rd Man Our tired heads have always haunted far too
low a level.

Ayamonn There's th' great dome o' th' Four Courts
lookin' like a golden rose in a great bronze bowl! An' th'
river flowin' below it, a purple flood, marbled with ripples
o' scarlet; watch th' seagulls glidin' over it – like restless
white pearls astir on a royal breast. Our city's in th' grip o'
God!

1st Man (*emotionally*) Oh, hell, it's grand!

Eeada Blessed be our city for ever an' ever.

Ayamonn (*lifting his right hand high*) Home of th'
Ostmen, of th' Norman, an' th' Gael, we greet you! Greet
you as you catch a passing hour of loveliness, an' hold it
tightly to your panting breast! (*He sings.*)

Fair city, I tell thee our souls shall not slumber
Within th' warm beds of ambition or gain;
Our hands shall stretch out to th' fullness of labour,
Till wondher an' beauty within thee shall reign.

The Rest (*singing together*)
We vow to release thee from anger an' envy,
To dhrive th' fierce wolf an' sly fox from thy gate,
Till wise men an' matrons an' virgins shall murmur
O city of splendour, right fair is thy fate!

Ayamonn (*singing*)
Fair city, I tell thee that children's white laughter,
An' all th' red joy of grave youth goin' gay,
Shall make of thy streets a wild harp ever sounding,
Touch'd by th' swift fingers of young ones at play!

The Rest (*singing*)
We swear to release thee from hunger an' hardship,
From things that are ugly an' common an' mean;
Thy people together shall build a brave city,
Th' fairest an' finest that ever was seen!

*Finnoola has been swaying her body to the rhythm of
the song, and now, just as the last part is ending, she
swings out on to the centre of the bridge in a dance. The
tune, played on a flute by someone, somewhere, is that
of a Gavotte, or an air of some dignified and joyous
dance, and, for a while, it is played in fairly slow time.
After some time it gets quicker, and Ayamonn dances
out to meet her. They dance opposite each other, the
people around clapping their hands to the tap of the
dancers' feet. The two move around in this spontaneous
dance, she in a golden pool of light, he in a violet-
coloured shadow, now and again changing their
movements so that she is in the violet-coloured shadow,
and he in the golden pool.*

Eeada (*loudly*) The finest colours God has to give are all around us now.

Finnoola (*as she dances*) The Sword of Light is shining!

1st Man (*exultantly*) Sons an' daughters of princes are we all, an' one with th' race of Milesius!

The dance comes to an end with Ayamonn and Finnoola having their arms round each other.

Eeada Praise God for th' urge of jubilation in th' heart of th' young.

1st Man An' for th' swiftness of leg an' foot in th' heart of a dance.

2nd Man An' for th' dhream that God's right hand still holds all things firmly.

The scene darkens slightly. Ayamonn loosens his hold on Finnoola and raises his head to listen to something. In the distance can be heard the sound of many feet marching in unison.

Finnoola (*a little anxiously*) What is it you're listenin' to?

Ayamonn I must go; goodbye, fair maid, goodbye.

Finnoola Is it goin' to go you are, away from the fine things shinin' around us? Amn't I good enough for you?

Ayamonn (*earnestly*) You're lovely stayin' still, an' brimmin' over with a wilder beauty when you're dancin'; but I must go. May you marry well, an' rear up children fair as Emer was, an' fine as Oscar's son; an' may they be young when Spanish ale foams high on every hand, an' wine from th' royal Pope's a common dhrink! Goodbye.

He kisses her, and goes across the bridge, passing out of sight on the farther bank of the river. The figures left behind have shrunk a little; the colours have faded a

good deal, and all look a little puzzled and bewildered.
The loungers have fallen back to the walls of the houses,
and, though they do not lie against them, they stand
close to them, as if seeking their shelter. There is a fairly
long pause before anyone speaks. They stand apart, as if
shy of each other's company.

Eeada (*murmuringly*) Penny each, th' ripe apples. Who
was it that spoke that time? Jasus! I musta been dhreamin'.

Dympna (*in a bewildered voice*) So must I, th' way I
thought I was lost in a storm of joy, an' many colours,
with gay clothes adornin' me.

Finnoola (*puzzled and dreamy*) Dhreamin' I musta been
when I heard strange words in a city nearly smothered be
stars, with God guidin' us along th' banks of a purple
river, all of us clad in fresh garments, fit to make Osheen
mad to sing a song of the revelry dancin' in an' out of
God's own vision.

Eeada (*murmuringly, but a little peevishly*) For God's sake
give over dwellin' on oul' songs sung by Osheen, th' way
you'd be kindlin' a fire o' glory round some poor bog-
warbler chantin' hoarse ditties in a sheltered corner of a
windy street. (*very sleepily*) Th' dewy violets, here, on'y
tuppence a bunch – Jasus, apples I mean!

Now the tramp-tramp of marching men is heard more
plainly.

Dympna (*a little more awake*) Tuppence each, the bunch
of vio– What can that be, now?

1st Man (*gloomily, but with a note of defiance in his*
voice) Th' thramp of marchin' soldiers out to prevent our
meetin' an' to stop our sthrike.

2nd Man (*in a burst of resolution*) We'll have both, in
spite of them!

*The scene darkens deeply now. In the pause following
the 2nd Man's remark, nothing is heard but the sound
of the tramping feet; then through this threatening
sound comes the sound of voices singing quietly, voices
that may be of those on and around the bridge, or of
those singing some little distance away.*

Voices (*singing quietly*)
   We swear to release thee from hunger and hardship,
   From things that are ugly and common and mean;
   Thy people together shall build a great city,
   The finest and fairest that ever was seen.

   Curtain.

Act Four

Part of the grounds surrounding the Protestant church of St Burnupus. The grounds aren't very beautiful, for they are in the midst of a poor and smoky district; but they are trim, and, considering the surroundings, they make a fair show. An iron railing running along the back is almost hidden by a green and golden hedge, except where, towards the centre, a fairly wide wooden gate gives admittance to the grounds. Beyond this gateway, on the pathway outside, is a street lamp. Shrubs grow here and there, and in the left corner, close to the hedge, are lilac and laburnum trees in bloom. To the right is the porch of the church, and part of the south wall, holding a long, rather narrow window, showing, in coloured glass, the figures of SS Peter and Paul. Some distance away from the porch is a rowan tree, also in blossom, its white flowers contrasting richly with the gay yellow of the laburnum and the royal purple of the lilac. The rest of the grounds are laid out in grass, except for the path leading from the gateway to the entrance of the church. It is a warm, sunny evening, the Vigil of Easter, and the Rector is sitting on a deck-chair, before a table, on which are some books and papers. He is evidently considering the services that are to be held in the church on the following day.

The Rector is wearing a thick black cassock lined with red cloth, and at the moment is humming a verse of a hymn softly to himself, as he marks down notes on a slip of paper before him. A square black skull-cap covers his head.

Rector (*singing to himself, softly*)

As Thou didst rise from Thy grim grave,
So may we rise and stand to brave
Th' power bestow'd on fool or knave;
We beseech Thee!

*The verger comes out from the porch and walks
towards the Rector. He is bald as an egg, and his
yellowish face is parched and woebegone-looking. He is
a man of sixty, and shows it. His ordinary clothes are
covered with a long black mantle of thin stuff, with a
small cape-like addition or insertion of crimson velvet
on the shoulders.*

Rector (*noticing the verger beside him*) Hymn 625: we
must have that as our opening hymn, Samuel.

Samuel It's got to go in, sir.

Rector As you say – it's got to go in. Did you want to
speak to me, Samuel?

Samuel Excuse me, sir, for what I'm agoin' to say.

Rector (*encouragingly*) Yes, yes, Samuel, go on.

Samuel (*mysteriously*) Somethin's afther happenin', sir,
that I don't like.

Rector (*turning a little in his chair*) Oh! What's that,
Sam?

Samuel Mr Fosther was here this mornin' runnin' a hand
through th' daffodils sent for Easther, an' found somethin'
he didn't like.

Rector Yes?

Samuel It's not for me to remark on anything that
manoeuvres out in front o' me, or to slip in a sly word on
things done, said, or thought on, be th' pastors, masthers,
or higher individuals of th' congregation; but, sometimes,

291

sir, there comes a time when a true man should, must speak out.

Rector (*with a sigh*) And the time has come to say something now – what is it, Sam?

Samuel (*in a part whisper*) This mornin', sir, and th' dear spring sun shinin' through th' yellow robes of Pether an' th' purple robes o' Paul, an' me arrangin' th' books in th' pews, who comes stealin' in, but lo and behold you, Fosther an' Dowzard to have a squint round. Seein' they're Select Vesthrymen, I couldn't ask them why they were nosin' about in th' silence of th' church on an ordinary week-day mornin'.

Rector (*patiently*) Yes; but a long time ago, you said something about daffodils.

Samuel I'm comin' at a gallop to them, sir.

Rector Good; well, let's hear about the daffodils.

Samuel Aha, says I, when I seen th' two prowlers with their heads close together, whisperin', aha, says I, there's somethin' on th' carpet.

Rector Is what you have to tell me something to do with Dowzard and Foster, or the daffodils?

Samuel Wait till you hear; sometimes Fosther an' Dowzard'll be to th' fore, an' sometimes th' daffodils. What can these two oul' codgers be up to? says I, sidlin' up to where they were, hummin' a hymn.

Rector Humming a hymn? I'm glad to hear it; for I'd be surprised to hear either of them humming a hymn.

Samuel Me it was, sir, who was hummin' th' hymn; for in a church, I like me thoughts to go with th' work I'm doin', if you know what I mean.

Rector (*impatiently*) It'll be nightfall before you get to the daffodils, man.

Samuel Wait till you hear, sir. There I was gettin' close to them be degrees, when, all of a sudden, didn't Fosther turn on me, shoutin' 'Are you goin' to be a party to th' plastherin' of Popish emblems over a Protestan' church?'

Rector Popish emblems?

Samuel Th' daffodils, sir.

Rector The daffodils? But they simply signify the new life that Spring gives; and we connect them in a symbolic way, quite innocently, with our Blessed Lord's Rising. And a beautiful symbol they are: daffodils that come before the swallow dares, and take the winds of March with beauty. Shakespeare, Sam.

Samuel (*lifting his eyes skywards and pointing upwards*) Altogether too high up for poor me, sir. (*He bends down close to the Rector's ear.*) When he seen the cross o' daffodils made by Breydon, he near went daft.

   A pause, as if Samuel expected the Rector to speak, but he stays silent.

God knows what'll be th' upshot if it's fixed to the Communion Table, sir. (*Another slight pause.*) Is it really to go there, sir? Wouldn't it look a little more innocent on th' pulpit, sir?

Rector (*in a final voice*) I will place it myself in front of the Communion Table, and, if Mr Foster or Mr Dowzard ask anything more about it, say that it has been placed there by me. And, remember, when you say Mr Foster and Mr Dowzard, it's to be Mr Breydon too. (*He hands some leaflets to Samuel.*) Distribute these through the pews, Sam, please. The arranging of the flowers is finished, is it?

Samuel Yessir; all but the cross.

Rector I will see to that myself. Thanks, Sam.

Samuel goes off into the church, and the Rector, leaning back in his chair with a book in his hand, chants softly.

Rector (*chanting*)
May wonders cease when we grow tame,
Or worship greatness in a name;
May love for man be all our fame,
We beseech Thee!

As he pauses to meditate for a moment, Mrs Breydon is seen coming along, outside the hedge. She enters by the gate, and comes over to the Rector. Sheila has come with her, but lags a little behind when they enter the grounds. The Rector rises quickly from his chair to greet Mrs Breydon.

(*Warmly*) My dear Mrs Breydon! Hasn't it been a lovely day? The weather promises well for Easter.

Mrs Breydon It would be good if other things promised as well as the weather, sir.

Rector We must be patient, and more hopeful, my friend. From the clash of life new life is born.

Mrs Breydon An' often new life dies in th' clash too. Ah, when he comes, sir, speak th' word that will keep my boy safe at home, or here.

Rector (*laying a gentle hand on her arm*) I wish I could, dear friend; I wish I could.

Mrs Breydon His mind, like his poor father's, hates what he sees as a sham; an' shams are powerful things, mustherin' at their broad backs guns that shoot, big jails that hide their foes, and high gallows to choke th' young cryin' out against them when th' stones are silent.

Rector Let those safely sheltered under the lawn of the bishop, the miniver of the noble, the scarlet and ermine of the judge, say unto him, this thing you must not do; I won't, for sometimes out of the mouths of even babes and sucklings cometh wisdom.

Sheila If what's against him be so powerful, he is helpless; so let this power go on its way of darkened grandeur, and let Ayamonn sit safe by his own fireside.

To the left, on the path outside the hedge, the Inspector, in full uniform, appears, evidently coming to see the Rector; on the right, followed by the men and women of the previous scenes, appears Ayamonn. He and the Inspector meet at the gate. The Inspector and he halt. The Inspector indicates he will wait for Ayamonn to pass, and Ayamonn comes into the grounds towards the Rector. The Inspector follows, but, in the grounds, stands a little apart, nearer the hedge. The men and women spread along the path outside, and stay still watching those in the grounds from over the hedge. They hold themselves erect, now; their faces are still pale, but are set with seams of resolution. Each is wearing in the bosom a golden-rayed sun. Brennan comes in and, crossing the grass, sidles over to sit down on the step of the porch.

Rector (*shaking Ayamonn's hand*) Ah, I'm so glad you've come; I hope you'll stay.

Ayamonn (*hastily*) I come but to go. You got the cross of daffodils?

Rector Your mother brought it to us; it will hang in front of our church's greatest promise. Come and place it there with your own loyal hands, Ayamonn.

Inspector Loyal hands engaged in rough rending of the law and the rumpling-up of decency and order; and all for

what? For what would but buy blacking for a pair of
boots, or a sheet of glass to mend a broken window!

Brennan (*from his seat on the porch's step*) He's right,
Ayamonn, me son, he's right: money's the root of all evil.

Ayamonn (*to the Inspector*) A shilling's little to you, and
less to many; to us it is our Shechinah, showing us God's
light is near; showing us the way in which our feet must
go; a sun-ray on our face; the first step taken in the march
of a thousand miles.

Inspector (*threateningly*) I register a lonely warning here
that the people of power today will teach a lesson many
will remember for ever; though some fools may not live
long enough to learn it.

Mrs Breydon Stay here, my son, where safety is a green
tree with a kindly growth.

Men and Women (*in chorus – above*) He comes with us!

Sheila Stay here where time goes by in sandals soft, where
days fall gently as petals from a flower, where dark hair,
growing grey, is never noticed.

Men and Women (*above*) He comes with us!

Ayamonn (*turning towards them*) I go with you!

Inspector (*vehemently*) Before you go to carry out all your
heated mind is set to do, I warn you for the last time that
today swift horses will be galloping, and swords will be
out of their scabbards!

Rector (*reprovingly – to Inspector*) I hope you, at least,
will find no reason to set your horses moving.

Inspector (*stiffly*) I'll do my duty, sir; and it would be a
good thing if someone we all know did his in that state of
life unto which it has pleased God to call him.

Rector (*losing his temper*) Oh, damn it, man, when you repeat the Church's counsel, repeat it right! Not *unto which it has pleased God to call him*, but *unto which it shall please God to call him.*

Inspector (*losing his temper too*) Damn it, man, do you believe that what the fellow's doing now is the state of life unto which it has pleased God to call him?

Rector (*hotly*) I have neither the authority nor the knowledge to deny it, though I have more of both than you, sir!

The Inspector is about to answer angrily, but Sheila catches his arm.

Sheila Oh, cancel from your mind the harder things you want to say, an' do your best to save us from another sorrow!

Inspector (*shaking off Sheila's hand roughly, and going to the gateway, where he turns to speak again*) Remember, all! When swords are drawn and horses charge, the kindly Law, so fat with hesitation, swoons away, and sees not, hears not, cares not what may happen.

Mrs Breydon (*angrily – up to the Inspector*) Look at th' round world, man, an' all its wondhers, God made, flaming in it, an' what are you among them, standing here, or on a charging horse, but just a braided an' a tasselled dot!

The Inspector hurries off, to pause, and stands outside the hedge, to the right, the men and women shrinking back a little in awe to give him a passage.

(*To Ayamonn*) Go on your way, my son, an' win. We'll welcome another inch of the world's welfare.

Rector (*shaking his hand*) Go, and may the Lord direct

you! (*He smiles.*) The Inspector's bark is louder than his
bite is deep.

Ayamonn For the present – goodbye! (*Ayamonn hurries
away through the gate, pausing, outside the hedge to the
left, turning to give a last look at the Inspector.*)

Inspector Bear back, my boy, when you see the horsemen
charging!

> *He goes out by the right, and Ayamonn goes out left,
> followed by the men and the women. There is a slight
> pause.*

Rector (*briskly – to banish a gloomy feeling*) Now, Mrs
Breydon, you run along to the vestry, and make us a good
cup of tea – I'm dying for one. (*To Sheila*) You'll join us,
Miss Moorneen, won't you?

Sheila (*immediately anxious*) Oh no, thanks. I . . . I
shouldn't even be here. I'm a Catholic, you know.

Rector I know, and I'd be the last to ask you do anything
you shouldn't; but rest assured there's no canonical law
against taking tea made by a Protestant. Off you go, and
help Mrs Breydon. I'll join you in a moment.

> *Sheila and Mrs Breydon go off by the south wall of the
> church.*

Brennan (*as the Rector is gathering his books and papers
from the table*) Hey, sir; hey there, sir! It won't shatther th'
community at large this disturbance, will it, eh?

Rector I hope not.

Brennan (*with a forced laugh*) No, no, of course not.
Bank of Ireland'll still stand, eh? Ay. Ravenous to break in,
some of them are, eh? Ay, ay. Iron doors, iron doors are
hard to open, eh?

Rector (*going off to get his tea*) I suppose so.

Brennan Ay, are they. He supposes so; only supposes – there's a responsible man for you!

The verger comes into the porch and bends over Brennan.

Samuel (*in a hoarse whisper*) Come in an' have a decko at our grand cross.

Brennan Cross? What cross?

Samuel One o' daffodils for Easther, to be put in front of th' Communion Table.

Brennan Popery, be God!

Booing is heard a little distance away, followed by the rattling fall of a shower of stones.

What's that; what's happenin'?

Samuel (*going to back, and looking down the street*) A crowd flingin' stones; flingin' them at two men runnin' for their life.

Brennan (*nervously*) Let's get into the church, quick. Throuble's beginnin' already.

They both go into the church, and Samuel closes the door. A crowd can be heard booing. Men and women, among them Eeada, Finnoola, Dympna, the Railwaymen, and the Lurchers who were on the bridge, pass across outside the hedge. The Leader carries a red flag, and all march with determination. They are all singing the following song:

Leaders (*singing*)
If we can't fire a gun, we can fire a hard stone,
Till th' life of a scab shrivels into a moan;

Crowd (*chorusing*)
    Let it sink in what I say,
    Let me say it again –
    Though the Lord made an odd scab, sure. He also
       made men!

Leaders (*singing*)
    Th' one honour he'll get is a dusty black plume,
    On th' head of th' nag taking him to the tomb;

Crowd (*chorusing*)
    Let it sink in what I say,
    Let me say it again:
    Th' scab's curs'd be th' workers, book, candle an' bell!

*They cross over and disappear. After a pause, Dowzard
and Foster come running in; they hurry through the
gateway, and dash over to the church's porch.*

    *Dowzard is a big, beefy, red-faced man, rolls of flesh
pouring out over the collar of his coat. His head is
massive and bald, with jet-black tufts behind his ear, and
a tiny fringe of it combed across high over his forehead.
Foster is small and scraggy, with aggression for ever
lurking in his cranky face, ready to leap into full view at
the slightest opportunity. His cheeks and lips are shaven,
but spikes of yellowish whiskers point defiantly out from
under his chin. His voice is squeaky and, when it is
strengthened in anger, it rises into a thin piping scream.
Both are dressed in the uniforms of railway foremen,
blue cloth, with silver buttons, and silver braid on
Dowzard's peaked hat and coat-sleeves, and gold braid
on those of Foster. Both have their coats tightly buttoned
up on them. They take off their peaked caps and wipe
sweat from their foreheads. Dowzard pushes the door.*

Dowzard We're safe here in th' grounds; Church grounds
sacred. Unguarded, verminous villains – Papists, th' lot o'
them!

Foster (*venomously*) On' one o' their leaders a Select
Vestryman. On' thot domned Rector stondin' by him.
Steeped in Popery: sign o' th' cross; turnin' eastward sayin'
th' Creed; sung Communion – be Gud, it's a public
scondal!

Dowzard Some o' them stones scorched me ear passin' by.
We shouldn't have worn our uniforms. Gave us away. I
knew we were in for it when they called us scabs.

Foster Scobs themselves! Smoky, vonomous bastards! I
tull you I'd wear me uniform in th' Vutican. (*He unbuttons
his coat and shows that he is wearing a vivid orange sash,
bordered with blue.*) Thor's me sash for all tae see. You
should ha' stud with me, mon; stud like th' heroes o'
Dully's Brae!

Dowzard (*shouting and knocking at door*) Ey, there, in
there, come out, open th' blasted door an' help a half-dead
man!

*The church door is opened, and the Rector, followed by
Samuel and Brennan, comes out into the grounds.*

Rector What's wrong; what has happened?

Dowzard Th' Pope's bullies with hard stones have smitten
us sore. Honest men, virtuous an' upright, loyal to th' law
an' constitution, have this day been smitten sore with
Popish stones – oh, me poor head!

Foster St Bartholomew's Day's dawnin' again, I'm tullin'
yous, an' dismumbered Protestants'll lie on all th' sthreets!

Rector You can't be badly hurt when you complain so
grandly.

Foster Stand up for th' ruffians be makin' luttle of our
hurts, so do, ay, do. (*Noticing Brennan who has edged
towards the gate and is about to go away*) Eh, you, aren't

you goin' to stay an' put tustimony to the fullness o' th'
Protestan' feth?

Brennan (*with slight mockery*) Ay, I would, an' welcome,
if I hodn't to go, forbye, at this hour of on uvery day, I
mak' ut a rule tae be sturdy in th' readin' of a chapther o'
God's word so's I won't hold on tae worldly things too
strongly. (*He goes out.*)

Foster (*fiercely*) A jully-fush Protestant! (*To the Rector*)
Look see, I tull you th' fires o' Smithfield 'ull be blazin'
round Protestant bodies again, an' coloured lights 'ull be
shown in th' Vatican windows soon!

Dowzard An' we'll be th' first to go up in th' flames.

Rector (*laughing contemptuously*) Nonsense, oh, nonsense.

Foster (*almost screaming*) It's not nonsense, mon! Every
sable-robed Jesuit's goin' about chucklin', his honds
twitchin' to pounce out on men like me here, an' Eddie
Dowzard there, tae manacle us, head, hond, and fut, for
th' wheel, th' thumbscrew, an' th' rack, an' then finish us
up at th' stake in a hoppy Romish auto-dey-fey! The
Loyola boyos are out to fight another buttle with th' men
o' King Bully!

Rector (*amused*) Well, let the Loyola boyos and King
Bully fight it out between them. I'm too busy to join either
side. Goodbye.

Foster (*catching his arm as he is going – viciously*) You're
no' goin' tae be lut slide off like thot, now, with your
guilty conscience, mon. There's things to be done, and
things tae be ondone in yon church, there; ay, ay.

Rector (*quietly*) Indeed?

Foster (*angrily – to Dowzard*) Uh, speak, speak a word,
mon, on' don't leave ut all tae me.

Dowzard First, sir, we want you to get rid o' Breydon from the vesthry an' from th' church.

Rector Oh, indeed?

Foster (*almost screaming*) It's no' oh, indeed; answer th' question – plain yes or no!

Rector (*coldly*) Gentlemen, Mr Breydon stays in the Vestry till the parishioners elect someone else; as for the church, God has seen fit to make him a member of Christ, and it is not for me, or even for you, gentlemen, to say that God did wrong.

Dowzard (*sneeringly*) An' when did that wondherful thing hoppen?

Rector At his baptism, as you yourself should know.

Foster (*with an agonized squeal*) Popery, Popery, nothin' but Popery! Th' whole place's infusted with it!

The verger appears at the porch door with the cross of daffodils in his hand. It has a Keltic shape, the shafts made of the flowers, and the circle of vivid green moss. Samuel shows it to Dowzard, behind the Rector's back, and Dowzard sidling over, takes it from him, Samuel returning into the church again.

Rector And now be good enough, Mr Foster, to let my arm go.

In the distance, a bugle-call sounding the charge is heard. Foster lets go of the Rector's arm; and they all listen.

Foster (*gleefully*) Aha, there's the bugle soundin' th' charge, an' soon the King's horses an' th' King's men'll be poundin' th' riothers undher their feet! Law an ordher in th' State an' law an' ordher in th' Church we must have. An' we're fightin' here as they're fightin' there – for th' Crown an' ceevil an' releegious liberty!

The sound of galloping horses is heard, followed by several volleys of rifle-fire. They all listen intently for a few moments.

Foster (*gleefully*) Hear that now? Your Breydon fullow'll soon be doshin' in here for th' church to hide him.

Rector The cross of Christ be between him and all harm!

Dowzard (*dancing out in front of the Rector, holding out the cross – with exultant glee*) The cross – a Popish symbol! There y'urre, see? A Popish symbol flourished in th' faces o' Protestant people! (*With a yell*) Ichabod!

Foster (*venomously*) I'll no' stick it, no; I'll no' stick it. Look-see, th' rage kindlin' godly Luther is kindlin' me! Here, go, gimme a holt of thot. (*He snatches the cross of flowers from Dowzard, flings it on the ground, and dances on it.*) Th' bible on' th' crown! The twa on' a half, th' orange on' blue; on' th' Dagon of Popery undher our Protestant feet!

Dowzard (*wildly*) Th' dhrum, th' dhrum, th' Protestant dhrum!

While Foster and Dowzard have been dancing about and shouting their last few words, the men and women have run frightened along the path, behind the hedge. Those running from the right, turn, and run back to the left; those running from the left, turn, and run back to the left again, passing each other as they run. They suddenly see the men and women running about behind the hedge, and at once plunge into the porch, almost knocking the Rector down.

Foster (*as they fly – to the Rector*) Out uh th' way, mon, out uh th' way!

After a pause Eeada comes running through the gate, into the garden, over to the Rector.

Eeada (*beseechingly*) Oh, sir, please let me into the church, till all th' sthrife is over – no place's safe with the soldiers firin' an' th' police runnin' mad in a flourish o' batons!

Rector (*reassuringly*) Be calm, be quiet, they won't touch a woman. They remain men, however furious they may be for the moment.

Eeada Arra, God help your innocence! You should ha' seen them sthrikin' at men, women, an' childher. An' me own friend, Dympna, in hospital gettin' her face laced with stitches, th' way you'd lace a shoe! An' all along of followin' that mad fool, Breydon!

Rector Go in, then. (*To the verger, who has come to the entrance*) See her safe.

Eeada and the verger go into the church. Finnoola comes slowly along the path outside the hedge, holding on to the railings as she moves, step by step. When she comes to the gateway, she sinks down to the ground and turns a white and distorted face towards those in the grounds.

Finnoola (*painfully*) For th' love o' God, one of you tell me if th' Reverend something Clinton's here, or have I to crawl a long way further?

Rector (*hurrying over to her*) He's here; I'm he, my good woman. What is it you want of me?

Finnoola I've a message for you from Ayamonn Breydon.

Rector (*eagerly*) Yes, yes; where is he?

Finnoola He's gone.

Rector Gone? Gone where?

Finnoola Gone to God, I hope.

A rather long pause.

Rector (*in a low voice*) May he rest in peace! And the message?

Finnoola Yes. He whispered it in me ear as his life fled through a bullet-hole in his chest – th' soldiers, th' soldiers. He said this day's but a day's work done, an' it'll be begun again tomorrow. You're to keep an eye on th' oul' woman. He wants to lie in th' church tonight, sir. Me hip's hurt; th' fut of a plungin' horse caught me, an' I flat on th' ground. He sent a quick an' a long farewell to you. Oh, for Christ's sake, get's a dhrink o' wather! (*The verger runs for a drink.*) We stood our groun' well, though. (*The verger comes back with the water, and she drinks.*) Now I can have a thrickle of rest at last. (*She stretches herself out on the ground.*)

Rector Where did you leave him? Where is he lying now?

She lies there, and makes no answer. He picks up the broken cross of flowers and is silent for a few moments.

(*With head bent low – sorrowfully*) Oh, Ayamonn, Ayamonn, my dear, dear friend. Oh Lord, open Thou mine eyes that I may see Thee, even as in a glass, darkly, in all this mischief and all this woe!

The curtain comes down to indicate the passing of some hours. When it rises again, it is evening. The lamp over the porch door is lighted, and so is the church, the light shining through the yellow robe of St Peter and the purple robe of St Paul from the window in the church's wall. The church organ is playing, very softly, a dead march. The lamp on the path, outside the hedge, isn't yet lighted. The dark figures of men and women can be faintly seen lining themselves along the hedge. Mrs Breydon is standing in the grounds, near to the gateway. Foster and Dowzard stand on the steps of the porch. A little in front, with his back turned towards them, stands

the Rector, now with white surplice over his cassock, his
stole around his neck, and the crimson-lined hood of a
Doctor of Divinity on his shoulders. Sheila, holding a
bunch of crimson roses in her hand, stands under the
rowan tree. Partly behind the tree, the Inspector is
standing alone. A lamplighter comes along the path,
carrying his pole with the little flower of light in the
brass top. He lights the lamp on the path, then comes
over to peer across the hedge.

Lamplighter What's up? What's on? What's happenin'
here? What's they all doin' now?

1st Man Bringin' th' body o' Breydon to th' church.

Lamplighter Aw, is that it? Guessed somethin' was goin'
on.

1st Man He died for us.

Lamplighter Looka that, now! An' they're all accouthered
in their best to welcome him home, wha'? Aw, well, th'
world's got to keep movin', so I must be off; so long! (*He*
goes.)

Dowzard (*speaking to the Rector's back*) For th' last time,
sir, I tell you half of the Vestry's against him comin' here;
they don't want our church mixed up with this venomous
disturbance.

Rector (*without moving, and keeping his eyes looking*
towards the gateway) All things in life, the evil and the
good, the orderly and disorderly, are mixed with the life of
the Church Militant here on earth. We honour our
brother, not for what may have been an error in him, but
for the truth for ever before his face. We dare not grudge
him God's forgiveness and rest eternal because he held no
banner above a man-made custom.

Foster (*savagely*) Aw, looksee, I'm no' a mon to sut down on' listen to a tumblin' blether o' words – wull ye, or wull ye not, give intil us?

In the distance a bagpipe is heard playing 'Flowers of the Forest'. Mrs Breydon's body stiffens, and Sheila's head bends lower on her breast.

Rector It is a small thing that you weary me, but you weary my God also. Stand aside, and go your way of smoky ignorance, leaving me to welcome him whose turbulence has sunken into a deep sleep, and who cometh now as the waters of Shiloah that go softly, and sing sadly of peace.

As he is speaking, the lament ceases, and a moment after, a stretcher bier, bearing the covered-up body of Ayamonn, appears at the gateway. It is carried down towards the church, and the Rector goes to meet it.

(*Intoning*) Lord, Thou hast been our refuge from one generation to another. For a thousand years in Thy sight are but as yesterday. (*He chants.*)

All our brother's mordant strife
Fought for more abundant life;
For this, and more – oh, hold him dear.
Jesu, Son of Mary, hear!

Gather to Thy loving breast
Ev'ry laughing thoughtful jest,
Gemm'd with many a thoughtful tear.
Jesu, Son of Mary, hear!

When Charon rows him night to shore,
To see a land ne'er seen before,
Him to rest eternal steer.
Jesu, Son of Mary, hear!

The bier is carried into the church, and, as it passes, Sheila lays the bunch of crimson roses on the body's breast.

Sheila Ayamonn, Ayamonn, my own poor Ayamonn!

The Rector precedes the bier, and Mrs Breydon walks beside it, into the church, the rest staying where they are. There is a slight pause.

Dowzard We'd betther be goin'. Th' man's a malignant Romaniser. Keep your eye on th' rabble goin' out.

Foster (*contemptuously*) There's little fight left in thom, th' now. I'll no' forgive thot Inspector fur refusin' to back our demond.

They swagger out through the gateway and disappear along the path outside the hedge, as those who carried the bier come out of the church.

2nd Man That's the last, th' very last of him – a core o' darkness stretched out in a dim church.

3rd Man It was a noble an' a mighty death.

Inspector (*from where he is near the tree*) It wasn't a very noble thing to die for a single shilling.

Sheila Maybe he saw the shilling in th' shape of a new world.

The 2nd and 3rd Men go out by the gateway and mingle with the rest gathered there. The Inspector comes closer to Sheila.

Inspector Oughtn't you to go from this gloom, Sheila? Believe me, I did my best. I thought the charge would send them flying, but they wouldn't budge; wouldn't budge, till the soldiers fired, and he was hit. Believe me, I did my best. I tried to force my horse between them and him.

Sheila (*calmly*) I believe you, Inspector Finglas.

Inspector (*gently catching her by the arm*) Tom to you, dear. Come, Sheila, come, and let us put these things away from us as we saunter slowly home.

Sheila (*with a quiver in her voice*) Oh, not now; oh, not tonight! Go your own way, and let me go mine, alone tonight.

Inspector (*taking her hand in his*) Sheila, Sheila, be sparing in your thought for death, and let life smile before you. Be sparing in thought of death on one who spent his life too rashly and lost it all too soon. Ill-gotten wealth of life, ill-gone for ever!

Sheila (*withdrawing her hand from his gently*) Oh, Tom, I hope you're right; you are right, you must be right.

> *They have walked to the gateway, and now stand there together, the men and women along the hedge eyeing them, though pretending to take no notice.*

Inspector You'll see it clearer, dear, when busy Time in space has set another scene of summer's glory, and new-born spring's loud voice of hope hushes to silence th' intolerant dead.

Sheila (*musingly*) He said that roses red were never meant for me; before I left him last, that's what he said. Dear loneliness tonight must help me think it out, for that's just what he said. (*Suddenly – with violence*) Oh, you dusky-minded killer of more worthy men!

> *She runs violently away from him, and goes out, leaving him with the men and women, who stand idly by as if noticing nothing.*

Inspector (*after a pause*) What are ye doing here? Get home! Home with you, you lean rats, to your holes and haunts! D'ye think th' like o' you alone are decked with th' dark honour of trouble?

> *Men and women scatter, slowly and sullenly, till only Brennan, with his melodeon on his back, is left, leaning by the gate.*

(*To Brennan*) Heard what I said? Are you deaf, or what?

Brennan (*calmly*) I'm a Protestant, an' a worshipper in this church.

Inspector One of the elect! So was Breydon. Well, keep clear of unruly crowds – my men don't wait to ask the way you worship when they raise their arms to strike.

> *He goes slowly away down the path. A few moments pass, then the Rector and Mrs Breydon come out of the church. He arranges a shawl round her shoulders.*

Rector There; that's better! My wife insists you stay the night with us, so there's no getting out of it.

Mrs Breydon She's kind. (*She pauses to look at the rowan tree.*) There's th' three he loved, bare, or dhrenched with blossom. Like himself, for fine things grew thick in his nature: an' lather come from the berries, th' red berries, like the blood that flowed today out of his white body. (*Suddenly – turning to face the church*) Is it puttin' out th' lights he is?

Rector Yes, before he goes home for the night.

Mrs Breydon Isn't it a sad thing for him to be lyin' lonesome in th' cheerless darkness of th' livelong night!

Rector (*going to the porch and calling out*) Sam, leave the lights on tonight.

> *The church, which had dimmed, lights up again.*

He's not so lonesome as you think, dear friend, but alive and laughing in the midst of God's gay welcome. Come.

> *They slowly go through the gate and pass out. Samuel comes from the church and swings the outer door to, to lock up for the night. Brennan comes down into the grounds.*

Samuel (*grumbling*) Light on all night – more of his Romanisin' manoeuvres.

Brennan Eh, eh, there; houl' on a second!

Samuel What th' hell do you want?

Brennan Just to sing a little song he liked as a sign of respect an' affection; an' as a finisher-off to a last farewell.

Samuel (*locking the door*) An what d'ye take me for? You an' your song an' your last farewell!

Brennan (*giving him a coin*) For a bare few minutes, an' leave th' door open so's th' sound'll have a fair chance to go in to him.

The verger opens the door.

That's it. You're a kind man, really.

Brennan stands facing into the porch, the verger leaning against the side of it. Brennan unslings his melodeon, plays a few preliminary notes on it, and then sings softly.

A sober black shawl hides her body entirely,
Touch'd be th' sun an' th' salt spray of th' sea;
But down in th' darkness a slim hand, so lovely,
Carries a rich bundle of red roses for me!

The rest of the song is cut off by the ending of the play. Curtain.

RED ROSES FOR ME

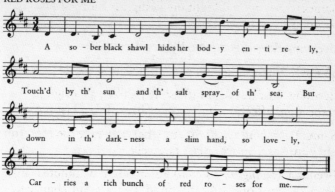

A so-ber black shawl hides her bod-y en-ti-re-ly,
Touch'd by th' sun and th' salt spray of th' sea; But
down in th' dark-ness a slim hand, so love-ly,
Car-ries a rich bunch of red ro-ses for me.

TH' BOULD FENIAN MEN

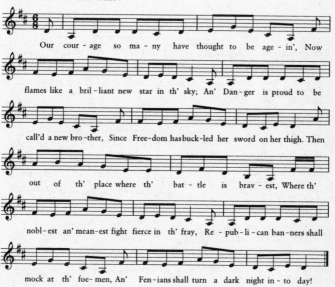

Our cour-age so ma-ny have thought to be age-in', Now
flames like a bril-liant new star in th' sky; An' Dan-ger is proud to be
call'd a new bro-ther, Since Free-dom has buck-led her sword on her thigh. Then
out of th' place where th' bat-tle is brav-est, Where th'
nobl-est an' mean-est fight fierce in th' fray, Re-pub-li-can ban-ners shall
mock at th' foe-men, An' Fen-ians shall turn a dark night in-to day!

SEAN O'CASEY

OH, QUEEN OF EBLANA'S POOR CHILDREN

Oh, Queen of Eb - la -na's poor child - ren, Bear swift - ly our woe a - way; An' give us a chance to live light - ly An hour of our life's_ dark day! Lift up th' poor heads ev - er bend - ing, An' light a lone star in th' sky, To show thro' th' dark - ness, de - scend - ing, A cheer - i - er way to die.

I TUCK'D UP MY SLEEVES

I stroll'd with a fine maid far out in th' coun - try, Th' blos - soms a - round us all cry - in' for dew;_ On a dai - sy deckt bench, sure, I sat down be - side her, An' tuck'd up my sleeves for to tie up her shoe. An' what's that to a - ny one wheth - er or no, If I came to th' fore when she gave me th' cue? She clos'd her eyes tight as she mur - mur'd full low, Be_ good e - nough, dear, for to tie up my shoe.___

RED ROSES FOR ME

FAIR CITY

Fair ci - ty,— I— tell thee our souls shall not slum - ber With -

- in th'— warm— beds of am - bi - tion or gain; Our

hands shall— stretch— out to th' full - ness of la - bour, Till

won - dher— an'— beau - ty with - in thee shall reign!

WE BESEECH THEE

As Thou didst rise from Thy— grim grave, So may we

rise to stand— and brave Th' pow'r be - stow'd on

fool— or knave.— We be - seech Thee!

THE SCAB

If we can't fire a gun, we can fire a hard stone, Till th' life of the

scab shriv - els in - to a moan. Let it sink in what I say, Let me

say it a - gain— Tho' th' Lord God made an odd scab He al - so made men!

BROTHERS

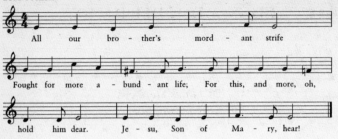

All our bro-ther's mord-ant strife
Fought for more a-bund-ant life; For this, and more, oh,
hold him dear. Je-su, Son of Ma-ry, hear!

COCK-A-DOODLE DANDY

*To James Stephens
the jesting poet
with a
radiant star
in's coxcomb*

Characters

The Cock

Michael Marthraun, a small farmer, now the owner of a lucrative bog

Sailor Mahan, once a sailor, now the owner of a fleet of lorries carrying turf from bog to town

Lorna, second young wife of Marthraun

Loreleen, Marthraun's daughter by his first young wife

Marion, helper in Lorna's house

Shanaar, a 'very wise old crawthumper', really a dangerous old cod

1st Rough Fellow } peasants working on the bog
2nd Rough Fellow }

Father Domineer, the parish priest of Nyadnanave

The Sergeant, of the Civic Guard

Jack, Mahan's foreman lorry driver

Julia, Lorna's sister, a paralytic on a visit to Lourdes

Her Father

One-eyed Larry, a peasant lad and potential sacristan

A Mayor

A Mace-bearer

The Messenger, in love with Marion

The Bellman, a kind of town crier

A Porter, of a general store in the nearby town

Scene One

*Part of the garden outside the house of Michael
Marthraun. It is rough and uncared-for, with tough
grass everywhere, sprinkled with buttercups and daisies.
It is surrounded by a stone wall, three to four feet high,
which is pierced by a wooden gate to the right of any
visitor entering the garden. To the left, a little way from
the gate, a clump of sunflowers, in full bloom, stand stiff
and stately, their blossoms big as shields, the petals
raying out widely and sharply, like rays from an angry
sun. Glancing farther to the left, a visitor would see the
gable-end of the house, with a porch jutting from it, and
a window above the porch. The porch is supported by
twisted pillars of wood, looking like snakes, which are
connected with lattice-work shaped like noughts and
crosses. These are painted a dazzling white. The
framework of the window above is a little on the skew,
and the sashwork holding the glass is twisted into
irregular lines. A little way from the porch, towards the
wall, is a dignified-looking bronze urn holding a stand-
offish, cynical-looking evergreen. Farther up, near the
wall, the Irish Tricolour flutters from a flagpole. The
house itself is black in colour, the sash and frame of the
window in it is a brilliant red.*

*It is a brilliantly fine day in summer, and as there is
nothing in the garden to provide a shade, the place is a
deep pool of heat, which, seemingly, has lasted for some
time, for the grass has turned to a deep yellow hue, save
where the house and porch throw a rich black shadow.
Stretching away in the distance, beyond the wall, is a bog
of a rich purple colour, dabbed here and there with black*

patches. The sky above it is a silvery grey, glittering like an Oriental canopy.

Some little distance away, an accordion is heard playing a dance tune, and, a few moments after, the Cock comes dancing in around the gable of the house, circles the dignified urn, and disappears round the farther end of the gable-end as the music ceases.

He is of a deep black plumage, fitted to his agile and slender body like a glove on a lady's hand; yellow feet and ankles, bright-green flaps like wings, and a stiff cloak falling like a tail behind him. A big crimson crest flowers over his head, and crimson flaps hang from his jaws. His face has the look of a cynical jester.

Michael Marthraun, followed by Sailor Mahan, comes into the garden by the porch. Each carries a kitchen chair, which they set down some way from the house. Michael is a man who is well over sixty years of age, clean-shaven, lean, and grim-looking. His lips twitch nervously whenever he forgets to keep his mouth tightly closed. He is dressed in a blackish tweed suit, and his legs are encased in black leggings. A heavy gold chain stretches across his waistcoat, and he wears a wide-leafed collar, under which a prim black bow is tied.

Sailor Mahan is a little over fifty, stouter than his companion, and of a more serene countenance. He has a short, pointed beard, just beginning to show signs of greyness. His face is of a ruddier hue, and shows that the wind and the stress of many storms have made it rugged, but in no way unpleasant. There is, maybe, a touch of the sea-breeze in his way of talking and his way of walking. He is wearing light grey flannel trousers, a double-breasted royal blue coat, and has a white scarf round his neck, over a light blue shirt. They come to the two chairs, and stand there facing each other.

Michael Come out here, come on out here, where a body

can talk free. There's whispers an' whispers in that house, upsettin' a man's mind.

Mahan (*puzzled*) Whispers? What kinda whispers?

Michael Sthrange kinds; whispers good for neither soul nor body.

Mahan But there's no one in the house but your wife, Lorna, Marion the maid, and your own girl Loreleen?

Michael Ay, so you think; but I know different.

Mahan (*breezily*) Nonsense, Mick; you're haulin' on a rope that isn't there!

Michael (*raising his voice*) You don't live in th' house, do you?

  Mahan is silent.

You don't live in th' house, do you?

Mahan (*raising his voice too*) I know I don't live in it, an' if it's like what you say, I don't want to live in it!

Michael Well, then, keep quiet when a man speaks of what he knows.

Mahan I know as much about a whisper as you do.

Michael You know about th' whispers of wind an' wave, harmless an' innocent things; but I'm talkin' about whispers ebbin' an' flowin' about th' house, with an edge of evil on them, since that painted one, that godless an' laughin' little bitch left London to come here for a long an' leering holiday.

Mahan Loreleen? Why, man, she's your own daughter by your first young wife!

Michael So it was said at th' time, an' so it's believed still; but I had me doubts then, and I've more doubts now. I

323

dhread meetin' her, dhread it, dhread it. (*With a frightened laugh*) Michael Marthraun's daughter! (*gripping Mahan's arm*) Is she anyone's daughter, man?

Mahan (*impatiently*) She must be somebody's daughter, man!

Michael (*impatiently*) Why must she be, man? Remember what th' Missioner said last night: Sthrange things are foisted by the powers of evil into th' life o' man. Since that one come back from England, where evil things abound, there's sinisther signs appearin' everywhere, evil evocations floatin' through every room.

Mahan (*puzzled*) What kinda evocation an' significality is there?

Michael (*looking suspiciously at the porch, then at the window above it, and drawing Mahan farther away from the house*) Looka, Sailor Mahan (*he speaks furtively*), there's always a stern commotion among th' holy objects of th' house, when that one, Loreleen, goes sailin' by; an invisible wind blows th' pictures out, an' turns their frenzied faces to th' wall; once I seen the statue of St Crankarius standin' on his head to circumvent th' lurin' quality of her presence; an' another time, I seen th' image of our own St Pathrick makin' a skelp at her with his crozier; fallin' flat on his face, stunned, when he missed!

Mahan (*doubtful, but a little impressed*) Good God, them's serious things, Michael Marthraun! (*Pause.*) Are you sure, now, Mick, you're not deludin' yourself?

Michael Have sense, man! An' me own wife, Lorna Marthraun, is mixin' herself with th' disordher, fondlin' herself with all sorts o' dismayin' decorations. Th' other day, I caught her gapin' into a lookin'-glass, an' when I looked meself, I seen gay-coloured horns branchin' from her head!

Mahan No! Oh, Mick, you're fancyin' things. Lorna's a fine, upstandin' woman, an' should be respected.

Michael Are you gone on her, too? I tell you, I seen the way th' eyes of young men stare at her face, an' follow th' movements of her lurin' legs – there's evil in that woman!

Mahan But there's nothin' evil in a pretty face, or in a pair of lurin' legs.

Michael Oh, man, your religion should tell you th' biggest fight th' holy saints ever had was with temptations from good-lookin' women.

Mahan (*getting nervous, and eager to change the subject*) Looka, let's sit down, an' thry to settle about what you're willin' to pay for th' cartage of th' turf.

Michael (*ignoring Mahan's attempt to change the tide of talk*) Up there in that room (*He points to the window above the porch.*) she often dances be herself, but dancin' in her mind with hefty lads, plum'd with youth, an' spurred with looser thoughts of love.

> *As he speaks, the sounds of a gentle waltz are heard, played by harp, lute, or violin, or by all three, the sounds coming, apparently, from the room whose window is above the porch.*

(*Bitterly*) There, d'ye hear that, man! Mockin' me. She'll hurt her soul, if she isn't careful.

Mahan She's young enough yet to nourish th' need o' dancin'. An' anyway, why did you insist on marryin' her, an' she so young; an' she so gay? She was all again' it herself.

Michael She consented to it, at last, didn't she?

Mahan Ay, when you, her father, an' th' priest had badgered th' girl's mind into disordered attention over th' catch she was gettin'.

Michael Oh, well you know, Sailor Mahan, that she had her blue eye on th' fat little farm undher me feet; th' taut roof over me head; an' th' kind cushion I had in th' bank, against a hard day.

Mahan I seen you meself throtting afther her from starboard to port, from poop to quarther-deck, hoistin' before her th' fancy of ribbon an' lace, silver-buckled shoes, an' a silk dhress for Sunday.

Michael An' what had she but a patched petticoat, a worn look, an' broken brogues to wear to Mass on Sundays? An' didn't I give her oul' fella fifty solid pounds so that her ailin' sisther could thravel to Lourdes to get undher th' aegis of th' Blessed Virgin? An' what did I get for them but a scraggy oul' bog of two hundhred acres?

Mahan An' you're makin' a good thing out of it since turf came into its own. It's made you a Councillor, a Justice of th' Peace, an' th' fair-haired boy of th' clergy.

Michael As you mentioned turf, we'd bether settle this question of you demandin', for carting it, an exthra amount I couldn't possibly pay.

Mahan (*stiffness coming into his voice*) You'll have to, Michael Marthraun, for it can't be done now for a cent less.

Michael We'll have a drink while we're discussin'. I have a bottle of th' best, ten years maturin', inside. Sit down there till I get it. (*He goes into the porch and, after a few moments, comes quickly out again, his mouth twitching, his voice toned to fear and hate.*) That one, Loreleen's comin' down th' stairs, an' I don't want to come too near her. We'll wait till she goes. Let's talk of our affairs, quietly, while she passes by. Th' thing to do, as Shanaar would tell you, when you hear a sound or see a shape of anything evil, is to take no notice of it. (*Whispering impatiently*) Sit down, man!

Mahan (*sitting down – dubiously*) Are you sure, Mick, you have a close-hauled comprehension of th' way you're thinkin'?

Michael Ay, am I sure; as sure as I am that a cock crows!

A cock suddenly crows lustily as Loreleen appears in the doorway of the porch. She is a very attractive young woman with an air of her own. A jaunty air it is, indicating that it is the sign of a handsome, gay, and intelligent woman. She is dressed in a darkish green dress, with dark red flashes on bodice and side of skirt. A saucy hat of a brighter green than the dress sports a scarlet ornament, its shape suggestive of a cock's crimson crest. Her legs – very charming ones – are clad in brown silk stockings; brown that flashes a golden sheen.

Michael, who has sat down, jumps startled to his feet at the sudden sound of the cock's crow and, stretching over the table, grips Mahan by the shoulder.

What's that, what's that?

Mahan (*startled by Michael's frightened movement*) What's what, man?

Michael (*trying to recover himself*) Nothin', I heard nothin'. What was it you were sayin'? (*In a whisper*) Get goin' on th' turf, man.

Mahan (*mystified, but doing his best*) You'll have to grant th' two shillin's additional on each load, Mick. I'd work me lorries at a loss if I took less. (*Placing an affectionate hand on Michael's shoulder*) An' you know well, you're such an oul' an' valued friend, I'd do it for affection's sake, if I only could.

Michael (*forgetting about Loreleen*) Don't I know that well, Sailor Mahan; an' I'd do th' same, an' more, be you;

327

but if I surrendhered two shillin's, I might as well give you th' bog as well. I have to live, Sailor Mahan.

Mahan Damn it, man, haven't I to live too? How th' hell am I goin' to give th' men a shillin' more without th' exthra two shillin's from you? Pray to th' saints to let them fall like rain from heaven, eh?

Michael (*putting his face closer to Mahan's, hotly*) Looka here, Sailor Mahan, you're not goin' to magicfy me into th' dhream of believin' you're not addin' every hurryin' week, a fine bundle o' notes to th' jubilant store you've there already, forcin' overtime on th' poor men o' th' bank, flickin' th' notes into imperial ordher.

Mahan (*as fiercely – standing up to say it, his face close to the face of Michael*) An' you yourself, Michael Marthraun, aren't worn away with th' punishment of poverty! Puttin' on a poor mouth, an' if you set out to count graciously all you have in hidlins, you'd be workin' many a long, glad day, without supper or sleep, be daylight an' candle-light, till your mind centhred on th' sum dominated be th' last note fluttherin' from your fingers!

Loreleen (*who has strolled slowly over to the gate, listening to the talk the while, turning at the gate to watch as well as listen*) Lay not up for yourselves treasures upon earth, where moth and rust doth corrupt, and where thieves break through and steal!

Michael (*in a frightened whisper*) Don't turn your head; take no notice. Don't pretend to hear her lyin' hallucinations!

> *A young, rough-looking Fellow, well-set and strong, comes running along the pathway to the gate. He is wearing dark brown corduroy trousers, belted at waist, grey shirt, and scarf of bright green, with yellow dots. He pushes Loreleen aside.*

1st Rough Fellow (*pushing Loreleen out of his way*) Outa me way, woman! (*He sees how charming she is as he swings her aside.*) Be God, but you're th' good-lookin' lass! What are you doin' in this hole?

Loreleen Seeking happiness, an' failing to find it.

1st Rough Fellow It isn't here you should be, lost among th' rough stones, th' twisty grass, an' th' moody misery of th' brown bog; but it's lyin' laughin' you should be where the' palms are tall, an' wherever a foot is planted, a scarlet flower is crushed; where there's levity living its life, an' not loneliness dyin' as it is here.

Loreleen (*dropping him a deep curtsy*) Thank you, sir knight, for th' silken compliments to your handmaiden.

She turns to go out, and the Rough Fellow hurries in through the gate, down to the two men.

1st Rough Fellow (*going through the gate down to where the two men are, and turning to speak up to Loreleen, still standing at the gate*) If you wait till I'm done with these fellas (*He indicates Michael and Mahan.*) I could go to th' bend o' th' road with you, for it's meself would surrendher a long spell of heaven's ease to go a long day's journey with a lass like you!

Another Rough Fellow hurries in along the pathway outside to the gate, pulling Loreleen aside when he finds her in his way. He wears light brown corduroy trousers, check shirt, and has a scarf of light yellow, with green stripes, round his neck.

2nd Rough Fellow (*pulling Loreleen out of his way*) Eh, there, woman – outa me way! (*He sees, as she swings around, how charming she is.*) Arra, what winsome wind blew such a flower into this dread, dhried-up desert? Deirdre come to life again, not to sorrow, but to dance! If

329

Eve was as you are, no wondher Adam fell, for a lass like you could shutther th' world away with a kiss! *(He goes through the gate, and down to the other men, pausing to look up at Loreleen again. To Loreleen).* Wait, lass, till I'm done with these fellas, an' I'll go with you till youth's a shadow a long way left behind!

Loreleen *(down to the two Rough Fellows)* I'm not for you, friends, for I'm not good for decent men. The two old cronies will tell you a kiss from me must be taken undher a canopy of dangerous darkness. *(She kisses a hand to them.)* Goodbye! *(She goes out.)*

Michael and Mahan *(together)* What d'ye th' two of yous want here? Why aren't yous at work?

1st Rough Fellow *(laying a hand sternly on the shoulder of Mahan)* Looka, you; you give us th' exthra shillin', or we leave your lorries standin', helpless an' naked on th' roads!

2nd Rough Fellow *(laying a hand sternly on Michael's shoulder)* Looka, you; looka that! *(He throws a cheque contemptuously on to the table.)* D'ye think a good week's wages is in a cheque for tuppence?

Michael You didn't work a week, because of th' rain, an' canteen contribution an' insurance brought your wage for the week to tuppence.

2nd Rough Fellow Tell me how I'm goin' to live a week on tuppence?

1st Rough Fellow Seein' th' both of them's Knights o' Columbanus, they should be able to say.

Michael That's a social question to be solved by th' Rerum Novarum.

2nd Rough Fellow Fifty years old; not worth much when

330

it was born, an' not worth a damn now. You give a guaranteed week, or th' men come off your bog! (*He goes off towards the gate.*)

1st Rough Fellow (*going to the gate – to Mahan*) Take our demand serious, or your lorries stand still on th' highways!

2nd Rough Fellow (*impatiently*) Looka, there she is! (*He points a finger in front.*) Let's hurry, an' we'll ketch up on th' fine, fair lady.

They hurry along the path, but suddenly stop to stare ahead.

1st Rough Fellow (*with awe in his voice*) What's happenin' to her? A cloud closin' in on her, flashes like lightning whirlin' round her head, an' her whole figure ripplin'!

2nd Rough Fellow (*frightened*) Jasus, she's changin' into th' look of a fancy-bred fowl! It's turnin' to face us; it's openin' its bake as big as a bayonet!

The crow of a cock is heard in the distance.

1st Rough Fellow (*frightened*) Here, man, th' other way for us! It's an omen, a warnin', a reminder of what th' Missioner said last night that young men should think of good-lookin' things in skirts only in th' presence of, an' undher th' guidance of, old and pious people.

The two of them hurry away in the opposite direction.

Michael (*to Mahan*) Did you hear that? I'm askin' you, Sailor Mahan, did you hear what them two graspin' rascals said?

Mahan I heard, but I can see no significality in it, unless th' two of them had dhrink taken.

Michael (*warningly*) Looka, Sailor Mahan, if you aren't careful, your wilful disbelief in things'll lead you asthray! Loreleen isn't me daughter; she isn't even a woman: she's either undher a spell, or she's a possessed person.

Mahan (*with contempt*) Aw, for God's sake, Mick, have sense, an' get that bottle o' whiskey out to put a spell on us.

Michael (*almost shouting*) Have you forgotten already th' case of th' Widow Malone who could turn, twinklin', into a dog or a hare, when she wanted to hide herself? An' how, one day, th' dogs followed what they thought was a hare that made for th' widow's cottage, an' dived through an open widow, one o' th' dogs snappin' a leg off before it could get through. An' when th' door was burst open, there was th' oul' witch-widow screamin' on her oul' bed, one leg gone, with blood spoutin' from th' stump, so that all th' people heard her last screechin' as she went sliddherin' down to hell!

Mahan I heard tell of it months after, when I come back from Valparaiso.

Michael Well, if you heard of it, you know it must have happened. An' here you are, thinkin' only of whiskey, and showin' how ready you are to ruin me be askin' more than I'm able to give. You, a good Christian, a Knight of St Columbanus, a student in th' Circle studyin' th' Rerum Novarum, you should show a sign of charity an' justice, recognizin' th' needs of th' people rather than your own. (*suddenly*) Here, I'll add thruppence, an' make th' offer ninepence. Hold out th' hand, an' clinch th' bargain.

Mahan I'll be scuppered if I will! You'll not use me like th' oul' father of th' good woman within, who sold you th' bog when he thought it was derelict, though you're makin' thousands out of it now.

Michael You forget I gave th' oul' cod enough to bring his other daughter to Lourdes for a cure!

Mahan You know th' way th' men are actin' now – goin' slow, an' doin' two journeys where they used to do three.

Michael An' aren't my men threatnin' to come off th' bog altogether? It's this materialism's doin' it – edgin' into revolt against Christian conduct. If they'd only judge o' things in th' proper Christian way, as we do, there'd be no disputes. Now let's be good sons of Columbanus – you thinkin' of my difficulties, an' me thinkin' of yours.

Mahan Make your offer one an' sixpence, an' I'll hoist th' pennant of agreement?

Michael I couldn't. Looka, Sailor Mahan, it would ruin me.

Mahan (*viciously*) You'd rather throw th' money after a tall-hat so that you could controvert yourself into a dapper disturbance th' time the president comes to view th' workin' of th' turf. Talk about Loreleen castin' a spell! Th' whole disthrict'll be paralysed in a spell when your top-hat comes out to meet the president's top-hat, th' two poor things tryin' to keep people from noticin' what's undher them! Two shillin's, now, or nothin'.

He sits down in disgust. Behind the wall, Shanaar is seen coming along the road; he opens the gate, and comes slowly down to where the two men are. He is a very, very old man, wrinkled like a walnut, bent at the shoulders, with longish white hair, and a white beard – a bit dirty – reaching to his belly. He is dressed peasant-wise, thin, threadbare frieze coat, patched blackish corduroy trousers, thick boots, good and strong, a vivid blue muffler round his neck, and a sack-cloth waistcoat, on which hangs a brass cross, suspended round his neck by twine. A round, wide-brimmed, black hat is on his head.

Shanaar (*lifting his hat as he comes in by the gate*) God save all here! God save all that may be in th' house, barrin' th' cat an' th' dog!

Michael (*with great respect*) An' you, too, Shanaar, old, old man, full of wisdom an' th' knowledge of deeper things.

Shanaar Old is it? Ever so old, thousands of years, thousands of years if all were told.

Michael Me an' Sailor Mahan here were talkin' some time ago, about th' sthrange dodges of unseen powers, an' of what the Missioner said about them last night, but th' easiness of his mind hasn't been hindhered.

Shanaar (*bending lower, and shoving his bearded face between the two men*) If it doesn't hindher th' easiness of his mind now, it will one day! Maybe this very day in this very place.

Michael (*to Mahan*) What d'ye say to that, now?

Mahan (*trying to be firm, but a little uneasy*) Nothin', nothin'.

Shanaar (*shoving his face closer to Mahan's*) Ah, me friend, for years an' years I've thravelled over hollow lands an' hilly lands, an' I know. Big powers of evil, with their little powers, an' them with their littler ones, an' them with their littlest ones, are everywhere. You might meet a bee that wasn't a bee; a bird that wasn't a bird; or a beautiful woman who wasn't a woman at all.

Michael (*excitedly*) I'm tellin' him that, I'm tellin' him that all along!

Mahan (*a little doubtfully – to Shanaar*) An' how's a poor body to know them?

Shanaar (*looking round cautiously, then speaking in a tense whisper*) A sure sign, if only you can get an all-round glimpse of them. (*He looks round him again.*) *Daemones posteriora non habent* – they have no behinds!

Michael (*frightened a lot*) My God, what an awe-inspiring, expiring experience!

Mahan (*frightened too, but trying to appear brave*) That may be, but I wouldn't put innocent birds or bees in that category.

Shanaar (*full of pitying scorn for ignorance*) You wouldn't! Innocent birds! Listen all: There was a cuckoo once that led a holy brother to damnation. Th' cuckoo's call enticed th' brother to a silent glade where th' poor man saw a lovely woman, near naked, bathin' her legs in a pool, an' in an instant th' holy man was taken with desire. Lost! She told him he was handsome, but he must have money if he wanted to get her. Th' brother entered a noble's house, an' demanded a hundhred crowns for his convent; but the noble was a wise old bird, an' said he'd have to see the prior first. Thereupon, th' brother up with an axe, hidden undher his gown, an' cleft th' noble from skull to chin; robbed th' noble, dhressed himself in rare velvets, an' searched out all th' rosy rottenness of sin with th' damsel till th' money was gone. Then they caught him. Then they hanged him, an', mind you (*the three heads come closer together*), while this poor brother sobbed on the scaffold, everyone heard th' mocking laughter of a girl and th' calling of a cuckoo!

> *As Shanaar is speaking the three last things, the mocking laughter of a girl is heard, the call of a cuckoo, and a young man's sobbing, one after the other, at first, then they blend together for a few moments, and cease. Shanaar stands as stiff as his bent back will allow, and the other two rise slowly from their chairs, stiff, too, and frightened.*

(*In a tense whisper*) Say nothing; take no notice. Sit down. Thry to continue as if yous hadn't heard!

Mahan (*after a pause*) Ay, a cuckoo, maybe; but that's a foreign bird: no set harbour or home. No genuine decent Irish bird would do a thing like that on a man.

Michael Looka here, Sailor Mahan, when th' powers of evil get goin', I wouldn't put anything past an ordinary hen!

Shanaar An' you'd be right, Mr Marthraun, though, as a rule, hens is always undher th' eye an' comprehension of a Christian. Innocent-looking things are often th' most dangerous. Looka th' lad whose mother had set her heart on him bein' a priest, an' one day, at home, he suddenly saw a corncrake flyin' into a house be an open window. Climbin' in afther it, he spied a glittherin' brooch on a table, an' couldn't resist th' temptation o' thievin' it. That lad spent th' next ten years in a reformatory; his mother died of a broken heart, and his father took to dhrink.

During the recital of Shanaar's story, the 'crek crek, crek crek' of a corncrake is heard.

Michael (*in a tense whisper – to Mahan*) D'ye hear that, Sailor Mahan?

Shanaar (*warningly*) Hush! Take no vocal notice. When yous hear anything or see anything suspicious, give it no notice, unless you know how to deal with it.

Michael (*solemnly*) A warnin' we'll remember. But supposin' a hen goes wrong, what are we to do?

Shanaar (*thoughtfully*) It isn't aysey to say, an' you have to go cautious. The one thing to do, if yous have the knowledge, is to parley with th' hens in a Latin dissertation. If among th' fowl there's an allusion of a hen from Gehenna, it won't endure th' Latin. She can't face th'

Latin. Th' Latin downs her. She tangles herself in a helluva disordher. She busts asundher, an' disappears in a quick column of black an' blue smoke, a thrue ear ketchin' a screech of agony from its centre!

Michael (*tremendously impressed*) Looka that now. See what it is to know!

A commotion is heard within the house: a loud cackling, mingled with a short, sharpened crow of a cock; the breaking of a delf; the half-angry, half-frightened cries of women. A cup, followed by a saucer, flies out through the open window, over the porch, past the heads of the three men, who duck violently, and then crouch, amazed, and a little frightened.

What th' hell's happenin' now?

Marion rushes to the door of the porch, frightened and alarmed. She is a young girl of twenty or so, and very good-looking. Her skirts come just to her knees, for they are nice legs, and she likes to show them – and why shouldn't she? And when she does so, she can add the spice of a saucy look to her bright blue eyes. Instead of the usual maid's cap, she wears a scarf-bandeau round her head, ornamented with silver strips, joined in the centre above her forehead, with an enamelled stone, each strip extending along the bandeau as far as either ear. She wears a dark green uniform, flashed with a brighter green on the sleeves and neck, and the buttons of the bodice are of the same colour. Her stockings and shoes are black. A small, neat, white apron, piped with green, protects her uniform.

Marion (*excitedly – to the men*) It's flyin' about th' house, an' behavin' outrageous! I guessed that that Loreleen's cluck, cluck, cluckin' would upset th' bird's respectable way of livin'!

Michael (*frightened*) What's wrong with you, girl; what's up?

Marion Will one of yous come in, an' ketch it, for God's sake, before it ruins th' house?

Mahan (*shouting*) Ketch what, ketch what, woman?

Marion A wild goose! It's sent th' althar light flyin'; it's clawed the holy pictures; an' now it's peckin' at th' tall-hat!

Michael A wild goose? Are you sure it was a wild one?

Marion (*in great distress*) I dunno, I dunno – maybe it's a wild duck. It's some flyin' thing tearin' th' house asundher.

Michael (*trembling – to Shanaar*) D'ye think it might be what you know?

Shanaar (*his knees shaking a little*) It might be, Mr Marthraun! it might be, God help us!

Mahan (*nervous himself*) Keep your heads, keep your heads! It's nothin'.

Michael (*beside himself with anxiety and dread – shaking Marion roughly by the shoulders*) Conthrol yourself, girl, an' speak sensibly. Is it a goose or a duck or a hen, or what is it?

Marion (*wildly*) It's a goose – no, it's a hen, it must be a hen! We thried to dhrive it out with flyin' cups and flyin' saucers, but it didn't notice them. Oh, someone should go in, or it'll peck th' place to pieces!

Shanaar (*prayerfully*) So long as it's not transmuted, so long as it's not been transmuted!

Michael (*shaking Marion again*) Where's Lorna, where's Lorna?

Marion (*responding to the shaking listlessly*) Last I seen of her, she was barricadin' herself undher th' banisters!

Michael (*pleadingly – to Mahan*) You've been free with whales an' dolphins an' octopususas, Sailor Mahan – you run in, like a good man, an' enthrone yourself on top of th' thing!

Mahan (*indignant*) Is it me? I'm not goin' to squandher meself conthrollin' live land-fowl!

Michael (*to Shanaar – half-commandingly*) In case it's what we're afraid of, you pop in, Shanaar, an' liquidate whatever it is with your Latin.

Shanaar (*backing towards the wall*) No good in th' house: it's effective only in th' open air.

Michael (*in a fury – to Marion – pushing her violently towards the gate*) You go, you gapin', frightened fool, an' bring Father Domineer quick!

All this time, intermittent cackling has been heard, cackling with a note of satisfaction, or even victory in it, interspersed with the whirring sound of wings.

As Marion rushes out through the gate, she runs into the arms of the Messenger, who carries a telegram in his hand. He clasps Marion tight in his arms, and kisses her. He wears a silvery-grey coat, buttoned over his breast, and trousers. On the right side of the coat is a flash of a pair of scarlet wings. A bright green beret is set jauntily on his head and he is wearing green-coloured sandals.

Michael and Mahan have moved farther from the house, and Shanaar has edged to the gateway, where he stares at the house, ready to run if anything happens. His hands are piously folded in front of him, and his lips move as if he prayed.

Messenger (*to Marion*) Ah, lovely one of grace an'

gladness, whose kiss is like a honied flame, where are you rushin' to in such a hurry?

Michael (*angrily – up to the Messenger*) Let her go, you – she's runnin' for th' priest!

Messenger Th' priest – why?

The cackling breaks into intensity, the whirring of wings becomes louder, and a plate flies out through the window, followed by a squeal from Lorna.

(*Astonished, but not startled*) What's goin' on in th' house?

Michael There's a wild goose, or somethin', asthray in th' house, an' it's sent th' althar bowl flyin'!

Marion An' it's peckin' th' holy pictures hangin' on th' walls.

Mahan Some think it's a wild duck.

Shanaar It may be a hen, only a hen.

Messenger (*releasing Marion, and handing the telegram to Michael*) Here's a telegram for you.

Michael takes it mechanically, and stuffs it in a pocket.

Is it losin' your senses yous are to be afraid of a hen? (*He goes towards the porch.*) I'll soon settle it!

Shanaar (*who is now outside, behind the wall*) If you value your mortal life, lad, don't go in, for th' hen in there isn't a hen at all!

Messenger If th' hen, that isn't a hen, in there, isn't a hen, then it must be a cock. I'll settle it! (*He rushes into the house.*)

Michael (*in agony*) If it's a cock, we're done!

Shanaar (*fervently*) Oh, *rowelum randee, horrida aidus, sed spero spiro specialii spam*!

> *The head of the Cock, with its huge, handsome crimson comb, is suddenly thrust through the window above the porch, and lets out a violent and triumphant crow. Shanaar disappears behind a wall, and Mahan and Michael fall flat in the garden, as if in a dead faint.*

Michael (*as he is falling*) Holy saints preserve us – it's th' Cock!

Shanaar (*from behind the wall*) Oh, *dana eirebus, heniba et galli scatterum in multus parvum avic asthorum*!

> *The Cock's head is as suddenly withdrawn, and a louder commotion is heard to be going on in the house; the Messenger shouting, a Woman's squeal. Then silence for a few moments as puffs of blue-black smoke jet out through the window. When the smoke has gone, the Messenger comes from the house into the garden. His cap is awry on his head, his face is a little flushed, and his mouth is smiling. He carries in his right hand what might have been a broomstick, but is now a silver staff, topped with a rosette of green and red ribbons. He is followed out by the Cock whom he is leading by a green ribbon, the other end circling the Cock's neck. The Cock follows the Messenger meekly, stopping when he stops, and moving when the Messenger moves.*

(*Peeping over the wall*) Boys an' girls, take no notice of it, or you're done! Talk only of th' first thing entherin' your minds.

Messenger (*looking with astonishment at the two men sitting up now on the ground, as far as possible from the house, and moving away when the Cock comes nearer*) What's th' matther with yous? Why are yous dodgin' about on your bums? Get up, get up, an' be sensible.

*Michael and Mahan scramble to their feet, hurry out
through the gate, and stand, warily, beside Shanaar.
Lorna's head appears at the window above the porch,
and it is at once evident that she is much younger than
her husband, very good-looking still, but the bright and
graceful contours of her face are somewhat troubled by
a vague aspect of worry and inward timidity. Her face
shows signs of excitement, and she speaks rather loudly
down to the Messenger.*

Lorna (*to the Messenger*) Robin Adair, take that bird
away at once. Hand him over to th' Civic Guard, or
someone fit to take charge of him.

Messenger (*up to Lorna*) Looka, lovely lady, there's no
danger, an' there never was. He was lonely, an' was only
goin' about in quest o' company. Instead of shyin' cups an'
saucers at him, if only you'd given him your lily-white
hand, he'd have led you through a wistful an' wondherful
dance. But you frightened th' poor thing!

Lorna Frightened him, is it? It was me was frightened
when I seen him tossin' down delf, clawin' holy pictures,
and peckin' to pieces th' brand new tall-hat that Mr
Marthraun bought to wear, goin' with the Mayor to meet
His Brightness, th' President of Eire, comin' to inaugerate
th' new canteen for th' turf workers.

Michael (*enraged*) Is it me new hat he's desthroyed?

Shanaar (*pulling Michael's arm in warning*) Damnit, man,
take no notice!

Michael (*turning indignantly on Shanaar*) How'd you like
your sumptuous, silken hat to be mangled into a
monstrosity!

Shanaar (*with concentrated venom*) Hush, man, hush!

Marion (*who has been looking at the Cock with*

admiration) Sure, he's harmless when you know him.

Messenger (*stroking its back*) 'Course he is! Just a gay bird, that's all. A bit unruly at times, but conthrollable be th' right persons. (*To the Cock*) Go on, comrade, lift up th' head an' clap th' wings, black cock, an' crow!

The Cock lifts up his head, claps his wings, and lets out a mighty crow, which is immediately followed by a rumbling roll of thunder.

Michael (*almost in a state of collapse*) Aw, we're done for!

Shanaar (*violently*) No notice, no notice!

Lorna (*from the window*) God bless us, what's that? (*down to the Messenger*) Robin, will you take that damned animal away, before things happen that God won't know about!

Messenger (*reassuringly – up to Lorna*) Lovely lady, you can let your little hands lie with idle quietness in your lap, for there's no harm in him beyond gaiety an' fine feelin'. (*To the Cock*) You know th' goose-step done be the Irish Militia in th' city of Cork more'n a hundhred years ago? Well, we'll go home doin' it, to show there's nothing undher th' sun Ireland didn't know, before th' world sensed it. Ready? One, two – quick march!

The Messenger and the Cock march off doing the goose-step. Marion follows them, imitating the step, as far as the end of the garden; then she stands looking after them, waving them farewell. Michael and Mahan come slowly and stealthily into the garden as the Cock goes out. They go to the chairs, on which they sit, exhausted, wiping their foreheads with their handkerchiefs. Shanaar comes towards them more slowly, keeping an eye in the direction taken by the Cock and the Messenger. When the place is clear, he anchors himself behind the table.

Lorna (*down to Marion*) Marion, dear, come on in, an'
help me to straighten things up a little. (*She goes away
from the window.*)

Marion (*going slowly towards the house, after having
given a last farewell – gleefully*) Wasn't it a saucy bird! An'
th' stately way he done th' goose-step! (*She playfully
shakes Michael's shoulder.*) Did you see it, sir?

   Michael takes no notice.

God forgive me, but it gave us all an hilarious time –
didn't it, sir?

Michael (*coldly*) Your misthress called you.

Marion I heard her, sir. What a clatther it all made! An'
yous all quakin', an' even Sailor Mahan there, shakin' in
his shoes, sure it was somethin' sinisther!

Mahan (*angrily*) You go in to your misthress, girl!

Marion (*giggling*) Th' bould sailor lad! An' he gettin'
rocked in th' cradle of th' deep! Me faltherin' tongue can't
impart th' fun I felt at seein' yous all thinkin' th' anchor
was bein' weighed for th' next world!

Michael (*loudly*) Go to your misthress when you're told.

Marion (*giggling more than ever*) An' oul' dodderin'
Shanaar, there, concoctin' his Latin, an' puttin' th' wall
between himself an' th' blast! Well, while yous sit all alone
there in th' gloamin', yous won't be in heart for singin'.
(*She chants.*) 'Only to see his face again, only to hear him
crow!' (*She runs in merrily.*)

Shanaar (*warily – in a warning whisper*) Watch that one!

Michael Th' ignorant, mockin', saucy face of her afther us
bein' in danger of thransportation to where we couldn't
know ourselves with agony an' consternation!

Shanaar (*fervently*) Sweet airs of heaven be round us all! Watch that one, Mr Marthraun. Women is more flexible towards th' ungodly than us men, an' well th' old saints knew it. I'd recommend you to compel her, for a start, to lift her bodice higher up, an' pull her skirt lower down; for th' circumnambulatory nature of a woman's form often has a detonatin' effect on a man's idle thoughts.

Michael (*pensively*) How thrue, how thrue that is!

Shanaar What we have to do now, is to keep thought from dwellin' on th' things seen an' heard this day; for dwellin' on it may bring th' evil back again. So don't let any thought of it, *ab initio extensio*, remain in your minds, though, as a precaution, when I'm passin' th' barracks, I'll acquaint the Civic Guard. Now I must be off, for I've a long way to thravel. (*He goes as far as the gate, and returns.*) Mr Marthraun, don't forget to have th' room, where th' commotion was manifested, *turbulenta concursio cockolorum*, purified an' surified be an understandin' clergyman. Goodbye. (*Again he goes as far as the gate, and returns.*) Be on your guard against any unfamiliar motion or peculiar conspicuosity or quasimodical addendum, perceivable in any familiar thing or creature common to your general recognizances. A cat barkin' at a dog, or a dog miaouin' be a fire would atthract your attention, give you a shock, but don't, for th' love of God, notice it! It's this scourge of materialism sweepin' th' world, that's incantatin' these evils to our senses and our doorsteps.

Mahan (*pensively*) That's th' way th' compass is pointin', Shanaar – everyone only thinkin', thinkin' of himself.

Shanaar An' women's wily exhilarations are abettin' it, so that a man's measure of virtue is now made with money, used to buy ornaments, bestowed on girls to give a gaudy outside to the ugliness of hell.

Michael (*fervently*) Oh, how thrue, how thrue that is!

Shanaar An' th' coruscatin' conduct in th' dance-halls is completin' th' ruin.

Mahan (*solemnly*) Wise words from a wiser man! Afther a night in one of them, there isn't an ounce of energy left in a worker!

Shanaar (*whispering*) A last warnin' – Don't forget that six thousand six hundhred an' sixty-six evil spirits can find ready lodgin's undher th' skin of a single man!

Michael (*horrified*) What an appallin' thought!

Shanaar So be on your guard. Well, goodbye.

Michael (*offering him a note*) Here's a pound to help you on your way.

Shanaar (*setting the note aside*) No, thanks. If I took it, I couldn't fuse th' inner with th' outher vision; I'd lose th' power of spiritual scansion. If you've a shillin' for a meal in th' town till I get to the counthry, where I'm always welcome, I'll take it, an' thank you.

   Michael gives him a shilling.

Thank you kindly. (*He goes out through the gate, and along the pathway outside. Just as he is about to disappear, he faces towards the two men, and stretches out a hand in a gesture of blessing. Fervently*) Ab tormentum sed absolvo, non revolvo, cockalorum credulum hibernica!

Michael (*with emotion*) You, too, Shanaar, oul' son; you too!

   Shanaar goes off.

Mahan (*after a pause – viciously*) That Latin-lustrous oul' cod of a prayer-blower is a positive danger goin' about th' counthry!

346

Michael (*startled and offended*) Eh? I wouldn't go callin' him a cod, Sailor Mahan. A little asthray in a way, now an' again, but no cod. You should be th' last to call th' man a cod, for if it wasn't for his holy Latin aspirations, you mightn't be here now.

Mahan (*with exasperation*) Aw, th' oul' fool, pipin' a gale into every breeze that blows! I don't believe there was ever anything engenderogically evil in that cock as a cock, or denounceable either! Lardin' a man's mind with his killakee Latin! An' looka th' way he slights th' women. I seen him lookin' at Lorna an' Marion as if they'd horns on their heads!

Michael (*doubtfully*) Maybe he's too down on th' women, though you have to allow women is temptin'.

Mahan They wouldn't tempt man if they didn't damn well know he wanted to be tempted!

Michael Yes, yes; but we must suffer th' temptation accordin' to the cognizances of th' canon law. But let's have a dhrink, for I'm near dead with th' drouth, an' we can sensify our discussion about th' increased price you're demandin' for carryin' th' turf; though, honest to God, Sailor Mahan, I can't add a ha'penny more to what I'm givin'.

Mahan A dhrink would be welcome, an' we can talk over th' matter, though, honest to God, Michael Marthraun, blast th' penny less I'll take than what I'm askin'.

Michael (*going to the porch, and shouting into the house*) Marion, bring th' bottle of ten years' maturin', an' two glasses! (*He returns.*) It's th' principle I'm thinkin' of.

Mahan That's what's throublin' me, too.

Marion comes in with the bottle of whiskey and the two glasses. She places them on the table, getting between the two men to do so.

347

(*Reading the label*) Flanagan's First! Nyav na Nyale – th' heaven of th' clouds! An' brought be a lass who's a Flanagan's first too!

Marion (*in jovial mood*) G'long with you – you an' your blarney!

Michael (*enthusiastically*) Had you lived long ago, Emer would have been jealous of you! (*He playfully pinches her bottom.*)

Marion (*squealing*) Ouch! (*She breaks away, and makes for the porch.*) A pair o' naughty men! (*She goes into the house.*)

Michael (*calling after her*) I forgot th' soda, Marion; bring th' siphon, lass.

Mahan (*complacently*) I could hold that one in me arms for a long time, Mick.

Michael Th' man would want to be dead who couldn't.

Mahan (*enthusiastically*) I'd welcome her, even if I seen her through th' vision of oul' Shanaar – with horns growin' out of her head!

> *Marion returns with the siphon which she places on the table. The two men, looking in front of them, have silly, sly grins on their faces.*
>   *The ornament, which Marion wears round her head, has separated into two parts, each of which has risen over her head, forming two branching horns, apparently sprouting from her forehead. The two men, shyly gazing in front, or at the table, do not see the change. Marion's face has changed too, and now seems to wear a mocking, cynical look, fitting the aspect of her face to the horns.*

Marion (*joking*) Two wild men – it's afraid I am to come near yous.

Michael puts his right arm round her waist, and Mahon his left one.

Mahan (*slyly*) What about a kiss on your rosy mouth, darlin', to give a honied tang to th' whiskey?

Michael An' one for me, too?

Marion (*with pretended demureness*) A thrue gentleman'll rise up an' never expect a thrue lady to bend down for a kiss. (*With vigour*) Up an' take it, before yous grow cold!

They rise from their chairs, foolish grins on their faces, settle themselves for a kiss, and then perceive the change that has taken place. They flop back on to the chairs, fright and dismay sweeping over their faces.

Mahan and Michael (*together*) Good God!

They slump in the chairs, overcome, their hands folded in front of their chests, palm to palm, as if in prayer. Marion looks at them in some astonishment.

Marion What ails yous? Was th' excitement too much for yous, or what?

Michael (*plaintively*) Saints in heaven help us now!

Marion What's come over yous? Th' way yous slumped so sudden down, you'd think I'd horns on me, or somethin'!

Michael (*hoarsely*) G'way, g'way! Shanaar, Shanaar, where are you now!

Marion (*going over to Mahan, and putting an arm round his neck*) What about you, gay one?

Mahan (*gurgling with fright*) You're sthranglin' me! G'way, g'way, girl!

Marion Looka, a kiss would do yous good. Yous think too much of th' world!

Mahan (*chokingly*) St Christopher, mainstay of mariners, be with me now!

Lorna thrusts her head out from the window over the porch.

Lorna (*down to Marion*) Let them two oul' life-frighteners fend for themselves, an' come in. From th' back window, I can see th' crowd gathered to give Julia a send-off to Lourdes, so come in to tidy if you want to join them with me.

Marion (*half to herself – as she runs into the house*) God forgive me – I near forgot! Here we are followin' laughter, instead of seekin' succour from prayer!

She runs in, and Lorna takes her head back into the room again.

Michael (*frightened and very angry*) Now, maybe, you'll quit your jeerin' at oul' Shanaar! Now, maybe, you'll let your mind concentrate on higher things! Now, maybe, you won't be runnin' loose afther girls!

Mahan (*indignantly*) Damnit, man, you were as eager for a cuddle as I was!

Michael (*lifting his eyes skywards*) Oh, d'ye hear that! I was only toleratin' your queer declivity, like a fool. An' afther all th' warnin's given be wise oul' Shanaar! Looka, Sailor Mahan, you'll have to be more on your guard!

Mahan (*trying to defend himself*) How could any man suspect such a thing? We'll have to think this thing out.

Michael (*with exasperation*) Think it out! Oh, man, Sailor Mahan, have you nothin' more sensible to say than that we'll have to think it out?

Mahan Let's have a dhrink, for God's sake, to steady us down!

Michael (*hurriedly putting bottle and glasses under the table*) What're you thinkin' of, Sailor Mahan? We can't dispense ourselves through a scene of jollification an' poor Julia passin' on her way to Lourdes!

Along the path, on a stretcher, carried by the two Rough Fellows, comes Julia, followed by her father. The stretcher is borne to the gate, and there laid down, so that the head of it is flush with the gate-posts, and the rest of it within the garden. The framework of the gate makes a frame for Julia, who is half sitting up, her head supported by a high pillow. Her face is a sad yellowish mask, pierced by wide eyes, surrounded by dark circles. Her father is a sturdy fellow of fifty, a scraggly greyish beard struggling from his chin. He is roughly dressed as a poorer peasant might be, and his clothes are patched in places. He wears a brown muffler, and a faded black trilby hat is on his head. All the time, he looks straight in front with a passive and stony stare.

Before the stretcher walks the Mayor, rather stout, clean shaven, wearing a red robe over rough clothing; he has a very wide three-cornered hat, laced with gold, on his head. Behind him walks the Mace-bearer, a big silver and black mace on his shoulder. He is tall, and wears a bright blue robe, trimmed with silver, on his head is a huge cocked hat, laced, too, with silver. These two do not enter the garden, but walk on, and stand waiting near the house, beside the flagpole, but without the wall.

Lorna, followed by Marion, comes out of the house. Instead of the bright headgear worn before, they have black kerchiefs, worn peasant-wise on their heads – that is, they have been folded triangularly, draped over their heads, with the ends tied beneath their chins.

Lorna runs over to the stretcher, kneels down beside it, and kisses Julia.

Lorna (*affectionately*) My sister, my little Julia, oh, how sorry I am that you have to go on this long, sad journey!

Julia (*her voice is low, but there is a hectic note of hope in it*) A long journey, Lorna darlin', but not a sad one; oh, no, not a sad one. Hope, Lorna, will have me be the hand all the long way. I go to kneel at the feet of the ever Blessed Virgin.

Lorna Oh, she will comfort you, me darlin'.

Julia Yes, she will comfort me, Lorna (*after a pause*); an' cure me too. Lorna, say she will cure me too.

Lorna (*stifling a sob*) An' cure you, too.

Julia (*to Michael*) Give me your good wishes, Mr Marthraun.

Michael (*with genuine emotion*) Julia, me best wishes go with you, an' me best prayers'll follow all th' long way!

Julia (*to Mahan*) An' you, Sailor Mahan – have you no good wish for the poor voyager?

Mahan (*fervently*) Young lass, may you go through healin' wathers, an' come back a clipper, with ne'er a spar, a sail, or a rope asthray!

Father Domineer comes quickly in on the path outside. He is a tall, rather heavily built man of forty. He has a breezy manner now, heading the forlorn hope. He is trying to smile now, but crack his mouth as he will, the tight, surly lines of his face refuse to furnish one. He is dressed in the usual clerical, outdoor garb, and his hard head is covered with a soft, rather widely brimmed black hat.

Father Domineer (*as happily as he can*) Now, now, no halts on th' road, little daughter! The train won't wait, an' we must have a few minutes to spare to make you comfortable. Bring her along, Brancardiers! Forward, in th' name o' God and of Mary, ever Virgin, ever blessed, always bending to help poor, banished children of Eve!

The two Rough Men take up the stretcher and carry it along the pathway outside, the Mayor, followed by his Mace-bearer, leading it on. Father Domineer follows immediately behind; then come Lorna and Marion, followed by Michael and Mahan.

As the stretcher moves along the pathway outside, a band in the distance is heard playing 'Star of the Sea', to which is added the voice of a crowd.

Crowd (*singing*)
Hail, Queen of Heaven, the ocean Star!
Guide of the wand'rer here below!
Thrown on life's surge, we claim thy care –
Save us from peril and from woe.
Mother of Christ, Star of the Sea,
Pray for the wanderer, pray for me.

Father Domineer (*enthusiastically*) Julia will bring us back a miracle, a glorious miracle! To Lourdes!

End of Scene One.

Scene Two

The scene is the same as before, though the sunshine isn't quite so bright and determined. The Irish Tricolour flies breezily from its flagpole; the table and chairs stand where they were, and the bottle and glasses are still under it.

No one is in the garden, all, apparently, having gone to see Julia away on her long, long journey. Away in the distance the band is playing 'Star of the Sea', and the tune can be softly heard from the garden.

After a few moments, Lorna and Marion come along the path outside, enter by the gate, and cross over into the house.

Marion (*anxiously*) What d'ye think of th' chance of a cure?

Lorna I'm afraid th' chance is a poor one; but we won't talk about it.

Marion (*piously*) Well, it was a grand send-off, an' God is good.

Lorna (*coldly*) An' th' devil's not a bad fella either.

They both go into the house, and, a few moments later, Michael and Mahan stroll along the path, come into the garden, and go to where the table and chairs are.

Mahan Well, th' anchor's weighed.

Michael It was an edifyin' spectacle, Sailor Mahan, thrustin' us outa this world for th' time bein'. Julia's asked for a sign, Sailor Mahan, an', believe me, she'll get it.

ahan She will, she will, though I wouldn't like to bet on it.

354

Michael She'll get what she's afther – a complete cure. Me own generous gift of fifty pounds for th' oul' bog'll be rewarded; an' th' spate o' prayin' goin' on, from th' Mayor to the Bellman, is bound to get th' higher saints goin', persuadin' them to furnish a suitable answer to all we're askin'.

Mahan (*impatiently*) Arra, man alive, d'ye think th' skipper aloft an' his glitterin' crew is goin' to bother their heads about a call from a tiny town an' disthrict thryin' hard to thrive on turf?

Michael (*indignantly*) Looka, if you were only versed in th' endurin' promulgacity of th' gospels, you'd know th' man above's concerned as much about Nyadnanave as he is about a place where a swarm of cardinals saunther secure, decoratin' th' air with all their purple an' gold!

Mahan (*as indignantly*) Are you goin' to tell me that th' skipper aloft an' his hierarchilogical crew are concerned about th' Mayor, the Messenger, Marion, me, an' you as much as they are about them who've been promoted to th' quarter-deck o' th' world's fame? Are you goin' to pit our palthry penances an' haltin' hummin' o' hymns against th' piercin' pipin' of th' rosary be Bing Bang Crosby an' other great film stars, who side-stepped from published greatness for a holy minute or two to send a blessed blast over th' wireless, callin' all Catholics to perpetuatin' prayer!

Michael (*sitting down on a chair*) Sailor Mahan, I ask you to thry to get your thoughts ship-shaped in your mind.

While they have been talking, the Messenger has come running along the path outside, and is now leaning on the gate, listening to the two men, unnoticed by them.

Mahan (*plumping down on the other chair – indignantly*) D'ye remember who you're talkin' to, man? Ship-shape in me mind! Isn't a man bound to have his mind fitted together in a ship-shape way, who, forced out of his thrue course be a nautical cathastrope, to wit, videliket, an act o' God, ploughed a way through th' Sargasso Sea, reachin' open wathers, long afther hope had troubled him no longer?

Michael (*wearily*) Aw, Sailor Mahan, what's them things got to do with th' things tantamount to heaven?

Messenger (*over to them*) Mick's right – them things can't be tantamount to anything bar themselves.

Mahan (*turning fiercely on the Messenger*) What do you want? What're you doin' here? Your coalition of ignorant knowledge can't comprehend th' things we talk about!

Messenger (*with some excitement*) Listen, boys – I've a question to ask yous.

Michael (*with a gesture signifying this isn't the time to ask it*) Ask it some time more convenient. An' don't refer to us as 'boys' – we're gentlemen to you!

Mahan (*to Michael*) Looka, Mick, if you only listened to Bing Crosby, th' mighty film star, croonin' his Irish lullaby, (*He chants.*) 'Tooral ooral ooral, tooral ooral ay', you'd have th' visuality to see th' amazin' response he'd have from millions of admirers, if he crooned a hymn!

Messenger I was never sthruck be Bing Crosby's croonin'.

Michael (*wrathfully – to Messenger*) You were never sthruck! An' who th' hell are you to be consulted? Please don't stand there interferin' with the earnest colloquy of betther men. (*To Mahan*) Looka, Sailor Mahan, any priest'll tell you that in th' eyes of heaven all men are equal an' must be held in respect an' reverence.

Mahan (*mockingly*) Ay, they'll say that to me an' you, but will they say it to Bing Crosby, or any other famous film star?

Messenger Will they hell! Honour be th' clergy's regulated by how much a man can give!

Michael (*furiously – to the Messenger*) Get to hell outa here! With that kinda talk, we won't be able soon to sit steady on our chairs. Oh!

 The chair he is sitting on collapses, and he comes down to the ground on his arse.

Mahan (*astonished*) Holy saints, what's happened?

Michael (*in a fierce whisper – to Mahan*) Take no notice of it, fool. Go on talkin'!

Mahan (*a little confused*) I'll say you're right, Mick; th' way things are goin' we won't be able much longer to sit serene on our chairs. Oh!

 The chair collapses under him, and he, too, comes down to the ground.

Michael (*in a fierce whisper*) Don't notice it; go on's if nothin' happened!

Messenger (*amused*) Well, yous have settled down now, anyhow! Will I get yous chairs sturdy enough to uphold th' wisdom of your talkin'?

Michael (*angrily – to Messenger*) There's nothin' wrong with th' chairs we have! You get outa here! Nothin's wrong with th' chairs at all. Get outa here – I don't trust you either!

Messenger I've somethin' important to ask yous.

Michael Well, ask it at some more convenient time. (*To Mahan*) It's a blessin' that so many lively-livin' oul' holy spots are still in th' land to help us an' keep us wary.

Messenger (*scornfully*) An' where are th' lively holy spots still to be found? Sure, man, they're all gone west long ago, an' the whole face o' th' land is pock-marked with their ruins!

Michael (*shouting at the Messenger*) Where are th' lost an' ruined holy places? We've always cared for, an' honoured, our holy spots! Mention one of them, either lost or ruined!

Messenger (*shouting back*) There are thousands of them, man; places founded by Finian, Finbarr, an' th' rest; places that are now only an oul' ruined wall, blighted be nettle an' dock, their only glory th' crimson berries of th' bright arbutus! Where's th' Seven Churches of Glendalough? Where's Durrow of Offally, founded by Columkille himself? Known now only be the name of the Book of Durrow!

Michael (*ferociously*) Book o' Durrow! It's books that have us half th' woeful way we are, fillin' broody minds with loose scholasticality, infringin' th' holy beliefs an' thried impositions that our fathers' fathers' fathers gave our fathers' fathers, who gave our fathers what our fathers gave to us!

Messenger Faith, your fathers' faith is fear, an' now fear is your only fun.

Mahan (*impatiently*) Let him go, Mick, an' let's have that dhrink you mentioned a year ago.

Marion's head appears at the window, looking down at the Messenger. The decorations on her head have now declined to their first place.

Marion (*down to the Messenger*) Hallo, Robin Adair! (*He looks up.*) Where are th' two oul' woeful wondhers? (*He points to where they are.*) Oh, they've brought the unsteady chairs out, and now they've broken them up! (*To Michael – angrily*) You knew well th' chairs in the hall were there only to present an appearance.

Messenger (*up to her*) Oh, Marion, Marion, sweet

Marion, come down till I give you a kiss havin' in it all the life an' longin' of th' greater lovers of th' past!

Marion (*leaving the window*) Now, now, naughty boy!

Michael (*sourly*) You'd do well to remember, lad, the month in jail you got for kissin' Marion, an' the forty-shillin' fine on Marion, for kissing you in a public place at th' cross-roads.

> *Marion comes from the house, goes towards the Messenger, who seizes her in his arms and kisses her.*

Messenger I'd do a year an' a day in a cold cell of pressed-in loneliness, an' come out singin' a song, for a kiss from a lass like Marion!

Marion Don't think too much of me, Robin Adair, for I've some of th' devil in me, an' th' two fostherers of fear, there, think I wear horns on holy days.

Michael (*impressively*) See – she's warnin' you, herself, young man!

Marion (*to the Messenger*) An' what has you here arguin' with them two oul' fools?

Messenger I came to ask a question of them, but they were buried in their prayers. Did you see him? Did he come this way?

Michael (*suddenly alarmed*) Come where?

Mahan (*alarmed*) See who?

Messenger Th' Cock.

Mahan and Michael (*together*) Th' Cock! (*They carefully creep away from the broken chairs, and stand up when they are some distance from them.*)

Messenger Ay. I thought he'd make for here first.

359

Michael (*echoing the Messenger*) Make for here first!

In the distance, the loud, exultant crow of the Cock is heard.

Messenger (*excitedly*) There he is! Away in the direction east of th' bog! I'll go get him, an' fetch him home.

Marion (*kissing the Messenger*) Bring him here first, Robin, an' I'll have a wreath of roses ready to hang round his neck.

Messenger (*rushing away*) I will, I will, fair one!

He goes off. She takes the broken chairs into the house.

Marion (*carrying in the chairs*) Next time, you boyos, take out two steady ones.

Michael (*horrified*) Did you hear what she said, Sailor Mahan? Hang a wreath of roses round his neck! Well, I'll have th' gun ready! Ay, now!

He goes over to the porch, but Mahan lays a restraining hand on his arm.

Mahan What good would th' gun be? Have you forgot what Shanaar told us? Your bullet would go clean through him, an' leave him untouched. Now that we're in peace here, let's have th' dhrink we were to have, an' which we both need.

Michael (*halting*) You're right, Sailor Mahan. If he comes here, what we have to do is to take no notice. Look through him, past him, over him, but never at him. (*He prepares the bottle of whiskey and the glasses.*) There's sinisther enchantments all around us. God between us an' all harm! We'll have to be for ever on our guard.

Mahan (*impatiently*) Yis, yis; fill out th' dhrink for God's sake!

Michael May it give us courage. (*He tilts the bottle over the glass, but none of it spills out.*) Good God, th' bottle's bewitched too!

Mahan Bottle bewitched? How could a bottle be bewitched? Steady your nerves, man. Thry givin' it a shake.

Michael (*who has left the bottle back on the table – retreating away from it*) Thry givin' it a shake yourself, since you're so darin'.

> *Mahan goes over to the table with a forced swagger, and reaches out a cautious hand for the bottle. As he touches it, its colour changes to a glowing red.*

Mahan (*fervent and frightened*) St Christopher, pathron of all mariners, defend us – th' bottle's changed its colour!

Michael There's evil things cantherin' an' crawlin' about this place! You saw th' seal on th' bottle showin' it was untouched since it left th' store. Flanagan's finest, Jamieson's best, ten years maturin' – an' look at it now.

Mahan How are we goin' to prevent ourselves from bein' the victims of sorcery an' ruin? You'd think good whiskey would be exempt from injury even be th' lowest of th' low.

Michael It's th' women who're always intherceptin' our good intentions. Evil things is threatenin' us everywhere. Th' one safe method of turnin' our back to a power like this is to go forward an' meet it half-way. (*He comes close to Mahan, and whispers hoarsely.*) Selah!

Mahan (*mystified and frightened at what he thinks may be something sinister*) Selah?

Michael (*emphatically*) Selah!

Mahan (*agonizingly*) Good God!

Michael Now, maybe, you'll believe what th' Missioner said last night.

Mahan (*a little dubiously*) He might have been exaggeratin' a bit, Mick.

Michael Look at th' bottle, man! Demons can hide in th' froth of th' beer a man's dhrinkin'. An' all th' time, my turf-workers an' your lorry drivers are screwin' all they can out of us so that they'll have more to spend on pictures an' in th' dance halls, leavin' us to face th' foe alone.

Mahan (*abjectly*) What's a poor, good-livin', virtuous man to do then?

Michael He must always be thinkin' of th' four last things – hell, heaven, death, an' th' judgement.

Mahan (*pitifully*) But that would sthrain a man's nerves, an' make life hardly worth livin'.

Michael It's plain, Sailor Mahan, you're still hankerin' afther th' things o' th' world, an' the soft, stimulatin' touch of th' flesh. You're puttin' th' two of us in peril, Sailor Mahan.

Mahan (*protesting*) You're exaggeratin' now.

Michael I am not. I seen your eyes followin' that Loreleen when she's about, hurtin' th' tendher muscles of your eye squintin' down at her legs. You'll have to curb your conthradictions, for you're puttin' us both in dire peril, Sailor Mahan. Looka what I've lost already! Me fine silk hat torn to shreds, so that Lorna's had to telephone th' Firm for another, that I may suitably show meself when I meet his Brightness, the President; an' looka th' whiskey there – forced into a misundherstandin' of itself be some minor demon devisin' a spell on it! Guess how much good money I surrendhered to get that bottle, Sailor Mahan?

Mahan I've no idea of what whiskey is a gallon now.

Michael (*impatiently*) What whiskey is a gallon now? Is there some kinda spell on you, too, Sailor Mahan? You can't think of whiskey in gallons now; you have to think of it in terms of sips; an' sips spaced out from each other like th' holy days of obligation.

Mahan An' how are we goin' to get rid of it? We're in some danger while it's standin' there.

Michael How th' hell do I know how we'll get rid of it? We'll have to get Shanaar to deal with it, an', mind you, don't go too near it.

> *The Porter appears on the sidewalk outside the wall. He is a middle-aged man with an obstinate face, the chin hidden by a grizzled beard. He is wearing a pair of old brown trousers, an older grey coat, and an old blue shirt. On his head is a big cap, with a long, wide peak jutting out in front of it. The crown of the cap is a high one, and around the crown is a wide band of dazzling scarlet. He is carrying a parcel wrapped in brown paper, either side of which is a little torn. He looks north, south, west, and then, turning east, he sees the two men in the garden.*

Porter (*to the two men*) Isn't it handy now that I've clapped eyes on two human bein's in this god-forsaken hole! I've been trudghin' about for hours thryin' to find th' one that'll claim what's in this parcel I'm bearin', an', maybe, th' two of yous, or maybe, one of yous, can tell me where I'll find him. I'm on th' thrack of an oul' fella callin' himself a Councillor an' a Jay Pee.

Michael What's his name?

Porter That's more than I can say, for th' chit of th' girl in th' shop, who took th' ordher, forgot to write down th' name, an' then forgot th' name itself when she started to write it down. All I know is that in this disthrict I'm seekin' a Mr Councillor So-an'-so; one havin' Councillor at his head an' Jay Pee at his tail.

Michael (*with importance*) I'm a Councillor and a Jay Pee.

Porter (*with some scorn*) D'ye tell me that now? (*He bends over the wall to come closer to Michael.*) Listen, me good man, me journey's been too long an' too dangerous for me to glorify any cod-actin'! It would be a quare place if you were a councillor. You'll have to grow a few more grey hairs before you can take a rise outa me!

Michael (*indignantly*) Tell us what you've got there, fella, an', if it's not for us, be off about your business!

Porter (*angrily*) Fella yourself! An' mend your manners, please! It's hardly th' like of you would be standin' in need of a silky, shinin' tall-hat.

Michael If it's a tall-hat, it's for me! I'm Mr Councillor Marthraun, Jay Pee – ordhered to be sent express by th' firm of Buckley's.

Porter (*with a quick conciliatory change*) That's th' firm. I guessed you was th' man at once, at once. That man's a leadher in th' locality, I said, as soon as I clapped me eye on you. A fine, clever, upstandin' individual, I says to meself.

Michael (*shortly*) Hand over th' hat, and you can go.

Porter Hould on a minute, sir; wait till I tell you: I'm sorry, but th' hat's been slightly damaged in thransit. (*He begins to take the hat from the paper.*)

Michael Damaged? How th' hell did you damage it?

Porter Me, is it? No, not me, sir. (*He stretches over the*

wall towards them.) When I was bringin' it here, someone
shot a bullet through it, east be west!

Michael Nonsense, man, who'd be shootin' bullets round
here?

Porter Who indeed? That's th' mystery. Bullet it was.
People told me the Civic Guards were out thryin' to shoot
down an evil spirit flyin' th' air in th' shape of a bird.

Michael (*alarmed*) Th' Cock!

Porter (*placing the tall-hat on the wall carefully*) An' seein'
how things are, an' th' fright I got, it's welcome a dhrink
would be from th' handsome bottle I see paradin' on th'
table.

Michael (*in a loud whisper*) To touch it is to go in danger
of your life – th' bottle's bewitched!

Porter Th' bottle bewitched? What sort of a place have me
poor, wandherin' feet sthrayed into at all? Before I
ventured to come here at all, I should have stayed at home.
I'm already as uneasy as th' place itself!

*A shot is heard, and the tall-hat is knocked from the
wall on to the road.*

Saints in glory, there's another one!

Mahan (*excitedly*) It's your hat, man, th' red band on
your hat!

Porter (*to Michael – speaking rapidly, picking the tall-hat
from the road and offering it to Michael*) Here, take your
hat, sir, an' keep it safe, an' I'll be goin'.

Michael (*frightened and angry*) Take it back; it's damaged;
take it back, fella!

Porter (*loudly and with anger*) Fella yourself! Is it takin'
th' risk I'd be of a bullet rushin' through me instead of th'

oul' hat? (*He flings it towards the two men.*) Here, take your oul' hat an' th' risk along with it! Do what you want with it; do what you like with it; do what you can with it – I'm off!

He runs off in the direction he came from, while the two men gaze doubtfully at the hat lying in the garden.

Michael (*tremulously*) The cowards that are in this counthry – leavin' a poor man alone in his dilemma! I'd be afraid to wear it now.

Mahan Aw, give yourself a shake, Mick. You're not afraid of a poor tall-hat. An' throw away ten good pounds.

He goes toward where the hat is, but Michael holds him by the arm.

Michael (*with warning and appeal*) No, don't touch it till we see further.

The Sergeant appears on the pathway outside. He has a rifle in his hands; he leans against the wall looking towards the two. He is obviously anxious, and in a state of fear.

Sergeant Yous didn't see it? It didn't come here, did it?

Michael (*breathless with the tension of fear*) No, no; not yet. (*With doleful appeal*) Oh, don't be prowlin' round here – you'll only be attractin' it to th' place!

Sergeant (*ignoring appeal*) Three times I shot at it; three times th' bullets went right through it; and twice th' thing flew away crowing.

Michael (*excitedly*) Did you get it th' third time, did you get it then?

Sergeant Wait till I tell yous: sthrange things an' unruly are happenin' in this holy land of ours this day! Will I ever forget what happened th' third time I hit it! Never, never. Isn't it a wondher an' a mercy of God that I'm left alive afther th' reverberatin' fright I got!

Michael (*eagerly*) Well, what happened when you hot it then?

Mahan (*eagerly*) When you hot it for th' third time?

Sergeant Yous could never guess?

Michael (*impatiently*) Oh, we know we'd never guess; no one can go guessin' about demonological disturbances.

Mahan Tell us, will you, without any more of your sthructural suggestions!

Sergeant As sure as I'm standin' here; as sure as sure as this gun is in me left hand; (*He is holding it in his right one.*) as sure as we're all poor, identified sinners; when I hot him for th' third time, I seen him changin' into a –

Michael and Mahan (*together*) What?

Sergeant (*whisperingly*) What d'ye think?

Mahan (*explosively*) Oh, we're not thinkin'; we can't think; we're beyond thinkin'! We're waitin' for you to tell us!

Sergeant Th' soul well-nigh left me body when I seen th' unholy novelty happenin': th' thing that couldn't be, yet th' thing that was. If I never prayed before, I prayed then – for hope; for holy considheration in th' quandary; for power to be usual an' spry again when th' thing was gone.

Michael What thing, what thing, man?

Mahan (*despairingly*) Thry to tell us, Sergeant, what you said you said you seen.

Sergeant I'm comin' to it; since what I seen was seen by no man never before, it's not easy for a man to describe with evidential accuracy th' consequential thoughts fluttherin' through me amazed mind at what was, an' what couldn't be, demonstrated there, or there, or anywhere else, where mortals congregate in ones or twos or crowds astoundin'.

Michael (*imploringly*) Looka, Sergeant, we're languishin' for th' information that may keep us from spendin' th' rest of our lives in constant consternation.

Sergeant As I was tellin' you, there was th' crimson crest of th' Cock, enhancin' th' head lifted up to give a crow, an' when I riz th' gun to me shouldher, an' let bang, th' whole place went dead dark; a flash of red lightning near blinded me; an' when it got light again, a second afther, there was the demonized Cock changin' himself into a silken glossified tall-hat!

Michael (*horrified*) A silken tall-hat!

Mahan A glossified tall-hat!

Michael (*to Mahan – viciously*) Now you'll quit undherestimatin' what th' holy Missioner said last night about th' desperate an' deranging thrickeries of evil things loose an' loungin' among us! Now you can see the significality of things?

Mahan (*going away as far as he can from the tall-hat lying in the garden*) Steer clear of it; get as far away from it as we can! Keep well abaft of it!

Sergeant (*puzzled*) Keep clear from what?

Mahan (*pointing to the hat*) Th' hat, man, th' hat!

Sergeant (*seeing the hat beside him, and jumping away from it*) I was near touchin' th' brim of it! Jasus! Yous should have warned me!

Michael (*close to the Sergeant – in a whisper*) Does it look anything like th' thing you shot?

Sergeant (*laying a shaking hand on Michael's arm*) It's th' dead spit of what I seen him changin' into durin' th' flash of lightning! I just riz th' gun to me shouldher – like this (*he raises the gun to his shoulder*) to let bang.

> *The garden is suddenly enveloped in darkness for a few moments. A fierce flash of lightning shoots through the darkness; the hat has disappeared, and where it stood now stands the Cock. While the lightning flashes, the Cock crows lustily. Then the light as suddenly comes back to the garden, and shows that the Cock and the hat have gone. Michael and Mahan are seen to be lying on the ground, and the Sergeant is on his knees, as if in prayer.*

Holy St Custodius, pathron of th' police, protect me!

Michael (*in a whisper*) Are you there, Sailor Mahan?

Mahan (*in a whisper*) Are you there, Michael Marthraun?

Michael I'm done for.

Mahan We're both done for.

Sergeant We're all done for.

Mahan Th' smell of th' sulphur an' brimstone's burnin' me.

Michael Now you'll give up mockin' Shanaar, if it's not too late. You seen how Marion's head was ornamented, an' it'll not be long till Lorna has them too.

Sergeant (*now sitting down, so that he is to the left of Michael, while Mahan sits to the right of him, so frightened that he must blame someone*) We'll have to curtail th' gallivantin' of th' women afther th' men. Th' house is their province, as th' clergy's tired tellin' them. They'll have to realize that th' home's their only proper place.

Michael An' demolish th' minds that babble about books.

Sergeant (*raising his voice*) Th' biggest curse of all! Books no decent mortal should touch, should never even see th' cover of one!

Michael (*warningly*) Hush! Don't speak so loud, or th' lesser boyo'll hear you!

Sergeant (*startled*) Lesser boyo? What lesser boyo?

Mahan (*whispering and pointing*) Th' boyo in th' bottle there.

Sergeant (*noticing it for the first time*) Why, what's in it?

Michael Th' best of whiskey was in it till some evil spirit put a spell on it, desthroyin' its legitimate use.

Sergeant (*unbelievingly*) I don't believe it. Nothin' could translate good dhrink into anything but what it was made to be. We could do with a dhrink now. (*He advances cautiously towards the table.*)

Michael (*excitedly*) Don't meddle with it, man; don't stimulate him!

The Sergeant tiptoes over to the table, stretches his hand out, and touches the bottle. He immediately lets out a yelp, and jumps back.

Sergeant Oh! Be God, it's red-hot!

Mahan (*angrily*) You were told not to touch it! You're addin' to our dangers.

Michael (*shouting*) Good God, man, couldn't you do what you're told! Now you've added anger to its impositional qualities!

Sergeant (*nursing his hand*) Aren't we in a nice quandary when an evil thing can insconce itself in a bottle!

Michael Th' whole place's seethin' with them. You, Sergeant, watch th' road north; you, Sailor Mahan, watch it south; an' I'll keep an eye on th' house.

Mahan goes to one end of the wall, the Sergeant to the other, and both stretch over it to look different ways along the road. During the next discussion, whenever they leave where they are, they move cautiously, crouching a little, as if they were afraid to be seen; keeping as low as possible for security.

One of us'll have to take th' risk, an' go for Father Domineer at once. (*He waits for a few moments, but no one answers.*) Did yous hear me, or are yous lettin' on to be deaf? I said one of us'll have to go for Father Domineer.

There is no reply.

Are you listenin' to me be any chance, Sailor Mahan?

Mahan I heard you, I heard you.

Michael An' why don't you go, then?

Mahan (*coming down towards Michael – crouching low*) Nice thing if I met th' Cock barrin' me way? Why don't you go yourself?

Michael What about th' possibility of me meetin' him? I'm more conspicuous in this disthrict than you, an' th' thing would take immediate recognizance of me.

Sergeant (*coming down towards them – crouching too*) Me an' Sailor Mahan'll go together.

Michael (*indignantly*) An' leave me to grapple with *mysteriosa Daemones* alone? (*He turns his face skywards.*)

Oh, in this disthrict there's not a sign of one willin' to do unto another what another would do to him!

Mahan (*fiercely*) That's a lie: there isn't a one who isn't eager to do to others what others would do to him!

The Bellman, dressed as a fireman, comes in, and walks along on the path outside. He has a huge brass fireman's helmet on his head, and is wearing a red shirt and blue trousers. He has a bell in his hand which he rings loudly before he shouts his orders. The three men cease their discussion, and give him their full attention.

Bellman (*shouting*) Into your houses all! Bar th' doors, shut th' windows! Th' Cock's comin'! In the shape of a woman! Gallus, Le Coq, an' Kyleloch, th' Cock's comin' in th' shape of a woman! Into your houses, shut to th' windows, bar th' doors!

He goes out in the opposite direction, shouting his orders and ringing his bell, leaving the three men agitated and more frightened than ever.

Sergeant (*frantically*) Into the house with us all – quick!

Michael (*hindering him – ferociously*) Not in there, you fool! Th' house is full o' them. You seen what happened to the whiskey? If he or she comes, th' thing to do is to take no notice; if he or she talks, not to answer; and take no notice of whatever questionable shape it takes. Sit down, quiet, th' three of us.

The three men sit down on the ground – Michael to the right, the Sergeant to the left, and Mahan in the centre.

(*Trembling*) Now, let th' two of yous pull yourselves together. An' you, Mahan, sing that favourite of yours, quietly, as if we were passing th' time pleasantly. (*As Mahan hesitates*) Go on, man, for God's sake!

Mahan (*agitated*) I can't see how I'll do it justice undher these conditions. I'll thry. (*He sings, but his voice quavers occasionally.*)

> Long time ago when men was men
> An' ships not ships that sail'd just to an' fro-o-o,
> We hoisted sail an' sail'd, an' then sail'd on an' on to
>   Jericho-o-o;
> With silks an' spice came back again because we'd
>   nowhere else to go!

Michael and Sergeant (*together*) Go, go!

Mahan (*singing*)
> Th' captain says, says he, we'll make
> Th' pirates where th' palmtrees wave an' grow-o-o,
> Haul down their sable flag, an' pray, before we hang
>   them all, heave yo-ho-ho;
> Then fling their bodies in th' sea to feed th' fishes down
>   below!

Michael and Sergeant (*together*) Low, low!

A golden shaft of light streams in from the left of the road, and, a moment afterwards, Loreleen appears in the midst of it. She stands in the gateway staring at the three men squatted on the ground.

Loreleen (*puzzled*) What th' hell's wrong here?

Michael (*in a whisper – motioning Mahan to continue*) Go on, man.

Mahan (*singing – with more quavers in his voice*)
> An' when we've swabb'd th' blood away,
> We'll take their hundhred-ton gunn'd ship in tow-o-o;
> Their precious jewels'll go to deck th' breasts of women,
>   white as snow-o-o;
> So hoist all sail an' make for home through waves that
>   lash an' winds that blow!

373

Michael and Sergeant (*together*) Blow, blow!

> *Loreleen comes into the garden, and approaches the men. The golden light follows her, and partly shines on the three singers.*

Loreleen (*brightly*) Singin' is it the three of you are? Practisin' for the fancy-dress ball tonight, eh? Ye do well to bring a spray of light, now and again, into a dark place. The Sergeant's eyes, too, whenever Lorna or me passes by, are lit with a light that never was on sea or land. An' th' bould Sailor Mahan is smiling too; only dad is dour. (*She glances at the bottle on the table.*) The song is heard, th' wine is seen, only th' women wanting. (*She runs over to the porchway, and shouts into the house.*) Lorna, Marion, come on down, come out here, an' join th' enthertainment!

> *Lorna and Marion come trotting out of the house into the garden. They are both clad in what would be called fancy dress. Lorna is supposed to be a gypsy, and is wearing a short black skirt, low-cut green bodice, with a gay sash round her waist, sparkling with sequins. Her fair arms are bare. Her head is bound with a silver and black ornament, similar in shape to that already worn by Marion. Her legs are encased in black stockings, and dark red shoes cover her feet. Marion is dressed as a Nippy, a gay one. She has on a short, bright green skirt, below which a black petticoat peeps; a low-cut bodice of a darker green, and sports a tiny black apron to protect her costume. She wears light brown silk stockings and brown shoes. Outside the white bandeau round her head she wears the ornament worn before. The two women stare at the three men.*

Lorna (*vexatiously*) Dhrunk is it? To get in that state just when we were practisin' a few steps for tonight's fancy-dress dance! (*She notices the bottle.*) Looka th' dhrink left out in th' sun an' air to dhry! (*She whips up the bottle, and*

places it inside on the floor of the porch.) An' even th'
Sailor Mahan is moody too! (*She goes over to the
Sergeant, stands behind him, and lays a hand on his head.
She is now in the golden light which shines down on the
Sergeant too.*)

> I saw a ship a-sailing, a-sailing on th' sea;
> An' among its spicy cargo was a bonny lad for me!

*The Sergeant rises slowly, as if enchanted, with a foolish
look of devotion on his face, till he stands upright beside
Lorna, glancing at her face, now and again, very shy
and uncertain. While this has been happening, Loreleen
has gone to Sailor Mahan, and now stands behind him
with a hand on his head.*

Loreleen (*down to Sailor Mahan*)
> I saw a man come running, come running o'er th' lea,
>   sir,
> And, lo, he carried silken gowns
> That couldn't hide a knee
> That he had bought in saucy towns;
> An' jewels he'd bought beyond th' bounds
> Of Asia's furthest sea.
> And all were lovely, all were fine,
> An' all were meant for me!

*Sailor Mahan rises, as if enchanted, till he stands upright
beside Loreleen, slyly looking at her now and again.*

Marion Aw, let's be sensible. (*She sees the gun.*) What's th'
gun doin'? Who owns th' gun?

Sergeant It's mine. I'm on pathrol lookin' to shoot down
th' demon-bird loose among innocent people.

Marion Demon-bird loose among innocent people! Yous
must be mad.

Sergeant (*indignantly*) We're not mad! It's only that we were startled when th' darkness came, th' lightning flashed, an' we saw Mr Marthraun's tall-hat turnin' itself into th' demon-bird!

Lorna (*mystified*) Th' darkness came, th' lightning flashed? A tall-hat changin' into a demon-bird!

Michael (*springing to his feet*) Ay, an' this isn't th' time for gay disturbance! So go in, an' sthrip off them gaudy things, an' bend your mind to silent prayer an' long fastin'! Fall prostrate before God, admittin' your dire disthress, an' you may be admitted to a new dispensation!

Lorna (*to Michael*) Nonsense! Your new tall-hat was delivered an hour ago, an' is upstairs now, waitin' for you to put it on. (*To Marion*) Take that gun in, dear, outa th' way, an' bring down th' tall-hat to show him he's dhreamin'.

> *Marion takes up the gun, and goes into the house with it, as Michael, in a great rage, shoves Mahan aside to face Lorna fiercely.*

Michael (*loudly*) Who are you, you jade, to set yourself up against th' inner sight an' outer sight of genuine Christian men? (*He shouts.*) We seen this thing, I tell you! If you knew what you ought to know, you'd acknowledge th' thrained tenacity of evil things. Betther had I left you soakin' in poverty, with your rags coverin' your thin legs, an' your cheeks hollow from mean feedin'. Through our bulgin' eyes, didn't we see th' horrification of me tall-hat turnin' into th' demonized cock? Me tall-hat, you bitch, me own tall-hat is roamin' round th' counthry, temptin' souls to desthroy themselves with dancin' an' desultory pleasures!

Mahan (*gripping Michael's arm*) Aw, draw it mild, Mick!

Michael (*flinging off Mahan's hold*) Go in, an' take them things, showy with sin, off you, an' dhress decent! (*He points to Loreleen.*) It's you who's brought this blast from th' undherworld, England, with you! It's easy seen what you learned while you worked there – a place where no God is; where pride and lust an' money are the brightest liveries of life! (*He advances as if to strike her, but Mahan bars his way.*) You painted slug!

Marian comes from the house, carrying a fresh, dignified tall-hat, noble in its silken glossiness. She offers it to Michael who jumps away from it.

No, no, take it away; don't let it touch me.

Marion puts the hat on the table, and the three men stare at it, as if expecting something to happen.

Lorna (*darting into the porch, and returning with the bottle; it has gone back to its former colour*) Let's have a dhrink to give us courage to fight our dangers. Fetch another glass, Marion.

Marion goes in, and returns with a glass. Lorna uncorks the bottle, and takes up a glass to fill it.

Michael (*warningly*) Don't meddle with that dhrink, or harm may come to us all!

Lorna (*recklessly*) If I can't wrap myself in th' arms of a man, I'll wrap myself in a cordial. (*She fills the glass, then she fills another one, and gives it to Loreleen; then she fills a third, and gives it to Marion.*) Here, Loreleen.

Loreleen takes the glass.

Here, Marion.

Marion takes the glass from her.

Mahan (*doubtfully, and with some fear*) I wouldn't, Lorna, I wouldn't drink it – there's some kind of a spell on it.

Lorna Is there, now? I hope to God it's a strong one! (*raising her glass*) Th' Cock-a-doodle Dandy!

Marion and Loreleen (*raising their glasses – together*) Th' Cock-a-doodle Dandy!

The three women empty their glasses together. Lorna fills her glass again, and goes over to the Sergeant.

Lorna (*offering the glass to the Sergeant*) Dhrink, hearty man, an' praise th' good things life can give. (*As he hesitates*) Dhrink from th' glass touched by th' lips of a very fair lady!

Sergeant (*impulsively*) Death an' bedamnit, ma'am, it's a fair lady you are. (*He takes the glass from her.*) I'm not th' one to be short in salutin' loveliness! (*He drinks, and a look of delightful animation gradually comes on to his face.*)

Loreleen (*who has filled her glass again – going over to Sailor Mahan, and offering him the drink*) Here, Sailor Mahan, man of th' wider waters, an' th' seven seas, dhrink! (*As he hesitates*) Dhrink from th' glass touched by th' lips of a very fair lady!

Mahan (*taking the glass – impulsively*) Here's a one who always yelled ahoy to a lovely face an' charmin' figure whenever they went sailin' by – *salud!* (*He drinks, and the look of animation gradually comes on to his face too.*)

Marion (*who has filled her glass the second time – going over to Michael and offering him the drink*) Dark man, let th' light come to you be dhrinkin' from a glass touched be th' red lips of a fair young maiden!

Michael (*who has been watching the others enviously – taking the glass from her*) Gimme it! I won't be one odd. Yous can't best me! (*He drinks it down greedily. A reckless look steals over his face.*)

During the last few moments, Lorna has been humming
a tune, which has been taken up by an accordion, very
softly. Then the Messenger appears on the pathway
outside, and it can be seen that he is the player. He sits
sideways on the wall, still playing softly a kind of a
dance tune.

(*To Marion*) In our heart of hearts, maid Marion, we care
nothin' about th' world of men. Do we now, Sailor
Mahan?

Mahan (*cautiously – though a reckless gleam is appearing*
in his eyes too) We all have to think about th' world o'
men at times.

Michael Not with our hearts, Sailor Mahan; oh, not with
our hearts. You're thinkin' now of th' exthra money you
want off me, Sailor Mahan. Take it, man, an' welcome!
(*enthusiastically*) An' more! You can have double what
you're askin', without a whimper, without a grudge!

Mahan (*enthusiastically*) No, damnit, Michael, not a
penny from you! We're as good as bein' brothers! Looka
th' lilies of th' field, an' ask yourself what th' hell's money!

Michael (*excitedly*) Dhross, be God! Dhross, an' nothin'
else! (*To Marion*) Gimme that hat there!

She gives it to him. He puts it on, puts an arm round her
waist, and they begin to move with the beat of the
music. As Michael puts his arm around her waist, the
ornament on her head rises into a graceful, curving
horn, but he does not notice it.
*   At the same time, the Sergeant, having put an arm*
round Lorna, moves in the dance, too. As he does so,
the ornament on her head, too, becomes a curving horn,
but he does not notice it. Then Mahan goes over
stealthily to Loreleen, who is watching the others, and
stabs her shyly in the ribs with a finger. She turns,

*smiles, takes hold of his arm, and puts it round her
waist. Then the two of them join the others in moving
round to the beat of the music, the cock-like crest in
Loreleen's hat rising higher as she begins to move in the
dance.*

*After a few moments, the dance quickens, the
excitement grows, and the men stamp out the measure
of the music fiercely, while the three women begin to
whirl round them with ardour and abandon. While the
excitement is at its height, a loud, long peal of thunder is
heard, and in the midst of it, with a sliding, rushing
pace, Father Domineer appears in the gateway, a green
glow enveloping him as he glares down at the swinging
dancers, and as a loud, lusty crow from the Cock rings
out through the garden.*

*The dancers, excepting Loreleen, suddenly stand
stock still, then fall on one knee, facing the priest, their
heads bent in shame and some dismay. Loreleen dances
on for some few moments longer, the music becoming
softer, then she slowly ends her dance to face forward
towards the priest, the Messenger continuing to play the
tune very softly, very faintly now.*

Father Domineer (*down to those in the garden – with
vicious intensity*) Stop that devil's dance! How often have
yous been warned that th' avowed enemies of Christianity
are on th' march everywhere! An' I find yous dancin'! How
often have yous been told that pagan poison is floodin' th'
world, an' that Ireland is dhrinkin' in generous doses
through films, plays, an' books! An' yet I come here to find
yous dancin'! Dancin', an' with th' Kyleloch, Le Coq,
Gallus, th' Cock rampant in th' disthrict, desthroyin' desire
for prayer, desire for work, an' weakenin' th' authority of
th' pastors an' masters of your souls! Th' empire of Satan's
pushin' out its foundations everywhere, an' I find yous
dancin', *ubique ululanti cockalorum ochone, ululo!*

Messenger (*through his soft playing of the accordion*) Th' devil was as often in th' street, an' as intimate in th' home when there was not film nor play nor book.

Father Domineer There was singin' then, an' there's singin' now; there was dancin' then, an' there's dancin' now, leadin' innocent souls to perjure their perfection. (*To Loreleen*) Kneel down, as th' others do, you proud an' dartin' cheat, an' beg a pardon!

Loreleen (*obstinately*) I seek no pardon for th' dance that's done.

Father Domineer (*turning away from her*) Seek for it then when pardon hides away.

Michael Oh, what have I done! I've bethrayed meself into a sudden misdoin'!

Mahan *Mea culpa*, me, too, Father!

Father Domineer Oh, Michael Marthraun, an' you, Sailor Mahan, Knights of Columbanus, I come to help yous, an' I catch yous in th' act of prancin' about with shameless women, dhressed to stun th' virtue out of all beholdhers!

Michael It was them, right enough, Father, helped be th' wine, that done poor me an' poor Sailor Mahan in! I should have remembered that a Columbanian knight told me a brother Columbanian knight told him another brother has said that St Jerome told a brother once that woman was th' gate of hell! An' it's thrue – they stab a man with a knife wreathed with roses!

Father Domineer Get up, get up, an' stand away from me; an' let ye never be loungers again in th' fight for good against evil.

They all rise up humbly, the women to one side, the men to the other, and go back some way, as the Priest comes into the garden. Loreleen strolls defiantly over to the table, and sits sideways upon it.

(*to Mahan*) An' now, Sailor Mahan, a special word for you. On my way here, I passed that man of yours who's livin' in sin with a lost an' wretched woman. He dodged down a lane to give me th' slip. I warned you, if he didn't leave her, to dismiss him – did you do so?

Mahan is silent.

I have asked you, Mahan, if you've dismissed him?

Mahan (*obstinately*) I see no reason why I should dismiss me best lorry driver.

Father Domineer (*coldly*) You don't see a reason? An' who are you to have any need of a reason in a question of this kind? (*Loudly*) I have a reason, an' that's enough for you!

Mahan (*defensively*) He's a fine worker, Father, an' th' nation needs such as him.

Father Domineer (*loudly*) We're above all nations. Nationality is mystical, maundering nonsense! It's a heresy! I'm the custodian of higher interests. (*Shouting*) Do as you're told – get rid of him!

Michael (*wheedling*) It's all right, Father – he'll do what your reverence tells him. Sailor Mahan's a thrue Columbanian.

Mahan (*angrily – to Michael*) He won't do what his reverence tells him!

Down the path outside comes the Lorry Driver, a man of thirty years of age. He doesn't look a giant, but there is an air of independence and sturdiness about him. He is wearing a leather jacket, a pair of soldier's khaki trousers, and an oily looking peaked cap. His face is

*tanned by the weather, and his upper lip is hidden by a
well-trimmed moustache. He hesitates for a moment
when he sees Father Domineer; but, stiffening a little, he
continues his walk to the gateway, into the garden. He
stands a little way from Mahan, looking at him,
evidently having something to say to him.*

Father Domineer (*sneeringly*) Ah, the gentleman himself
has arrived. (*To the Lorry Driver*) We were just talking of
you, my man. I have told Mr Mahan to dismiss you. You
know why. You're a scandal to th' whole place; you're a
shame to us all. Either leave this woman you're living
with, or go to where that sort of thing's permitted.
(*Loudly*) You heard me?

Lorry Driver (*surlily*) I heard you.

Father Domineer (*impatiently*) Well?

Lorry Driver I come to speak with Mr Mahan, Father.

Mahan (*quickly*) Me, Jack! Oh, yes; what's the throuble
now?

Lorry Driver Plenty, sir. The turf-workers have left th'
bog, an' we've no turf to load. Th' delegate says he sent a
telegram to Mr Marthraun, sayin' th' men would leave th'
bog, if no answer came within an hour.

Messenger He did, an' I delivered it.

Michael Damnit, but I forgot about it! The tension here
put it out of me mind!

Father Domineer (*catching the Lorry Driver by an arm*)
Never mind turf or tension now. Are you going to go from
here?

Lorry Driver (*obstinately*) I'll go, if Mr Mahan tells me to
go.

Father Domineer (*in a fury*) Isn't it a wondher God doesn't strike you dead! I tell you to give the wretched woman up, or go, an' that's enough for either Sailor Mahan or you. (*He shakes the Lorry Driver's arm.*) Will you give that wretched woman up; will you send that woman of yours away?

Lorry Driver (*resentfully*) Eh, don't be pullin' th' arm outa me!

Father Domineer (*his fury growing*) Did you send that woman away; are you going to do it?

Lorry Driver (*shaking his arm free, and stepping back*) Aw, let go! I didn't an' I won't!

Father Domineer (*in an ungovernable burst of fury*) You wretch, would you dare to outface your priest? Get out of me sight!

He lunges forward, and strikes the Lorry Driver swiftly and savagely on the side of the head. The man falls heavily; lies still for a moment; tries feebly to rise; falls down again, and lies quite still.

Mahan (*frightened*) He's hurted, Father; you hot him far too hard.

Father Domineer (*frightened too – with a forced laugh*) Nonsense! I just touched him. (*He touches the fallen man with his foot.*) Get up, get up – you're not that much hurt.

Mahan (*bending over the Lorry Driver, and placing a hand on his breast*) I'm afraid he's either dyin' or dead, Father! (*Father Domineer runs over agitatedly to the fallen man, kneels down beside him, and murmurs in his ear. Then he raises his head to face the others.*)

Father Domineer (*to the others*) Yous all saw what happened. I just touched him, an' he fell. I'd no intention

384

of hurting him – only to administer a rebuke.

Sergeant (*consolingly*) Sure, we know that, Father – it was a pure accident.

Father Domineer I murmured an act of contrition into th' poor man's ear.

Messenger (*playing very softly*) It would have been far fitther, Father, if you'd murmured one into your own.

End of Scene Two.

Scene Three

It is towards dusk in the garden now. The sun is setting, and the sky shows it. The rich blue of the sky has given place to a rich yellow, slashed with green and purple. The flagpole stands black against the green and yellow of the sky, and the flag, now, has the same sombre hue.

The big sunflowers against the wall have turned into a solemn black, too; the house has a dark look, save where a falling shaft from the sun turns the window above the porch into a golden eye of light. Far away, in the depths of the sky, the evening star can be faintly seen.

In the distance, for some time, the sounds of drumming, occasionally pierced by the shrill notes of a fife, can be heard.

Mahan is sitting at the table, busy totting up figures on papers spread out before him, his face knotted into creases of anxiety and doubt.

Lorna and Marion are leaning against the wall, away from the gateway, and near the house. Their gay garments are covered with dark hooded cloaks to temper the coolness of the evening air.

Lorna They all seem to be out on th' hunt – police an' soldiers, with th' bands to give them courage. Th' fools!

Marion D'ye think they'll get him? Th' place'll lose its brightness if th' Cock's killed.

Lorna How can they desthroy a thing they say themselves is not of this world? (*She goes over to Mahan, and stares at him for a moment.*) It's cooler. The sun's settin'.

Mahan (*hardly noticing*) Is it? I didn't notice. I'm busy.

Everything thrust through everything else, since that damned Cock got loose. Th' drouth now dhryin' everything to dust; the turf-workers refusin' to work, th' women thinkin' only of dancin' an' dhress. But we'll lay him low, an' bury him deep enough to forget he ever came here!

Lorna Th' men on th' bog work hard; they should get all you've got to give them.

Mahan (*resentfully*) An' why th' hell shouldn't they work hard? Who'd keep th' fires of th' nation burning, if they didn't?

Lorna They work for you, too; an' for Michael. He's got a pile in th' bank, an' rumour says you've got one too.

Mahan (*whining*) Michael may; I never had, an' I'm losin' th' little I had since I lost me best lorry dhriver – blast th' hand that hot him!

The Cock suddenly glides in, weaving a way between Mahan at the table, and Lorna, circling the garden, and finally disappearing round the gable-end of the house; the dance tune softly keeps time with his movements.

(*Jumping to his feet*) What was that? I thought I saw him prancin' by me!

Lorna (*startled too*) What was what?

Mahan Th' Cock in his black plumage, yellow legs, an' crimson crest!

Marion (*who has gone tense*) You put th' heart across me! I thought you meant th' poor dead man. (*She turns to look along the road again.*)

Lorna (*to Mahan*) There's little use worryin' over figures till you settle with th' men.

Mahan (*irritably*) That's Mick's business, that's Mick's business!

Marion (*running over to whisper excitedly to Lorna*) Here they are – Father Domineer an' Mr Marthraun comin' along th' road!

Mahan (*irascibly*) Aw, what does that Father Domineer want comin' here when we've so much to think about! Delayin' things! I want to get away from here before it gets dark.

Lorna Didn't you know they're goin' to purge th' poor house of its evil influences?

Mahan (*irritably*) Oh, can't they do first things first?

Along the pathway outside come Father Domineer and Michael, followed by a lad. The lad is One-eyed Larry. His face is one alternately showing stupidity or cunning, according to whomsoever may be speaking to him. Where his left eye was is a black cavity, giving him a somewhat sinister look. He is lanky and rather awkward-looking. He is wearing a black cassock or soutane, piped with red braid, and is bare-headed. He is carrying a small bell, a book, and an unlighted candle. He shuffles along after the two men, and follows them into the garden.

Father Domineer We'll banish them, never fear, Michael, before I have to leave th' parish because of that unhappy accident. I've faced worse. Be staunch. Th' bell is powerful, so is th' book, an' th' blessed candle, too. (*He glances at the women.*) Let yous women keep to th' farther end of th' garden. (*He glances at Mahan.*) We won't be long, Sailor Mahan. (*Suddenly, as he, Michael, and One-eyed Larry reach the porch*) Where's that other one?

Michael Is it Loreleen, me daughter, Father?

Father Domineer She's no daughter of yours, Michael. (*Bending down to whisper warningly*) Get rid of her, get rid of her – she's dangerous!

Michael How get rid of her, Father?

Father Domineer Pack her off to America!

Michael (*respectfully – as they are about to go into the house*) I'll go first, Father.

Father Domineer (*setting him gently aside*) No, no; mine th' gap of danger.

The three of them go in, the Priest first, then Michael, and, lastly, One-eyed Larry. Marion and Lorna move over to the farther side of the garden.

Lorna It's all damn nonsense, though Michael has me nerves in such a way that I'm near ready to believe in anything.

Mahan Waste of time, too. It'll take a betther man than Father Domineer to dhrive evil things outa Eire.

Marion Messenger says he's only addin' to their number, an' soon a noddin' daffodil, when it dies, 'll know its own way to hell.

The roll of a drum is heard and a great booing. Marion runs to the wall to look over it, and up the road.

(*Excitedly*) A girl runnin' this way, hell for leather. My God, it's Loreleen!

After a few moments, Loreleen runs along the pathway outside, and dashes in through the gateway to Lorna, who catches her in her arms. Clumps of grass and sods of turf, and a few stones follow Loreleen in her rush along the road.

Loreleen (*out of breath*) God damn th' dastards of this vile disthrict! They pelted me with whatever they could lay hands on – th' women because they couldn't stand beside me; th' men because there was ne'er a hope of usin' me as they'd like to! Is it any wondher that th' girls are fleein' in their tens of thousands from this bewildhered land? Blast them! I'll still be gay an' good-lookin'. Let them draw me as I am not, an' sketch in a devil where a maiden stands!

Lorna (*soothingly*) Be calm, child! We can't go in, for Father Domineer's inside puttin' things in ordher. (*Releasing Loreleen*) I'll run along th' road to them disturbers, an' give them a bit o' me mind! (*She catches hold of Marion's arm.*) Come on, Marion!

  She and Marion rush out along the road, and pass out
  of sight.

Loreleen (*staring at the house*) He's inside, is he? That's not where th' evil is, th' gaum, if he wants to know.

Mahan (*seriously*) Come here, Loreleen; nearer, for I've something to say to you. (*As she does not stir, he grips her arm, and draws her farther from the house.*) We might be heard.

Loreleen (*suspiciously*) What do you want, Sailor Mahan? You're not of one mind with them who chased me?

Mahan (*a little embarrassed*) Aw, God, no! Me sails of love are reefed at last, an' I lie quiet, restin' in a lonely harbour now. I'm too old to be flusthered with that kinda folly. I just want to warn you to get outa this disthrict.

Loreleen (*bitterly*) Why must I go? Is it because I'm good-lookin' an' gay?

  But the bold Mahan isn't indifferent to the charms of
  Loreleen. So he goes on to show Loreleen the
  youthfulness of his old age; that his muscles are still
  strong, his fibres flexible. He becomes restless, and

walks about, occasionally glancing at the house,
nervous at what may be happening inside. When he
comes to a chair, he nonchalantly swings a leg over the
back of it, turning on the foot of the same leg to swing
the other one back again. These actions, like the
conversation, though not done in a hurry, are done
quickly, as if he wanted to say all he had to say before
any interruption.

Mahan (*swinging a leg over a chair*) Partly because you're
good-lookin' an' partly because of th' reckless way you
talk. Remember what happened to poor Jack. I'd clear out
if I were you. (*He vaults on to the table, swings round it*
on his backside, and vaults from it on the opposite side, a
little stiffly.)

Loreleen How'm I to clear out? I've no money left. Th'
forty pounds I had, Dad put into his bank for me, an'
now won't give me a penny of it, because he says if I
got it, I'd go to England; an' if I went to England, I'd
lose me soul, th' shaky, venomous lout! An' I keep quiet
because of Lorna. (*Hurriedly, as Mahan is stiffly*
climbing a few feet up the flagpole) Oh, don't be doin'
th' monkey on a stick! Maybe you could help me?
Could you, would you?

Mahan (*sliddering from the pole, swinging a leg over a*
chair, and coming closer to her) Now that's what I'd
hoped you'd say. This is th' first time I've caught you
alone. I'll give you what you need, an' you can weigh
anchor, an' be off outa this damned place. Listen, darlin':
you steal out tonight to th' Red Barn, west of th' Holy
Cross, an' I'll dhrive there with what'll get you as far as
you want to go. (*He suddenly puts an arm round her in a*
kind of clutch.) Jasus, you have lovely eyes!

Loreleen (*trying to pull his arm away*) Oh, Sailor Mahan,
don't do that! Let me go – someone may see us!

Mahan (*recklessly*) You deserve to be ruffled a bit! Well, will you come to th' Red Barn, while th' rest are goin' to th' dance, an' save yourself? Yes or no!

Loreleen Maybe, maybe; yes, yes, I'll go. Let go your clutch!

> *The house shakes, a sound of things moving and crockery breaking comes from it; several flashes of lightning spear out through the window over the porch; and the flagpole wags drunkenly from side to side.*
>
> *Marion and Lorna appear on the pathway outside the wall, and hurry along into the garden just as One-eyed Larry comes running out of the house, his face beset with fear. His one eye takes in the picture of Loreleen breaking away from Mahan. Loreleen turns aside from One-eyed Larry, while Mahan, embarrassed, turns to face him.*

One-eyed Larry (*excitedly*) It's startin' in earnest! There's a death-sthruggle goin' on in there! Poor Father Domineer's got a bad black eye, an' Micky Marthraun's coat is torn to tatthers!

Lorna (*hurrying into the garden*) What's happened, what's happenin'?

Mahan (*with dignity – to One-eyed Larry*) Misther Marthraun in your mouth, me lad.

Loreleen (*mischievously*) Let th' lad tell his funny story.

One-eyed Larry (*turning on Loreleen*) It's funny to you because you're in league with th' evil ones! (*To the others*) One o' Father Domineer's feet is all burned be a touch from one o' them, an' one o' Micky's is frozen stiff be a touch from another. (*To Mahan*) Maybe you'd ha' liked me to have lost me other eye while you were warmin' yourself in that one's arms! (*He points to Loreleen.*)

Mahan (*furiously*) You one-eyed gett, if you had two, I'd cyclonize you with a box!

Loreleen (*unmoved – a little mockingly*) An' how did th' poor lamb lose his eye?

Mahan (*indifferently*) Oh, when he was a kid, he was hammerin' a bottle, an' a flyin' piece cut it out of his head.

One-eyed Larry (*venomously*) You're a liar, that wasn't th' way! It was th' Demon Cock who done it to me. Only certain eyes can see him, an' I had one that could. He caught me once when I was spyin' on him, put a claw over me left eye, askin' if I could see him then; an' on me sayin' no, put th' claw over th' other one, an' when I said I could see him clear now, says he, that eye sees too well, an' on that, he pushed an' pushed till it was crushed into me head.

Loreleen (*mockingly*) What a sad thing to happen!

The house shakes worse than before, and seems to lurch over to one side. The flagpole wags from side to side merrily; there is a rumble of thunder, and blue lightning flashes from the window. All, except Loreleen, cower together at the far end of the garden. She stands over by the wall, partly framed by the sable sunflowers.

Marion (*full of fright*) Sacred Heart! Th' house'll fall asundher!

Loreleen (*gleefully*) Let it! It's th' finest thing that could happen to it!

One-eyed Larry (*trembling violently*) It's now or never for them an' for us. They're terrible powerful spirits. Knocked th' bell outa me hand, blew out th' candle, an' tore th' book to threads! Thousands of them there are, led be th' bigger ones – Kissalass, Velvethighs, Reedabuck, Dancesolong, an' Sameagain. Keep close. Don't run. They might want help.

393

*Screeches like those of barn owls are heard from the
house, with the 'too-whit too-whoo' of other kinds, the
cackling of hens, and the loud cawing of crows.*

(*Frantically pushing his way to the back of the others*)
Oooh! Let me get back, get back!

*The house shakes again; the flagpole totters and falls
flat; blue and red lightning flashes from the window,
and a great peal of thunder drums through the garden.
Then all becomes suddenly silent. They all hang on to
each other, shivering with fear, except Loreleen, who
lights a cigarette, puts a foot on a chair, leans on its
back, looks at the house, and smokes away serenely.*

Lorna (*tremulously*) Why has th' house gone so silent
suddenly?

One-eyed Larry (*from the rear*) They've either killed th'
demons, or th' demons has killed them.

Marion God save us, they must be dead!

Loreleen (*with quiet mockery*) Welcome be th' will o'
God.

Lorna (*suddenly – with great agitation*) Get back, get
back! Run! There's something comin' out!

*She, Marion, and One-eyed Larry race for the gateway,
rush on to the sidewalk, and bend down, so that only
their heads can be seen peeping over the wall. Mahan
shrinks back to the far end of the garden, and Loreleen
remains where she is.*
*From the house, sideways, through the now lurching
porch, come Father Domineer and Michael. Both are
limping, Father Domineer on his left foot, Michael on
his right one. Domineer has a big black eye, his coat is
awry on his back, and his hair is widely tossed.
Michael's coat hangs in tatters on him. Father*

*Domineer's face is begrimed with the smudges of
smoke, and both look tired, but elated.*

*One-eyed Larry at once runs out, and takes his place
reverently behind them, standing with his hands folded
piously in front of his breast, his eyes bent towards the
ground. Mahan straightens up, and Lorna and Marion
return to the garden. Loreleen remains as she was.*

Father Domineer (*as he enters with Michael*) Be assured,
good people, all's well, now. The house is safe for all. The
evil things have been banished from the dwelling. Most of
the myrmidons of Anticlericus, Secularius, an' Odeonius
have been destroyed. The Civic Guard and the soldiers of
Feehanna Fawl will see to the few who escaped. We can
think quietly again of our Irish Sweep. Now I must get to
my car to go home, and have a wash an' brush up. (*To
Marion and Lorna*) Off you go into the house, good
women. Th' place, th' proper place, th' only place for th'
woman. Straighten it out, and take pride in doing it. (*He
shoves Marion towards the porch.*) Go on, woman, when
you're told! (*To Michael*) You'll have to exert your
authority more as head of the house.

Michael (*asserting it at once – to Lorna*) You heard what
Father Domineer said. Go on; in you go, an' show yourself
a decent, God-fearin' woman.

Father Domineer (*trying to be gracious – to Lorna*) Th'
queen of th' household as th' husband is th' king.

*Marion has gone into the house with a sour-looking
face, and Lorna now follows her example, looking
anything but charmed.*

(*Turning to Loreleen*) And you – aren't you going in to
help?

Loreleen (*quietly*) No, thanks; I prefer to stay on in the
garden.

Father Domineer (*thunderously*) Then learn to stand on the earth in a more modest and suitable way, woman! (*Pointing to ornaments on crest of hat and breast of bodice*) An' do you mind that th' ornaments ye have on of brooch an' bangle were invented be th' fallen angels, now condemned to everlastin' death for worshippin' beauty that faded before it could be clearly seen? (*Angrily*) Oh, woman, *de cultus feminarum malifico eradicum*!

Michael That one's mind is always mustherin' dangerous thoughts plundered outa evil books!

Father Domineer (*startled*) Books? What kinda books? Where are they?

Michael She has some o' them in th' house this minute.

Father Domineer (*roaring*) Bring them out, bring them out! How often have I to warn you against books! Hell's bells tolling people away from th' thruth! Bring them out, *in annem fiat ecclesiam nonsensio*, before th' demoneens we've banished flood back into th' house again!

Michael and One-eyed Larry jostle together into the porch and into the house to do Father Domineer's bidding.

Loreleen (*taking her leg down from the chair, and striding over to Father Domineer*) You fool, d'ye know what you're thryin' to do? You're thryin' to keep God from talkin'!

Father Domineer You're speakin' blasphemy, woman!

Mahan What do people want with books? I don't remember readin' a book in me life.

Michael comes back carrying a book, followed by One-eyed Larry carrying another. Father Domineer takes the book from Michael, and glances at the title-page.

Father Domineer (*explosively*) A book about Voltaire! (*To Loreleen*) This book has been banned, woman.

Loreleen (*innocently*) Has it now? If so, I must read it over again.

Father Domineer (*to One-eyed Larry*) What's th' name of that one?

One-eyed Larry (*squinting at the title*) Ullisississies, or something.

Father Domineer Worse than th' other one. (*He hands his to One-eyed Larry.*) Bring th' two o' them down to th' Presbytery, an' we'll desthroy them.

Loreleen snatches the two books from One-eyed Larry. One-eyed Larry tries to prevent her, but a sharp push from her sends him toppling over. Loreleen, with great speed, darts out of the gateway, runs along the pathway, and disappears.

(*Standing as if stuck to the ground*) Afther her, afther her!

Michael (*astonished*) Me legs won't move!

Mahon and One-eyed Larry (*together*) Nor mine, neither.

As Loreleen disappears, the Cock suddenly springs over the wall, and pirouettes in and out between them as they stand stuck to the ground.
  Cute ears may hear the quick tune, played softly, of an accordion, as the Cock weaves his way about. The Sergeant appears running outside, stops when he sees the Cock, leans over the wall, and presents a gun at Michael.

Michael (*frantically – to Sergeant*) Not me, man, not me!

Terribly excited, the Sergeant swings the gun till it is pointing at Mahan.

Mahan (*frantically*) Eh, not me, man!

After the Cock has pirouetted round for some moments, while they all remain transfixed, the scene suddenly goes dark, though the music continues to sound through it. Then two squib-like shots are heard, followed by a clash of thunder, and, when the garden enjoys the light of early dusk again, which comes immediately after the clap of thunder, the music as suddenly ceases.

The returning light shows that Father Domineer is not there; that Michael and Mahan are stretched out on the ground; and that One-eyed Larry is half over the wall, his belly on it, his legs trailing into the garden, his head and shoulders protruding into the road.

Michael (*moaning*) Shot through the soft flesh an' th' hard bone!

Mahan (*groaning*) Shot through th' hard bone an' th' soft flesh!

One-eyed Larry (*shouting*) Mrs Marthraun, Marion, we're all killed be th' Cock an' th' Sergeant!

Lorna and Marion come running out of the house over to the two prostrate men.

Lorna What's happened? Where's th' Sergeant?

One-eyed Larry (*sliddering over the wall, frantic with fear*) I seen him runnin' off when he'd shot us all! I'm goin' home, I'm goin' home! Father Domineer's been carried off be th' Demon Cock – I'm off! (*He runs swiftly down the road, and disappears.*)

Lorna (*bending over Michael*) Where were you hit? D'ye think there's a chance of you dyin'?

Michael (*despairingly*) I'm riddled!

Lorna (*feeling his body over*) I can't see a speck of damage on you anywhere, you fool.

Marion (*who has been examining Mahan*) No, nor on this fella either.

Michael I tell you th' bullet careered through me breast an' came out be me back!

Mahan An' then tore through me back an' came out be me breast!

Lorna What darkness was One-eyed Larry talkin' about? An' Father Domineer carried off be the Cock! Me nerves are all gettin' shatthered. It's all very thryin'. (*She pokes Michael roughly with her foot.*) Here, get up, th' both of yous. There isn't a thing wrong with either of you.

Mahan (*sitting up cautiously, and feeling in his breast pocket*) What th' hell's this? (*He pulls out a bullet bigger than a cigar.*) Looka, Michael Marthraun, th' size of th' bullet that went tearin' through you an' then through me! (*Very devoutly*) Good angels musta gone along with it, healin' all at th' same time that it tore our vitals.

Michael (*as devoutly*) Some higher an' special power musta been watchin' over us, Sailor Mahan. Sharin' a miracle, now, Sailor Mahan, we're more than brothers.

Mahan (*fervently*) We are that, now; we are indeed. I'll keep this bullet till th' day I die as a momento of a mementous occasion!

Lorna (*impatiently*) Get up, get up. An' don't disturb us again while we're practisin' for the fancy-dhress dance tonight in th' hope of winning a spot prize.

Michael (*furiously to her*) You'll win no spot prize, an' there'll be no dance till that Demon Cock's laid low! (*To Mahan – piously*) Thrue men we are, workin' in a thruly

brotherly way for th' good of th' entire community –
aren't we, Sailor Mahan? That's what saved us!

Mahan (*as piously*) We are that, Michael; we are indeed;
especially now that we've settled th' question finally so
long disputed between us.

Michael (*suspiciously, a note of sharpness in his voice*)
How settled it?

Mahan Be you arrangin' to give me, not only what I was
askin', but twice as much.

Michael (*sarcastically*) Oh, did I now? That was damned
good of me! (*Angrily*) No, nor what you were askin'
either. D'ye want me to ruin meself to glorify you? An'
didn't I hear a certain man promisin', nearly on his oath,
he'd give his lorries for next to nothin' to serve th'
community?

Mahan (*shouting*) When I was undher a spell, fosthered
on me here! I'm goin', I'm goin'. I'll argue no more! (*He
goes out by the gate and along the road, pausing as he is
about to disappear.*) For th' last time, Michael Marthraun,
are you goin' to do th' decent for th' sake of th' nation, an'
give me what I'm askin'?

Michael (*with decision – quietly*) No, Sailor Mahan, I'm
not. (*He shouts.*) I'd see you in hell first!

Mahan (*as he goes*) A sweet goodbye to you, an' take a
dhrug to keep from stayin' awake o' nights thinkin' of the
nation's needs!

Lorna (*persuasively*) Be reasonable, Michael. You're
makin' enough now to be well able to give him all he
asks.

Michael (*savagely seizing her arm*) Listen, you; even
though you keep th' accounts for me, it's a law of nature

an' a law of God that a wife must be silent about her husband's secrets! D'ye hear me, you costumed slut?

Lorna (*freeing herself with an effort*) Don't tear th' arm out of me! If you want to embalm yourself in money, you won't get me to do it!

The sound of the wind rising is heard now – a long, sudden gust-like sound, causing Michael to do a sudden rush towards the gate, pressing himself back all the time, and gripping the wall when he gets to it. The two women do not notice the wind.

Michael Jasus! that was a sudden blast!

Lorna (*wondering*) Blast? I felt no blast.

Marion (*shaking her head*) He's undher a spell again.

One-eyed Larry comes running along the road outside, excited and shouting. He is holding on tensely to the waist-band of his trousers.

One-eyed Larry (*without the wall*) A miracle, a miracle! Father Domineer, outa th' darkness, was snatched from th' claws of the Demon Cock, an' carried home safe on th' back of a white duck!

Lorna (*amazed*) On th' back of a white duck? When will wondhers cease! They're all goin' mad!

Michael (*clapping his hands*) Grand news! Was it a wild duck, now, or merely a domestic one?

One-eyed Larry Wild or tame, what does it matther? It carried him cheerily through th' sky, an' deposited him dacently down on his own doorstep!

Michael (*with deep thought*) It might well have been one of me own sensible ducks that done it.

One-eyed Larry (*coming to the gate*) Wait till I tell yous.

Th' Demon Cock's furious at his escape, an' he's causin' consthernation. He's raised a fierce wind be th' beat of his wings, an' it's tossin' cattle on to their backs; whippin' th' guns from th' hands of Civic Guard an' soldier, so that th' guns go sailin' through th' sky like cranes; an' th' wind's tearin' at the clothes of th' people. It's only be hard holdin' that I can keep me own trousers on!

Michael (*eagerly*) Th' wind near whipped me on to th' road a minute ago.

The Bellman enters on the pathway outside, and meets One-eyed Larry at the gateway, so that the two of them stand there, the one on the left, the other to the right of it.

The collar and one arm are all that are left of the Bellman's coat, and his shirt has been blown outside of his trousers. He is still wearing the brass hat. His right hand is gripping his waist-band, and his left carries the bell that he is ringing.

Bellman (*shouting*) Get out, get in! Th' Demon Cock's scourin' th' skies again, mettlesome, menacin', molestifyin' monsther! Fly to your houses, fall upon your knees, shut th' doors, close th' windows! In a tearin' rage, he's rippin' th' clouds outa th' sky, because Father Domineer was snatched away from him, an' carried home, fit an' well, on th' back of a speckled duck!

One-eyed Larry (*startled into anger*) You're a liar, it wasn't a speckled duck! What are you sayin', fella? It was a pure white duck that carried th' Father home!

Bellman (*angrily – to One-eyed Larry*) Liar yourself, an' you're wrong! It was a speckled duck that done it; speckled in black, brown, an' green spots. I seen it with me own two eyes doin' th' thrick.

One-eyed Larry (*vehemently*) I seen it with me one eye in concentration, an' it was a duck white as th' dhriven snow that brought him to his domiceel.

Lorna I'd say white's a sensible colour, an' more apter for th' job.

Michael I'd say a speckled duck would look more handsome landin' on a doorstep than a white fowl.

Marion (*thoughtfully*) I wondher, now, could it have been Mr McGilligan's tame barnacle goose?

Michael (*explosively*) No, it couldn't have been Mr McGilligan's tame barnacle goose! Don't be thryin' to scatther confusion over a miracle happenin' before our very eyes!

The Sergeant comes rushing in along the pathway outside the wall, and runs into the garden through the gateway, roughly shoving the Bellman and One-eyed Larry out of his way. His cap is gone, a piece of rope is tied round his chest to keep his coat on; and, when he reaches the gate, all can see that he wears no trousers, leaving him in a long shirt over short pants. He is excited, and his face is almost convulsed with fear and shame.

Sergeant (*shoving One-eyed Larry and Bellman aside*) Outa me way, you fools! (*Rushing into the garden – to Michael*) Give me one of your oul' trousers, Mick, for th' love o' God! Whipped off me be a blast of th' wind me own were. When I seen them goin', me entire nature was galvanized into alarmin' anxiety as to what might happen next.

Michael A terrible experience! What's to come of us, at all!

Sergeant (*tearfully*) Why isn't Father Domineer here to help? He doesn't care a damn now, since he was carried home, safe an' sound on th' back of a barnacle goose!

One-eyed Larry (*dumbfounded and angry*) A barnacle goose? What are you sayin', man? It was a dazzlin' white duck that brought him home.

Bellman (*to One-eyed Larry*) I'm tellin' you it was a specially speckled duck that done it.

Sergeant (*emphatically*) It was a goose, I'm sayin'. Th' Inspector seen it through a field-glass, an' identified it as a goose, a goose!

Lorna (*amused – laying a hand on Marion's shoulder*) Look at him, Marion. All dollied up for th' fancy-dhress dance!

Marion (*hilariously*) It's lookin' like th' blue bonnets are over th' bordher!

Michael (*angrily – to the Sergeant*) Get into th' house, man, an' don't be standin' there in that style of half-naked finality! You'll find some oul' trousers upstairs. (*Turning on Lorna and Marion as the Sergeant trots timidly into the house*) You two hussies, have yous no semblance of sense of things past an' things to come? Here's a sweet miracle only afther happenin', an' there yous are, gigglin' an' gloatin' at an aspect in a man that should send th' two of yous screamin' away! Yous are as bad as that one possessed, th' people call me daughter.

The sound of the wind now rises, swifter, shriller, and stronger, carrying in it an occasional moan, as in a gale, and with this stronger wind comes the Messenger, sauntering along outside the wall, sitting down on it when he reaches the end farthest from the house. Nothing in the garden is moved by the wind's whistling violence, except Michael, the Bellman, and One-eyed Larry (who have been suddenly hustled into the garden by the wind). These three now grip their waist-bands, and begin to make sudden movements to

*and fro, as if dragged by an invisible force; each of
them trying to hold back as the wind pushes them
forward. The Messenger is coaxing a soft tune from
his accordion; while Marion and Lorna are unaffected
by the wind, and stand staring at the men, amused by
their antics.*

(*A little frantic*) Listen to th' risin' evil of th' wind! Oh, th'
beat of it, oh, th' beat of it! We know where it comes from
– red wind on our backs, black wind on our breasts,
thryin' to blow us to hell!

Bellman (*gliding about, pushed by the wind; holding on
to his trousers with one hand, while he rings his bell with
the other one*) Fly into th' houses, close th' windows, shut
th' doors!

One-eyed Larry (*gliding in opposite direction*) We can't,
we can't – we go where th' wind blows us!

Messenger What ails yous? I feel only th' brisk breeze
carrying the smell of pinewoods, or th' softer one carryin'
th' scent of th' ripenin' apples.

Michael (*to the women, while he holds fast to his waist-
band*) Get in, an' sthrip off them coloured deceits, smellin'
of th' sly violet an' th' richer rose, sequestherin' a lure in
every petal! Off with them, I say, an' put on a cautious
grey, or th' stated humbleness of a coal-black gown!

*The Sergeant comes from the house wearing Michael's
best black Sunday trousers. He comes from the porch
shyly, but the moment he steps into the garden, his face
flashes into a grim look, and he grabs hold of the waist-
band, and glides about as the others do.*

(*Seeing the trousers – with a squeal of indignation*) Me best
Sunday black ones! Couldn't your damned plundherin'
paws pounce on something a little lowlier to wear?

Bellman Get into th' houses, shut to th' doors, close th' windows!

Father Domineer suddenly appears on the pathway outside, and stands at the gateway looking into the garden. A gust of wind, fierce and shrill, that preceded him, declines in a sad wail, and ceases altogether, leaving a sombre silence behind it. Father Domineer's hair is tossed about; he has a wild look in his eyes, and he carries a walking-stick to help him surmount the limp from the hurt he got when warring with the evil spirits.

Father Domineer (*stormily*) Stop where yous are! No hidin' from the enemy! Back to hell with all bad books, bad plays, bad pictures, and bad thoughts! Cock o' th' north, or cock o' th' south, we'll down derry doh down him yet. Shoulder to shoulder, an' step together against th' onward rush of paganism! Boldly tread, firm each foot, erect each head!

One-eyed Larry, Michael, Bellman and Sergeant (*together – very feebly*) Hurraah!

Father Domineer Fixed in front be every glance, forward at th' word advance!

One-eyed Larry, Michael, Bellman and Sergeant (*together – very feebly*) Advance!

Father Domineer We know where we're goin', an' we know who's goin' with us.

Michael The minsthrel boy with th' dear harp of his country, an' Brian O'Lynn.

Bellman Danny Boy an' th' man who sthruck O'Hara.

One-eyed Larry Not forgettin' Mick McGilligan's daughter, Maryann!

Sounds of fifing and drumming are heard, mingled with the sound of booing, a little distance away.

Father Domineer (*jubilantly*) Listen to th' band! We're closin' in; we're winnin'! (*He puts a hand up to shade his eyes, and peers forward.*) They've collared one of them! Aha, a woman again! (*Pause.*) A fine, familiar one too. (*He shouts.*) Lead th' slut here, Shanaar, right here in front of me!

He goes through the gateway, and waits in the garden for things to come.

    Shanaar appears on the pathway, followed by the two Rough Fellows dragging Loreleen along. She is in a sad way. Her hair is tumbled about; her clothes are disarranged; her bodice unbuttoned, and her skirt reefed half-way up, showing a slim leg, with the nylon stocking torn. One of the Rough Fellows is carrying her hat with its cock-like crest in his hand. A blood-stained streak stretches from a corner of an eye half-way down a cheek. Her face is very pale, and intense fright is vividly mirrored in it. She is dragged by the arms along the ground by the men, led by Shanaar, to where the Priest is standing. When she is nicely placed before him, she hangs her head, ashamed of her dishevelled state, and of the way she has been pulled before him. Other men and women follow them in, but are checked from crowding the pathway by an order from the Priest. The Messenger rises from his seat on the wall, and comes near to where the men are holding Loreleen. He has placed the carrying straps of his accordion over his shoulders, and now bears the instrument on his back. Michael, the Bellman, and One-eyed Larry stand some way behind the Priest. Marion and Lorna have started to come to Loreleen's assistance, but have been imperiously waved back by Father Domineer, and have retreated back towards the house, where they stand to stare at what

*happens. Shanaar stands at the gateway, gloating over
the woeful condition of Loreleen.*

Father Domineer (*to those following the men dragging in
Loreleen*) Go back; keep back there! Give th' honied
harlot plenty of space to show herself off in.

Shanaar (*down to Father Domineer*) Tell her off, Father;
speak to her in th' name of holy Ireland!

Father Domineer (*to Sergeant*) You go, Sergeant, an' keep
them from coming too close; (*To Shanaar*) an' you,
Shanaar, stand at the opposite end to keep any others from
pressing in on us. (*To the men holding Loreleen*) Bring her
a little closer.

The men drag her closer.

Now, jerk her to her feet.

The men jerk her upright.

Well, me painted paramour, you're not looking quite so
gay now; your impudent confidence has left you to
yourself. Your jest with heaven is over, me lass! (*To the
men*) How did you ketch her?

1st Rough Fellow (*with pride*) We've been on her tail,
Father, for some time. We ketched her in a grand car with
a married man; with a married man, Father, an' he thryin'
to put an arm round her.

2nd Rough Fellow (*butting in to share the pride of
capture*) So we hauled her outa th' car, and hustled her
here to you.

Lorna (*running over to the man nearest to her, and
catching his arm*) Let th' poor lass go, you cowardly lout! I
know you: your whole nature's a tuft of villainies! Lust
inflames your flimsy eyes whenever a skirt passes you by. If

God had given you a tusk, you'd rend asundher every woman of th' disthrict!

Father Domineer (*angrily – to Lorna*) Get back to your place, woman! (*Shouting, as she hesitates*) Get back when I tell you!

> Lorna moves slowly away from Loreleen's side and goes into the house.

Marion (*as she follows Lorna into the house*) Dastard Knights of Columbanus, do noble work, an' do it well!

Loreleen (*to Father Domineer – appealingly*) Make them let me go, Father, an' let me get into th' house! It was Sailor Mahan promised me enough to take me away from here that made me go to him. I shouldn't have gone, but I wanted to get away; (*brokenly*) get away, away! Five pounds he gave me, an' they took them off me, with th' last two pounds of me own I had left.

Father Domineer (*savagely*) Sailor Mahan's a decent, honest soul, woman! A man fresh for th' faith, full of good works for clergy an' his neighbours. (*He bends down to hiss in her ears.*) An' this is th' man, you sinful slut, this is th' man you would pet an' probe into a scarlet sin!

Loreleen I only wanted to get away. I wanted to get away from Sailor Mahan as much as I wanted to get away from all here.

Father Domineer (*to the two Rough Fellows*) Where's Sailor Mahan?

1st Rough Fellow Th' people pelted him back to his home an' proper wife, Father, an' he's there now, in bed, an' sorry for what he thried to do.

Loreleen (*plaintively*) Make them give me back th' last few pounds I had.

Father Domineer (*to the Rough Fellows*) You shouldn't have handled Sailor Mahan so roughly. Where's the money?

2nd Rough Fellow We tore it up, Father, thinkin' it wasn't fit to be handled be anyone of decent discernment.

Loreleen (*emphatically*) They didn't; they kept it. (*Stifling a scream*) Oh, they're twisting me arms!

Father Domineer (*cynically*) Don't be timid of a little twinge of pain, woman, for, afther th' life you've lived, you'll welther in it later. (*To the two Rough Fellows*) Yous should have kept th' money to be given to th' poor.

Messenger (*coming over to the Rough Fellow on Loreleen's right – calmly*) Let that fair arm go, me man, for, if you don't, there's a live arm here'll twist your neck instead. (*With a shout*) Let it go!

> *After a nod from the priest, the 1st Rough Fellow lets Loreleen's arm go. The Messenger goes quietly round to the 2nd Rough Fellow.*

Let that fair arm go, me man, or another arm may twist your own neck! Let it go!

> *The 2nd Rough Fellow sullenly does so.*

Now stand a little away, an' give th' girl room to breathe.

> *The two Rough Fellows move a little away from Loreleen.*

Thank you. (*To the Priest*) Now, Father, so full of pity an' loving-kindness, jet out your bitther blessin', and let th' girl go. An' thry to mingle undherstandin' with your pride, so as to ease th' tangle God has suffered to be flung around us all.

Father Domineer (*fiercely – to the Messenger*) Keep

farther away, you, for th' crowd is angry and their arms are sthrong! We know you – enemy to th' glow of tradition's thruth, enemy to righteous reprobation, whose rowdy livery is but dyed in rust from th' gates of hell! (*To Loreleen*) An' you, you'd hook your unholy reputation to a decent man's life. A man, like Sailor Mahan, diligent in his duty, th' echo of whose last prayer can ever be heard when another worshipper enters th' church. You'd sentence him to stand beside you, you shuttle-cock of sin!

Loreleen (*roused to indignation*) Oh, end it, will you! You fail in honesty when you won't make them give me back what they robbed from me. When you condemn a fair face, you sneer at God's good handiwork. You are layin' your curse, sir, not upon a sin, but on a joy. Take care a divil doesn't climb up your own cassock into your own belfry!

Father Domineer (*furiously*) You'll dhribble th' blackness of sin no longer over our virtuous bordhers! (*He hisses the words out.*) *Stipendium peccati mors est*! Get away from here quicker than you came, or it's in your coffin you'll be – in your coffin, your coffin!

Shanaar (*from the gateway*) A merciful sentence, an aysey one, for a one like her!

Loreleen (*half defiantly*) How am I to go where I'd like to go, when they took all I had off me? How am I to go for miles with me clothes near rent from me back, an' frail shoes on me feet?

Father Domineer (*putting his face closer to hers*) Thrudge it; thrudge on your two feet; an' when these burn an' blister, go on your knees; an' when your knees are broken an' bruised, go on your belly; crawl in th' dust, as did th' snake in th' Garden of Eden, for dust is th' right cushion for th' like of you! (*He raises himself erect, and commands in a loud voice.*) Go now!

Loreleen turns away, goes slowly through the gateway, and along the road outside. As Loreleen reaches the gate, Lorna runs out of the house. She is wearing a dark red cloak, and carries a green one over her arm. She has a fairly large rucksack strapped on her back.

Lorna (*calling as she runs out of the house*) Loreleen!

Loreleen halts but does not turn her head.

Loreleen, I go with you! (*Lorna shoves Father Domineer aside at the gateway, nearly knocks Shanaar over, and hurries to Loreleen. Draping the green cloak over Loreleen's shoulders*) I go with you, love. I've got a sthrong pair of shoes in the sack you can put on when we're free from th' Priest an' his rabble. Lift up your heart, lass: we go not towards an evil, but leave an evil behind us!

They go out slowly together.

Father Domineer (*taking the Sergeant by the arm*) Let her go quietly to her own. We'll follow some of the way to prevent anyone from harming her. (*Down to Michael*) Be of good cheer, Michael; th' demon is conquered – you can live peaceful an' happy in your own home now.

He goes out with the Sergeant, followed by all who may be there, except Michael, the Messenger and Shanaar.
  The Messenger goes back to the wall, sits on it sideways, takes the accordion from his back, and begins to play, very softly, the air of 'Oh, Woman Gracious'. Shanaar leans on the wall from the outside, looking down at Michael, who is now seated gloomily on a chair beside the table, an elbow resting on it, his head resting on the hand.

Shanaar (*down to Michael*) His reverence never spoke a thruer word, Mick, than that of you'd have happiness an' peace now. You were a long time without them, but you have them now.

Michael (*doubtfully*) Maybe I have, Shanaar, an', God knows, I need them. (*He pauses for a moment, thinking.*) I wondher will Lorna come back?

Shanaar (*emphatically*) Oh, devil a come back! You need have no fear o' that, man. An' fortunate you are, for a woman's always a menace to a man's soul. Woman is th' passionate path to hell!

Messenger (*playing softly on his accordion and singing*)
   Oh, woman gracious, in golden garments,
   Through life's dark places, all glintin' go;
   Bring man, in search of th' thruth tremendous,
   Th' joy that ev'ry young lad should know.

   Then come out, darlin', in reckless raiment,
   We'll dance along through Ireland gay,
   An' clip from life life's rich enjoyments,
   An' never want for a word to say.

Marion has come into the porch, and now stands at the door, watching the Messenger. She is covered to her knees by a bright-blue cloak.

   Cling close to youth with your arms enthrancin',
   For youth is restless, an' loth to stay;
   So take your share of th' kisses goin',
   Ere sly youth, tirin', can slink away!

Marion crosses the garden towards the gate, and is about to go through it when the Messenger catches her by the arm.

Would you leave me here, alone, without a lass to love me?

Marion (*gently removing the hold of his hand on her arm*)

413

Your voice is dear to me; your arm around me near seals
me to you; an' I'd love to have –

Messenger (*quickly*) Your lips on mine!

Marion But not here, Robin Adair, oh, not here; for a
whisper of love in this place bites away some of th' soul!

> *She goes out by the gateway, and along the road taken
> by Lorna and Loreleen. The Messenger stays where he
> is, wistful and still.*

(*Just before she goes*) Come, if you want to, Robin Adair;
stay, if you will.

Shanaar (*to the Messenger*) Stay, Messenger. Take a
warnin' from a wise oul' man, a very wise oul' one, too.
(*He turns his head to look peeringly to the left along the
road.*) What's this I see comin'? If it isn't Julia, back from
Lourdes, an' she on her stretcher still! I'd best be off, for
I've no inclination to thry a chatter with a one who's come
back as bad as she was when she went.

> *He bends down nearly double, so as not to be seen, and
> slyly and quietly steals away.*
>   *After a pause, Julia comes in on her stretcher, carried
> by the two Rough Fellows as before, her father, silent
> and stony-faced, walking beside her. The stretcher is laid
> down in the garden just inside the gate. Julia is covered
> with a rug, black as a winter's sky, and its sombre hue is
> enlivened only by the chalk-white face of the dying girl.
> The Messenger has gone from the gateway, and now
> stands in a half-to-attention, military way, a little
> distance from the stretcher, looking down at Julia. Julia's
> father stands, as before, behind her head. Michael sits,
> unnoticing, elbow on table, his head resting on his hand.*

Julia (*in a toneless voice – to no one in particular*) Lorna, I
want Lorna.

Messenger (*gently*) She's gone, Julia.

Julia Gone? Gone where?

Messenger To a place where life resembles life more than it does here.

Julia She's a long way to go, then. It's th' same everywhere. In Lourdes as here, with all its crowds an' all its candles. I want Loreleen.

Messenger She's gone with Lorna, an' Marion's followed them both.

Julia Then there's no voice left to offer even th' taunting comfort of asking if I feel better.

Messenger There's Michael Marthraun there.

Julia (*after a long look at Michael*) He, poor man, is dyin' too. No one left, an' th' stir there was when I was goin' – th' Mayor there, with all his accouthered helpers; th' band playin'; Father Domineer spoutin' his blessin'; an' oul' Shanaar busy sayin' somersaultin' prayers; because they all thought I would bring a sweet miracle back. (*She pauses.*) There was no miracle, Robin; she didn't cure me, she didn't cure me, Robin. I've come back, without even a gloamin' thought of hope. (*She pauses again. With a wan smile*) I can see your whole soul wishin' you could cure me. Touch me with your questionable blessin' before I go.

Messenger (*very softly*) Be brave.

Julia Nothin' else, Robin Adair?

Messenger Evermore be brave.

Julia (*after a pause*) Dad, take me home.

The Rough Fellows take up the stretcher and carry it out, the stony-faced father following in the rear without a word.

Michael (*raising his head from his hand to look at the Messenger*) Maybe Lorna might come back. Maybe I mightn't have been so down on her fancy dhressin'.

Messenger (*tonelessly*) Maybe she will; maybe you mightn't.

Michael (*tonelessly too*) It'll be very lonely for me now. All have left me. (*He takes a set of rosary beads from his pocket, and fingers them.*) I've no one left to me but th' Son o' God. (*He notices the Messenger settling the accordion comfortably on his back, and watches him going to the gate.*) Are you goin' too?

Messenger (*shortly*) Ay.

Michael Where?

Messenger To a place where life resembles life more than it does here.

Michael (*after a pause*) What, Messenger, would you advise me to do?

Messenger (*turning at the gate to reply*) Die. There is little else left useful for the likes of you to do.

He swings his accordion comfortably before him, and plays a few preliminary notes. Then he starts to sing softly as he goes away along the pathway outside; while Michael leans forward on to the table, and buries his head in his arms.

(*Singing and accompanying himself on the accordion – as he is going off*):
She's just like a young star out taking the air –
Let others be good or be clever –

With Marion gay, a gay flower in her hair,
Life becomes but a pleasant endeavour.

When building a city or making the hay,
I'll follow her close as night follows day,

Or lads follow lasses out nutting in May,
For ever and ever and ever!

The End

SEAN O'CASEY

STAR OF THE SEA

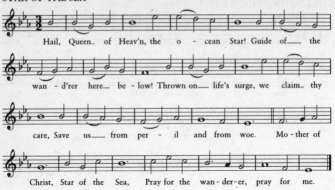

Hail, Queen of Heav'n, the o - cean Star! Guide of the
wan - d'rer here be - low! Thrown on life's surge, we claim thy
care, Save us from per - il and from woe. Mo - ther of
Christ, Star of the Sea, Pray for the wan - der - er, pray for me.

WHEN MEN WAS MEN

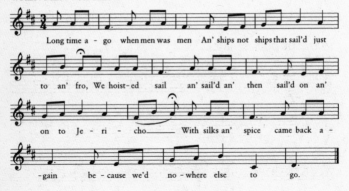

Long time a - go when men was men An' ships not ships that sail'd just
to an' fro, We hoist-ed sail an' sail'd an' then sail'd on an'
on to Je - ri - cho With silks an' spice came back a -
-gain be - cause we'd no - where else to go.

COCK-A-DOODLE DANDY

LORELEEN'S SHANTY

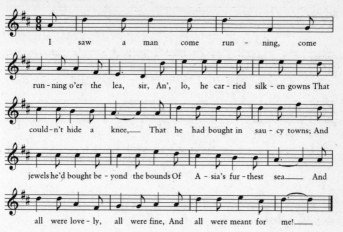

I saw a man come run-ning, come run-ning o'er the lea, sir, An', lo, he car-ried silk-en gowns That could-n't hide a knee,— That he had bought in sau-cy towns; And jewels he'd bought be-yond the bounds Of A-sia's fur-thest sea— And all were love-ly, all were fine, And all were meant for me!—

MUSIC FOR COCK'S DANCE

OH, WOMAN GRACIOUS

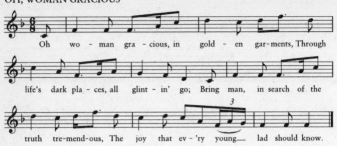

Oh wo - man gra - cious, in gold - en gar - ments, Through
life's dark pla - ces, all glint - in' go; Bring man, in search of the
truth tre-mend-ous, The joy that ev - 'ry young— lad should know.

MARION

She's just like a young star out ta-king the air— Let o-thers be good or be
cle - ver— With Mar - rion gay, a gay flow'r in her hair, Life be -
-comes but a pleas-ant en - dea - vour. When build-ing a ci - ty or
ma-king the hay, I'll fol-low her close— as night fol - lows day, Or
lads fol-low lass-es out nut-ting in May, For— ev - er and ev - er and ev - er.—